TENNYSON

ALFRED TENNYSON
1844

From a lithograph after the painting by Samuel Laurence

[*Frontispiece*

TENNYSON

A MODERN PORTRAIT

BY

HUGH I'ANSON FAUSSET

" *Proclaim the faults he would not show:*
Break lock and seal: betray the trust;
Keep nothing sacred: 'tis but just
The many-headed beast should know."

NEW YORK / RUSSELL & RUSSELL

REPRODUCED FROM THE FIRST, ILLUSTRATED, EDITION OF 1923
TO WHICH HAS BEEN ADDED THE PREFACE
WRITTEN BY THE AUTHOR FOR THE 1929 PRINTING
REISSUED, 1968, BY RUSSELL & RUSSELL
A DIVISION OF ATHENEUM HOUSE, INC.
BY ARRANGEMENT WITH THE ESTATE OF HUGH I'ANSON FAUSSET
L. C. CATALOG CARD NO: 68-11326
PRINTED IN THE UNITED STATES OF AMERICA

TO

MY FATHER

PREFACE

THIS book on its first appearance provoked considerable criticism from wounded "Tennysonians." Much of this criticism reflected only sentimental revulsion, but some of it, of which that of the late Sir Edmund Gosse was typical, calls for a brief reply. Sir Edmund wrote that I was concerned about matters which are of little or no concern to us while we are following the adventures of an artist. Of what importance can it be to enquire whether the author of "The Lotus Eaters" was "scared" by the "Disease of Doubt"? And he added that poetry should be "a matter complete in itself, like a statue or a rose, to be judged purely on its merits as a figure or a flower."

This is not the place to discuss such a doctrine of pure æstheticism. It is enough to say that all art reflects as it is conditioned by the personality which creates it, even if in the greatest art the personal achieves the impersonal, and that, as is stated in a Foreword, my aim was to draw a living portrait of a poet *and a man*. In this endeavour, I did not, indeed I could not, neglect technical criticism and appreciation. But the qualities of Tennyson's artistry have been so often and justly appraised, that to repeat such appraisement was superfluous. My purpose, as I clearly stated, was not to judge poetical "roses," but to explore the personality of a man, who was also a poet. Anyone may justly quarrel with the results of my enquiry into Tennyson's personality; but it is scarcely just to attack me for failing to reach an æsthetic rose-garden, to which I never undertook to direct my steps.

PREFACE

The second defect to which Sir Edmund drew attention was the undue prominence given to political and social vicissitudes, which had really little or nothing to do with literature.

Here again I must reply that I was not concerned with literature as a self-sufficient activity, but with Tennyson, with whom such political and social vicissitudes had, to his own injury it may be as a poet, much to do. Sir Edmund ended his criticism with the words: "I never met with so gratuitous an assertion....as that Tennyson was responsible for our late great war." He discovered such an assertion in the last paragraph of the book. But no such assertion was of course made. Tennyson, I have urged, allowed himself to float upon the impure stream of contemporary public opinion, and so to reflect, and at one time even to encourage, that combination of arrogance and panic, which the thoughtless have called "Patriotism" and the honest "Jingoism." That spirit and the repercussions it begot, in my opinion contributed to the catastrophe of 1914. All I have remarked is that Tennyson, with all his moral affirmations, never till his old age, when it was too late, and even then dubiously, raised his very public voice in protest.

Most indeed of the criticisms of my treatment of Tennyson are necessarily criticisms of my treatment of the Victorian age, of which Tennyson was in many ways the most representative voice. And I may say that I sympathise as little as many of my critics with that satirical exploitation of the morals and manners of the nineteenth century which has been, until recently, the fashion. Nevertheless, negative and merely clever as much of this has been, it has been dictated by something deeper than bad temper, envy of material prosperity, or picturesque perversity. The war would indeed have effected little, if it had not compelled the younger generation, whose credulous faith and generosity it took and mangled, to examine and arraign the values of a civilisation of which it was the logical and cumulative issue. Those values in different degrees poisoned Victorian literature and Victorian life, and nowhere can they be read more clearly than in the characteristics of Tennyson as man and artist. And although, perhaps, our generation has suffered too much from their consequences, not indeed in material impoverishment which is of small account, but in desolating human loss, to avoid those sneers of embitterment which must mar a just indictment, yet that indictment of a self-indulgent æsthetic, a commercial imperialism pretending to divine sanction, and of a patronising and self-interested morality is a primary duty which we owe to the living and the dead.

One of my critics remarked, "Shakespeare is much more an imperialistic 'Laureate' than Tennyson, and so is Mr. Kipling. Our Georgians do not mind them." He is strangely misinformed. Mr. Kipling's dynamic genius as revealed in his style commands our admiration as Swinburne's does. His jingoistic substance we deplore, but at least it speaks with a pagan candour; it does not lean upon a sanctimonious morality. Nor does Shakespeare's. The exuberant nationalism of "Henry VI" is little more to the taste of many of us than the ranting patriotism of "Maud," but it is clear which is the fruit of strength and which of weakness, which is honest and which is a lie in the soul. Imperialism, however, was only one issue and one which necessarily did not bulk large in my criticism of Tennyson. The fundamental issue between our age and the Victorian is between a creative and a possessive conception of life. We are convinced that behind all the moral talk and vast material and decorative output of the Victorian age, it was possessive instead of creative. That such an age should delude itself by professions of high-mindedness only aggravates the evil. In public policy and domestic relationship, in the style and substance of art, in religion and industrialism we see the self-regarding impulses clouding the moral atmosphere. Hence the fear alike of the senses and the mind and a consequent inability to submit the self to life without prejudice, without patronage, and without fear of a loss of dignity. Hence the decline of expression into adornment, of imagination into sentiment, and of religion into an interested morality.

That there were great exceptions in the Victorian age no one would be so foolish as to deny, but Tennyson was scarcely one of them, and the whole aim of my study of his personality was to discover, without having recourse to the many personal anecdotes which might lend an unfair, though telling, support to my diagnosis, how far he was too self-regarding to be true. For there can be no such "sympathetic readjustment of our times to the old century," as one of my critics suggested, until the false in it has been clearly winnowed from the true. That moment, it may be, is nearer now than when this book was written. But although to-day I should doubtless write it somewhat differently, it is rather the style than the substance which I should modify. For the substance I still believe to be essentially true.

H. I'A. F.

BRACKLESHAM,
CHICHESTER.

December, 1928.

FOREWORD

My aim in this book has been to create a living portrait of a poet and a man as I have conceived him after a close study both of his life and his poetry and of their intimate reactions.

For twenty years of middle life, the period contained in Part II. and some of Part III. of this book, Tennyson's poetry supplies the more vital and explicit evidence. In youth and in later life it exists rather as the implicit habit of his life, from which, therefore, I have been careful not to disentangle it.

I am, above all, anxious that it should not be thought by any reader that I have desired, in the happy but perverse fashion of youth, to engage in the service of cleverness against true greatness, or to mock virtue for the pleasure of trivial applause. We have read so often of late that the young criticise Tennyson merely out of a rather dissolute caprice. It is a libel, I am convinced, upon their sincerity, which in this book I have tried to attest, addressing myself to Tennyson's life and poetry intent only on the truth, eager only to discover where this man, whom previous biographers have agreed to honour with all reverent panegyric, can satisfy the scrutiny of those artistic and moral values which Plato named eternal and consistent, and where he fails, as all but the greatest must, to survive so searching an ordeal. I have tried to disengage the man's reality from his appearance, his spiritual significance from the sentimental picture before which for so long men and women prostrated themselves. For the biographical material upon which I have

FOREWORD

drawn I am, of course, primarily indebted to the Memoir of the poet compiled by his son. From among the many other sources which I have had occasion to consult I make particular mention of " Tennyson and His Friends," edited by Hallam, Lord Tennyson, and of " Tennyson, Ruskin and Browning," by Anne Thackeray Ritchie. For moments of illumination gleaned in passing from the writings of other biographers and memorialists I cannot, alas! make separate acknowledgment; they are become too involved in the processes of my own vision for that. Yet without them that vision would have lacked something of the confident outline which I believe it to possess.

H. I'A. F.

Newtown, Newbury.

CONTENTS

ILLUSTRATIONS

PART I

TENDENCIES

TENNYSON

TENDENCIES

I

ONE windy afternoon of March in the year 1827 a carriage might have been seen careering along a raised road in Lincolnshire. On either side were deep dykes, and the surrounding landscape showed grey and desolate. Nowhere was there sign of hedge or tree, except for some rows of shivering poplars that screened a group of farm buildings, red-bricked, blue-tiled, and very plain. Across this flat stretch of irrigated marsh the wind blew strongly, hissing through the shrunken stems of the reeds and filling the air with a sound as of the sea, monotonous and menacing.

The carriage, which had come over the wolds from Louth, had descended through Alford, and was now travelling over that strip of land known as " The Marsh " to Mablethorpe. Arrived here, two young men alighted, and, passing through the little village, they mounted the sea bank under which it sheltered, treading the tussocks of coarse grass and skirting the bushes of sea-buckthorn. At its summit a wide view awaited them. Below stretched a waste of sands, first smooth and dry, then wrinkled with countless little wave-channels which reflected the clouded light in a kind of dull silver. Beyond, half a mile distant, but every moment creeping nearer, was the sea, those dark waters, unevenly rimmed with foam, that sent forth a low reverberation, an anxious, all-pervading murmur. The afternoon sun, slanting suddenly through the clouds, burnished the moist sand as copper; and the two young men, in turn doffing their hats and lifting their faces skyward, began to chant rapidly sets of verses, apparently quite familiar to them. A sense of triumph showed alike in their features and gestures, and, by a certain wild distinction in their persons, they seemed in that exultant moment to belong to the elements and to challenge the power and permanence of the sea. Then, leaping down the bank over sand and shingle, with arms flung wide, they ran across the broad level, still declaiming and gesticulating in the face of heaven and the shore's solitude, until the distance dwarfed them. Far away, like two dancing specks, they showed against the sea, and the gusty echo of their voices died in the prevailing murmur.

These two young men, whose conduct on that afternoon might well have surprised a passing stranger, were Charles and Alfred Tennyson. Acting on the advice of an enterprising family coachman, concerned about their lack of pocket-money, they had submitted their occasional verses to a Mr. Jackson, a bookseller of Louth. He had offered £10 for the copyright, and on that day, under the title of " Poems by Two Brothers," the first-fruits of their sensibility had been given to the world.

" We have passed the Rubicon, and we leave the rest to fate," they had written in their Preface, and in the first enthusiasm of public authorship they had driven across the marsh to share their triumph with the winds and waves.

The book, it must be admitted, was rather an easy

morsel for fate to swallow, as the work of precocious schoolboys is apt to be. The *Literary Chronicle*, alone in noticing it, ran no undue risks in writing that " This little volume exhibits a pleasing union of kindred tastes, and contains several little pieces of considerable merit " ; but it failed to do justice to the mellow melancholy with which these two poets of eighteen and nineteen paid their debt of tears to long-lost youth, parted for ever, in Byronic grandeur, from love and hope to dare " the roaring blast," or bade farewell with a pathos possibly familiar to readers of Scott and Moore to the mythical harp and hall of their forefathers. But the affectations with which youth must always seek to veil its complete inexperience, to reconcile the yawning emptiness of its matter with the urgency of its intention, were in this case exaggerated. For Alfred Tennyson, with a sensitiveness towards his public's requirements—whether dictated by humility or astuteness we do not know, but very unusual in so young a poet—had omitted from the volume any verses which seemed likely by their originality or personal sincerity to be " too much out of the common for the public taste." So early did he shrink from the ordeal of society's criticism.

But, apart from this undue respect for conventional opinion, Alfred Tennyson was at this time all that we like to fancy a young poet should be. His stature was striking both for its grace and power, his beauty remarkable. A figure rising to six feet was crowned by a head which already suggested the large kingliness notable in later years. Above the broad brow the hair lay dark and thick, falling in waves over the ears, with a hint of gold in it for the light to find. The face made a general impression of haughty fastidious-ness, of an intense sensibility balanced by a high preoccupation, the eyes being large, luminous, and heavy-lidded, the nose strong, even dictatorial, but slender also and rarely chiselled, the lips full, but so shapely in their curves as to suggest a scorn of license, which was reinforced by the pointed chin. Foreign and romantic in its swarthiness, the face was yet commandingly aristocratic; it was even more culti-vated than sublime. The aquiline nose, steady eyes, and somewhat deprecating mouth contended with the largeness of head and brow and the luxuriant hair to leave upon the onlooker a conflicting impression both of power and of preciosity.

Charles Tennyson had not the grandeur of feature remarked in his younger brother. His hair was dark and curling, his brown eyes gentler, his expression of a milder eloquence. One wrote of him in later years : " He was like something out of some other world, more holy, more silent than that in which most of us are living." Yet he, too, by his swarthy complexion and something dusky and untamed in face and bearing, suggested a Spanish rather than an English origin, and surprised those who saw him into curiosity, as towards one unique as well as lovable.

Both brothers had magnificent voices, deep, reso-nant and emotionally expressive. Circumstances had hitherto made them inseparable. The third and fourth sons in a family of twelve, they had grown up together in the old white Rectory at Somersby, in the closest communion of work and play. Few rumours or diversions from the outer world came to break the quiet intercourse of a very devoted family. There, in a little attic under the roof, Charles and Alfred had slept together from their earliest years, together had shared in bird's-nesting rambles on summer afternoons to Stockworth, Harrington or Scrivelsby, had vied with each other at " King of the Castle," or ridden together plumed and caparisoned through a world of faery and romance.

Daily they had walked to Cadney's village school, bent on the first adventure of learning, and later had accompanied their elder brother Frederick to the grammar school at Louth, where, under the influence of the Rev. J. Waite, they had learnt to regard the establishment with a definite and lasting antipathy. It would be interesting to know the sentiments entertained towards them by their fellow-scholars. These can hardly have been favourable, though mixed with awe both for the Tennysons' physical supremacy and their proud self-sufficiency. For the young Tennysons disdained the sports of the multitude. Their spare time they spent in wandering together over the wolds, reading works foreign to the school curriculum, and even in writing verses—a tendency which every respectable system of education seeks to eliminate. If they played, it was not at Prisoner's Base or the like in the schoolyard with their fellow-pupils, but at being Emperors of China in the exclusive circle of their Aunt Mary's garden. Probably, therefore, no universal regret was felt when, in 1817, they left the school, Frederick for Eton, Charles and Alfred for Somersby, where during eleven years they pursued in turn an earnest, desultory or fanciful existence under the direct, but not inquisitorial, eye of their parents.

The Reverend George Clayton Tennyson, the father of these remarkable boys, was himself a man of great height and emphatic appearance. He laboured at times under a sense of injury because, though head of the family, his rights to inheritance of property had been passed over in favour of a younger brother. A Hebrew and Syriac scholar, a brilliant talker, by nature somewhat haughty and passionate, yet tender at heart beneath a native gruffness, he had taken

Orders without any very strong leaning towards the service of souls. His parishioners certainly respected him for a gentleman rather than reverenced him for a saint. There was in him something of the gloomy genius, strenuous independence of character and erratic power which were manifest in his eldest son Frederick. He was large-minded, and greatly gifted socially, but, like many men of nervous temperament, subject to fits of profound despondency, which led people often to mistake a worried moodiness for stern displeasure. With his boys he was strict, both as parent and schoolmaster, but his dignity was unmixed, we feel, with any petty irritability. For clever and well-read as he was, he was built upon the grand scale, and his exact learning was balanced by a genial humanity. For his sons' better instruction he perfected his Greek, and his library, far from specialising in the Fathers or the sermons of divines, offered them a catholic selection of all that was most alive in English literature.

But if the father impressed his sons by learning, individuality and force of intellect, the mother was to them an example of tender, unassuming spirituality. More winning even than her beauty was the purity and innocence of her personality. In later years her son wrote of her as " one of the most angelick natures on God's earth, always doing good by a sort of intuition " ; and " the summer calm of golden charity," which he described as perpetually reigning on her lips, expressed itself practically, as is a woman's way, in many an act of consideration and keen insight, of quiet counsel in distress, in religious devotion, and a hate of gossip and meanness, and in a love of animals and a pity for wounded things, of which the unscrupulous were known to take advantage. Though harassed by the cares of a large family, she did not fail to instil in her sons a spirit of gentleness and courtesy, a watchful reverence towards and a lyric sympathy with nature, which in all of them, but particularly in Alfred, took early root. To her did he owe his consistent passion for close observation of birds and Nature's ways, and to her should the local gamekeepers have complained by rights, when they regularly found their traps sprung by her compassionate son.

To the home life, then, of her family, Mrs. Tennyson, in her small and gentle competence, brought such an example of radiant docility as influenced her son's ideal of womanhood for life ; while to his father he owed not only his early gift of versifying, but that wonder in the face of the mysterious, that moral questioning, which were to trouble so disastrously and ineffectually his eager sense of beauty in the world ; and lastly, those moods of darkness which were to come upon him from time to time, and cause him to flinch with proud but morbid agony from the stark reality in which he feared to feel himself alone.

But outside the circle of Somersby Rectory was another teacher, more influential, perhaps, over the latent poet in the boy than even his parents or his home. For the lessons of this authority were learnt so well that for sixty years syllables of its instruction were to be heard upon the lips of the affectionate pupil.

The Lincolnshire countryside, from Somersby to the sea, is unusually varied. It has three distinct characteristics, of wold, marsh and fen, and the native can choose whether he turn to upland or lowland ; he may seek the wooded hills rising out of deep valleys, their hollows filled with trees, their ridges spread for the passage of the cloud-shadows, where there is a peace more familiar than austere, or he may prefer the broad, rich fields of corn and pasture, the drained fenland sparsely populated, but with a " certain miracle of symmetry," or he may choose the marsh, so named from days before dykes and watercourses had rescued it from inundation. Here on this level tract he will find variety according to the season, and to his distance from the sea. Often it will seem over-luxuriant, a tangle of silvery creeks, where willows hang over reedy banks, the haunt of swallows dipping about drowsy mills and granges, of crowding cuckoo-flowers and marsh-marigolds. But the further east he goes, the more bare and open is the land; and in gloomy autumn or winter, on a windy afternoon or in a rainy twilight, the marsh can be indescribably desolate, a land of weariness and wailful reeds, or a solitude patient and resigned.

Alfred Tennyson loved best the wold and the marsh. The little village of Somersby itself lies cupped in green fields, surrounded by some half-dozen grey-towered churches, the bells of which

> " from hill to hill
> Answer each other in the mist."

Here he watched year by year the buds unfold upon lime, chestnut and sycamore, heard the " windy clamour " of the daws, and the brawling of the little brook that ran through a " brambly wilderness " at the foot of the Rectory garden, with its " cressy islets white with flowers." Here he observed the habits of the " careful robin," and later, when the summer woods " made a murmur in the land," or from the dry, dark wold the air blew cool " on the oat-grass and the sword-grass and the bulrush in the pool," he stood entranced by the nightingale singing in the leafy dusk beyond the high evergreen hedges that stood about his home.

Yet, though the appeal of such country to the senses is strong, it is seldom overpowering. It is an enchantment which invites surrender rather than a beauty

that has terror in it, and calls the imagination into
play. The beauty of the wolds with their broken lines
of cliff and dale, their gushing waters, bowery lanes
and overgrown villages, has a sumptuous quality that
enervates ; their broad streams are a little sluggish,
the meadows heavy with scent ; Nature's mood is complacent. The beauty of the marsh is often subdued
and even austere, but rarely majestic or dynamic.
Its half-tones of colour and allusive distances invite
rather a gentle melancholy, a temperate joy, or a faint
and spectral mysticism. Only upon the borders of
the sea, whose voice comes moaning inland when the
wind sets westerly, does Nature reveal her passion and
her cruelty with any candour. And even here, for
the flatness of the shore and the lingering distance
of the ebb-tide, she lulls more than threatens, is a
phantom of desolation rather than a monster of
destruction.

It was in the lap of such country that Tennyson's
boyhood was nursed. A shy, solitary-dreaming child,
both restive and reserved, we see him growing up in
an environment calculated to soothe his nerves and
excite his sensibility. Into the quiet of the Rectory
garden, with its sloping lawn overshadowed by wych-
elms, larch and sycamores, its walks of turf bordered
by lilies and roses, hollyhocks and sunflowers, its
plaited alleys and orchard where at dawn the apples
would lie like golden globes in the dewy grass, no
disagreeable sound would penetrate, but only the
familiar murmur of the brook, the vague voice of white
kine, of sheep, of pigeons in distant woods. Within
doors, too, was comfortable intimacy, whether in the
little yellow-curtained, book-lined drawing-room, its
two large windows level with the lawn, or in the Gothic
vaulted dining-room with groined roof, high ecclesiastical windows, carved stone chimney-piece and panelled

door, the scene of many a family festivity, or in the
bay-windowed nursery inside which the woodbine
climbed or the little attic under the roof where Charles
and Alfred slept.

The large family was never rowdy; a certain
studiousness, emanating probably from the father,
brooded over the household, and the children were apt
and diligent to encourage each other in literary studies,
even in the adventures of authorship. Their games
were rarely the mere physical expressions to which
boyhood's leisure is so commonly devoted. They were
rather the mimic enterprises of a romance in which the
boys played their knightly part. The spell of Arthur
was already upon them, summoned by the instinct of
chivalry in their blood; and even their childish play
resolved itself into the duels of kings and their champions, and the shock of fantastic jousts. To this must
be added a passion for story-telling, for endless diffuse
fictions, of which each would in turn place a new
instalment underneath the potato-bowl at dinner-
time, or in winter evenings perpetuate over the fire.

Alfred was the kindest of elder brothers to the
younger children, and a scene has been preserved for
us, typical doubtless of many an evening hour, when,
taking his little sister Cecilia on his knee, with Arthur
and Matilda sprawling against him on either side and
the baby, Horatio, between his legs, he fascinated them
with legends of knights and heroes among untravelled
forests, rescuing distressed damsels from dragon,
demon or witch. So early did the " Idylls of the
King " begin to germinate, while perhaps it is not idle
to see a connection between the pastoral poems of
later days and that early story of tender sentiment,
entitled " The Old Horse," which he used to tell for
months on end.

But beautiful as such a home was as a haunt of peace

and charmed domestic unity, we may question whether Alfred or Charles benefited altogether by their long years of unbroken seclusion beneath its roof. Conditions invited self-absorption, the perpetual gratification of easy experiences to an unhealthy degree. No call was made upon their initiative; there was no need to struggle against odds or accept the bitter occasional defeats which profit boyhood so much. Even their education lacked the discipline of competitive strife, which is not without its uses in forging the metal of intellect and deepening the cravings of culture.

It is not good for the young soul to be too much at peace with itself and life—it learns too early to take its ease in a " Paradise of Dainty Devices," to drowse indolently upon the breast of Nature and idly hymn the beauty of its mistress. Especially was this true of the Tennyson brothers, whose sensibility was abnormally keen and their temperaments highly nervous. It is noticeable that Frederick, who went to Eton from Louth, preserved to the end of his life a character of robust and strenuous originality, a passionate detestation of cant and a power of genuine imagination in marked contrast with his younger brother. Alfred, however, through these years absorbed Nature and books with passive delight. In the affectionate circle of his home he had no hard battles to fight, and no rude reality threatened him at any time with pain or discomfort. Rather, his talents were applauded and every sign of originality encouraged, while his position as elder brother invited an attitude of precocious dignity and kindly patronage, which only a natural modesty preserved from priggishness.

That his sensibility felt the strain of so guarded and gratifying an existence is sufficiently evident in the

fits of depression by which, even in boyhood, he was
known to be troubled ; the truth being that at such
times he laboured under a weight of absorbed and
accumulated impressions which stifled a healthy
activity of mind and body.   He was a prey of melancholy idleness, because his appetite was indulged
beyond his powers of assimilation.   We cannot say
how much he owed to the circumstances of his
upbringing this incapacity to see the branches of the
tree of life for the leaves, this failure to live intensely
with all his faculties and pierce to the reality of life
beyond its vesture.   Yet, whether native to him or
induced by circumstances, a preponderance of recep-
tivity over initiative was to limit his activity all his
days.

His virtue and high-mindedness, constant as they
were, suffered under the same disability ; they had
not been put to school with life, nor had they
stood the test of association with laxity or vice—and
so they remained rather a sincere but unquestioned
convention than a passion purged and enlarged by
experience.   This his poetry, that candid confessional
of character, was in its good time to prove, yet in the
boy rising to adolescence a poet's temperament and
powers were apparent enough.

The child who, at five years, swept by a March
storm down the garden, had cried with arms ecstati-
cally spread wide, " I hear a voice that's speaking in
the wind," and over whom the phrase " Far, far
away " exercised a strange charm, was a portent of
poetry waking from the sleep of Nature.   By his
eighth year a slate covered on two sides with
Thomsonian blank verse in praise of flowers shows the
measure of advancing sophistication ; his twelfth
birthday hails him arrived in the borderland of heroic
romance with an epic poem of five thousand octo-

syllabic lines in the manner of Sir Walter Scott; at fifteen he is come to the drama of passion and intrigue in iambics, and the news of Byron's death, filtering through so incongruously from the world of hasty fashion to the decorous rusticity of Somersby, brings a day " when the whole world seemed to be darkened " for him, a day of devastating dejection, devoted to the carving on a rock of the pregnant epitaph " Byron is dead." To one at least in England it was a tragedy deliciously unalloyed.

But behind the normal and mechanical process of these imitations, inevitable to a poetical youth with time on his hands and few other interests, he was possessing himself of the riches of Nature's household. His energies expended themselves on mimicry, his senses battened peacefully on the countryside, as he dawdled by Stockworth Mill, or gazed, amid drenched furze, from the high wolds forty miles across a fertile plain to the minster towers of Lincoln. Only at Mablethorpe, in the cottage under the sea-bank where the family spent their holidays, did the naked elements at times come to chasten the sweet pleasure of life with the spectacle of

> " Gray sand-banks, and pale sunsets, dreary wind,
> Dim shores, dense rains, and heavy-clouded sea."

Here, scanning the North Sea in wild weather, tufted with spray, or at night when a full tide flowed in to shore like a sinister army advancing with muffled tread, or when in a high swell the shock of a great wave on the flat was like a clap of thunder close at hand, the young Tennyson tasted a passion beyond the scope of Byronic melodrama, one in which his alarmed senses gave place to his exultant spirit. The cloistered calm of wooded hollows and blossomy vales, where Nature squandered her wealth to enhance her charms, was forgotten as he stood on the sand-built ridge and watched her, stark, cruel, and triumphant, sap the outposts of the land.

At night here, to him who has seen on one hand the setting sun pave the marsh with rainbow colour, on the other the rising moon light a track of gold upon the sands, the stars when they come seem to be set in a wider heaven than is elsewhere to be found. The active peace of that infinite prospect, so different from indolent meadow and lawn, Tennyson experienced at Mablethorpe. It was the one passion in which, losing himself utterly, he found himself truly. Through all the years of earnest effort, application, and various poetical output, he would return in moments of ecstasy to this scene, and however prosaic the context or apparently fortuitous the metaphor, never did the vital music fail. He did not observe the sea as he observed Nature elsewhere, with the eye of the connoisseur and epicure combined. The sea refused such refinements. It had spoken to him, as the wind spoke to the child of five, and its language, up to the last sigh of surrender in " Crossing the Bar," was poetically the most valid that ever passed his lips.

It was fitting, then, that the two brothers should celebrate their first public confession of poetry at Mablethorpe. Had they known it, that tireless prodigal, the sea, was the best physician for their muse, threatened as it was by a sickness which the close and cultivated life that lay before them could only accentuate. The root of this malady was spiritual passivity combined with an avid sensuousness. And the morbid germs of self-satisfaction, moral compromise and indulgence of fancy were even then ready to multiply on a ground from which candid passion and bold intellectuality had been unconsciously debarred. In a fragment of an early play we read

" Ha ! by St. James
Mine was no vulgar mind in infancy,
Ev'n then the force of nature and high birth
Had writ nobility upon my brow."

The words are those of a character by the young Tennyson, but so youthful a dramatist is rarely able to create puppets detached from himself. The waves with which he shared his triumph on that March day of 1827 would have made short work of such lines as these, and yet, although Byron's shade may have guided the pen, they have their significance. Already exclusiveness, the negation of vital truth, had begun to prey upon the poet's universal province, and Cambridge, to which the brothers went in the following year, was not likely to recall the author to the paths of liberty.

2

In February, 1828, Charles and Alfred Tennyson matriculated at Trinity College, Cambridge. A university is a problem in opposites. For thither in the dawn of conscious life comes impressionable youth, eager for wonders, with a capacity for generous idealism as yet untutored by experience and intolerant of compromise. Youth is ready to remake the world as it should be, and supposes that it can be done with a noble gesture ; in the inspiration of young romance it will read into even an ugly life the poetry its ardent soul conceives ; and, indeed, what an illumination of the world might come from the persisting in such views by one single generation of men !

But the institution to which they bring their dreams has in the nature of things little use for generous sentiments, in short, for feeling at all, whether true or false. It is a mill through which the immature mind is passed, to issue stamped with the sign of efficiency in this branch of knowledge or that. University dons are apt to be just those upon whom the mill has most tyrannously made its impress—narrow pedants, the victims of mental specialisation, " mousing owls," " Sabbath drawlers of old saws," who, though loaded with academical honours, enter into life as Macaulay wrote, " with their education still to begin," and of necessity never to be begun. There are in every age exceptions to this rule of pedantry—noble, large-spirited men, through all the years " keeping the younger generation in hail," to whom, therefore, the young turn with gladness, knowing that they are not putting their ignorance to school with prejudice, or their hopes with shrivelled scepticism. But these are few : and Oxford and Cambridge have best served such poets as they have avoided expelling by the intercourse which they occasion between young men of liberal sentiments who have met together in college rooms and have crossed their minds. The truest culture of University life has always been won in this way, and not in the schools.

Alfred Tennyson went up to Cambridge charged with no excessive idealism. His desire for better things never threatened revolution ; his love of beauty was held within decorous bounds, and his intellectual curiosity was almost woefully discreet. And yet the university, as an institution, disappointed even him by its poverty of ideas and prosaic logic-chopping. Of its doctors, proctors, and deans he wrote, " you teach us nothing, feeding not the heart," and years later he said in conversation with Dr. Butler : " There was a want of love in Cambridge then." The want, we may safely say, was not peculiar to his time. But it had an unfortunate effect on the course of his personal development.

An association with large, active, and experienced

minds at this time would have been invaluable; backed by a programme of regular study, it might have led Tennyson on to the adventure of positive individual thought. He might have ceased to take a merely private pleasure in the exquisiteness of classical verse, to ruminate on the opinions of others, to reflect idly the beauties of Nature, or multiply regrets over " the golden days of Faerie " that were no more. The need to fight for his own point of view in an open arena might have put an end to the misery which he confessed haunted him, because of an inability " to consolidate our gossamer dreams into reality." At Somersby he had dreamed too much, floating agreeably in a backwater of life; at Cambridge he was drawn into a company of remarkable young men, but as a dignified spectator rather than an unprivileged partaker in the battle of their wits. At first he lived lonely and depressed, feeling " the country so disgustingly level, the revelry of the place so monotonous, the studies of the University so uninteresting, so matter-of-fact." So shy was he, too, that he was known to turn away from dinner in hall out of a sudden nervousness of facing people.

Yet one so striking in appearance could not long remain solitary. He was discovered by a band of young enthusiasts and enrolled in their society, of which he soon became the presiding spirit. He looked the poet with commanding conviction. Indeed, it is possible that the many distinguished societies which from this time to the end of his life were eager to enrol him in their company did so more out of reverence for his noble presence than for any vivid contribution which he made to the current of talk. It was his custom to sit silent, inserting only here and there a brief question or a sound summary of opinions already expressed. But this he did with an earnest dignity which rendered even the commonplace singularly impressive, and convinced the originators of opinions which he repeated that in truth he alone had fathered them. Never was there a pose, if pose it was, which so grandly silenced the voices of criticism or the scoffs of irreverence. Yet the regal attitude, we may believe, was in no way consciously assumed. There was a grandeur purely in his physical presence, which bore down all resistance and seemed to enfold a sorry world in its magnanimity. Six feet high, broad-chested, strong-limbed, long-fingered, he filled whatever room he entered with an impression of power and refinement. The face, which all agreed to call in a vague way Shakespearean, with its deep-lidded eyes brooding inward rather than distantly abstracted, its chaplet of swarthy hair, its sensitive lips and frequent look of puzzled melancholy, seemed to ponder godlike over the little affairs of men. His contemporaries were convinced that here was " a man at all points, of grand proportions and feature, significant of that inward chivalry becoming his ancient and honourable race."

That Tennyson should accept the unanimous verdict and do all in his power to justify it was natural enough. It was hard for a young man to support so inflated a reputation, to know that he was named by his associates " truly one of the mighty of the earth," and be compelled to conduct himself as the mighty do. Certainly a regal reticence best served his purpose, for no one was so small-minded as to probe the mystery of thought which this great man surely cherished within him, but was too exquisitely sensitive to render explicit. It was enough that he should sit in front of the fire smoking and meditating, rarely mingling in conversation, except with one terse phrase to sum up the issue of the arguments.

In his case alone was the rule of this informal society waived, by which members proposed, in turn, a subject for discussion and, standing before the mantelpiece, read their essays in regular succession. Tennyson was excused, that his poetry and wisdom might remain unfettered, and although he once attempted an essay on the subject of " Ghosts," he was too shy to deliver it. A study, however, of the preface to this essay, which alone survives, wakens conjecture as to whether shyness was in truth the cause of the last-moment withdrawal; for we can hardly credit that a society of keen minds would have been impressed by the arguments of one who not only confessed that he stood " as it were upon a vantage ground," but had apparently nothing to offer concerning the spiritual world, which he had chosen as his subject, but phrases of sentimental vagueness.

Moreover, in the less serious moments of life, when the cloud of thought was lifted and the necessity for divination removed, his peculiar sensitiveness and moody melancholy were apt to pass away. Humorously would he take quiet note of things, his conversation no longer languid but abounding, as the talk of normal natural men, in hearty expressions of common sense, and showing, too, a strength and self-reliance which was in strange contrast with his timidity in intellectual argument.

The Cambridge society which adopted this " kind of Hyperion " as its presidential image was named " The Apostles." It had been founded by John Sterling, and the trend of its thought was towards a sort of religious radicalism. Its members courted liberty within the bounds of legitimacy; theirs was a sentiment for freedom rather than a passion, and they indulged it within the strict limits of conventional decency. And yet the friends whom Tennyson made in this apostolic circle, who represented for him the whole reality of his Cambridge life, were an intensely human and various set, and to a rooted respect for the traditions in thought, art and life, added more than a dash of speculative daring. Unprepared as yet to question the basic premises of religion or society, they would argue frankly against the prejudices, superstitions and hypocrisies of the day ; search, too, with little practical success, it may be admitted, but much sincere sympathy, for measures which might relieve the ugliness, hunger and penury all too manifest in the world of hasty industrialism about them, and bring reason to the study of moral sentiments and metaphysics to the purging of their conception of God. That their rationality did not go very far is probable, for they stood in the vanguard of that great army of enquirers who, throughout the century, were ever more disinterestedly to examine the indentures of faith and sentiment. But for their time they were a gallant band, and seem to have pursued all their debate, whether political, religious or philosophic, with a high enthusiasm and a generous ardour worthy of fine spirits trying their first strokes on the turbid stream of life. Many of the Apostles were to remain Tennyson's intimate and lifelong friends, many were destined to attain positions of dignity, particularly in the Church.

Four claim at least a passing reference for their marked originality of character. Spedding, " old Spedding," as he was affectionately named, because he was recognised all his years as combining the best qualities of youth and age, devoted most of his working life to the study of Bacon. Tennyson called him " the wisest man I know," but he carried his wisdom lightly, being full of pleasant scoffs, calm and shrewd, " a

Socrates in life and in death." If, however, his
serenity signified mastery over his emotions, those
emotions were profound. He loved others with a deep
tenderness, and though he was too genial a man to be
embittered by life, pain lent at times a melancholy to
his composure. His death followed a street accident ;
he was run down by a cab, a situation of which he lived
long enough to record the humour.

Very different in temperament was Richard Monck-
ton Milnes (later Lord Houghton), a man of vast
versatility, and of such ebullient spirits " as always put
you in a good humour." A ready conversationalist on
every topic, with a whimsical love of paradox which he
would use to puzzle the dull or superficial, he was also
the kindliest of mortals. His sympathies, naturally
deep, and deepened by travel and experience, made
him the generous friend of unpopular causes and the
patron of many men of letters, while it is probable that
his conflicting interests, of which politics was para-
mount, alone prevented his taking a high place himself as poet or *littérateur*.

In subtle reasoning power, however, Brookfield
Blakesly was supreme in the society, as also in a gift
of dramatic humour, by which he would conduct
imaginary dialogues between characters real or fictitious, each one more droll than the last, until the whole
company was brought to the floor in the pains of
laughter. Yet over Blakesly, as over almost all this
brotherhood of sober enthusiasts, there hung a phantom cloud of melancholy, so that even his jesting
was not spontaneous, but rather that of a " kindlier,
trustier Jaques." This mood of reflective sadness,
as of those who heard the music of life always in the
minor key, was a little incongruous in a society so
youthful. Possibly it emanated from the chair in
which Tennyson sat and brooded ; certainly it seemed

to affect most of the members, so that they grew not only to contemplate life, but to crack jests and conduct religious or political arguments, with either a rueful raillery or a meditative tenderness, as if struggling against pervading depression. Their disputes, too, though conducted in high seriousness, almost, indeed, with elaborate ritual, seem to have lacked all the true fire of controversy, all fundamental antagonisms, and their arguments to have been assumed only for purposes of debate.

Least of all, however, did this melancholy damp the spirits of Arthur Hallam, and for that reason he was the most loved and reverenced, and impressed Tennyson from the beginning as one who " seemed to tread the earth as a spirit from some better world." His mind was of that attractive quality which, while capable if necessary of trading in facts, prefers to range curiously in the freer realm of ideas. His early bias towards the speculative and the metaphysical, and his interest in moral and political philosophy, tended to disperse the physical concentration and sublimate the eager hunger for sensation which it is necessary for the poet to preserve. Yet a poet he was in sympathy, as also in his passionate pursuit of the Absolute, the Eternal and the Beautiful. His taste in poetry was thus austere ; and, being a lover of Dante, convinced of the poet's religious office as revealer of universal truth through the medium of actuality, he disliked any mere trick of versifying, any flowery redundance, which bore little relation to genuine emotion. To him, poetry no more than life was an amusement, yet he did not allow his conception of its seriousness to cloud the natural sunniness of his disposition. From a child the combination in him of a sweet nature with subtle mental powers was remarkable. In no sense an exact scholar either at Eton or at Cambridge, he was that

ARTHUR HUGH HALLAM

From the painting at Eton College by Sir M. A. Shee, P.R.A., by kind permission of the Provost

[*To face p.* 24

better thing, a true one, in so far as he absorbed the spirit of whatever he studied, even to the point of forgetting the letter. He read widely and knew where to read discursively, and his familiarity with Greek, Latin and Italian, or with Elizabethan literature, and with the romantic poets of his own century, was of this intuitive kind ; though weak in memory he could assimilate abstruse ideas and master complicated dialectic with rapidity. Yet, like all men of true sympathy as well as keen understanding, he considered emotion in the last resort a truer arbiter than thought. His temperament was too earnest and human for casuistry, and politically he put his trust in a change of heart that would guarantee the triumph of right and justice, rather than in any tinkering from outside with an imperfect social mechanism. There were times even with him when all seemed dark, " irrecoverably dark," he wrote, when his sensitive soul was wounded by the cruelty of life, and his liberal heart disgusted by its meanness. But so pure and unquenchable was the fount of charity within him that worldly sediment could not long discolour it.

This temperate, eloquent, enthusiastic being came to Tennyson like a revelation of what he himself would be, but could not. Hallam had the constant high spirits which Tennyson rarely achieved, the large, lucid and eager speech which was never his, the pioneering energy, the questing individuality to which he could not rouse himself, while in common they shared a reflective love of virtue, of great thoughts, and of beautiful ideas not too curiously defined.

But the link which bound them indissolubly was that of spontaneous and admiring affection. They realised in each other (perhaps Tennyson the more, having the more dependent nature of the two) that desire for an intimate reciprocation of human sympathy and understanding, relieved of the fever and waste of passion which so often distorts the love of man and woman. The value of such a disinterested relationship can hardly be exaggerated. To Tennyson particularly, as, indeed, to all men engaged in a forlorn adventure and oppressed by a sense of loneliness and difficulty, the assurance of a friend's faith and his lavish encouragement meant, at the time, everything. The fits of melancholy from which Tennyson suffered were real enough, for during his first year of residence, discontented as he was with the University and its meagre-souled authorities, he was no less embittered with himself. Removed from the comfortable peace of Somersby and the transcendental music of the sea at Mablethorpe, involved also in a society of active minds pursuing, however darkly, new ideals of truth and duty, he was secretly troubled by an inability to grapple with ideas as did his companions. The give and take of argument, the gymnastics of individual speculation, which were a joy to them, were, he discovered, an exercise beyond his powers. It is true that he could sit quietly and observe and, if the need arose, condense the arguments of others with dignified assurance. No one doubted that his silence was the seal of wisdom, and not of cowardice or intellectual lassitude. But beneath the mask of sublimity was a very real disquiet. The life at Somersby had not led him to question his powers ; he had accepted gladly the world of Nature and studied it, now with sensuous exactness, now with abandon, while the literature which he had read had seemed to him only a lesson in refinement, a treasured tale of romance, a tapestry of fancy graced with noble phrases, exquisite gestures and heroic situations. The labour of a poet, as he had conceived it, was doubtless to suggest the beauty of virtue to men, but chiefly by perpetuating this lovely paradise, adding perhaps another rose-blown arbour, or a fresh fountain where the ageless nymphs might trip down and unveil their limbs in the noon of an eternal summer.

But the zeal of the Apostles speedily shattered so gentle an illusion. Blakesly, for example, assured him that " a volume of poetry written in a proper spirit, a spirit like that which a vigorous mind indues by the study of Wordsworth and Shelley, would be, at the present juncture, the greatest benefit the world could conceive." Trench had said to him with all the assurance of a future Archbishop, " Tennyson, we cannot live in art." It was a rousing call to action, and yet the " proper spirit " eluded his grasp. He admired Shelley for his music and his unworldliness, but his enthusiastic doctrine was hard to comprehend, and his ideal ecstasies were apt to escape the pursuer and vanish into air ; while even Wordsworth, he had to confess, seemed often very dull.

As a result he was merely unsettled. He doubted his right to cultivate sensations and convert them into beautiful words while failing dismally to quicken within himself the spirit of impassioned vision. Hallam's admiration, and, indeed, that of all his brother Apostles, was, under these circumstances, very encouraging. That so many eager-minded men should assume without question his poetic power went far to blunt the edge of his uneasy self-criticisms. The next year, 1829, brought further encouragement. The subject chosen for the Chancellor's prize poem was " Timbuctoo." It was a subject admirably suited to Tennyson's condition of mind at the time, in so far as it bore no relation whatever to reality. With infinite tact and simulated carelessness he patched up an old poem on " The Battle of Armageddon," and sent it in under the new title. It was

a piece of laboured decoration and fanciful extravagance, marked in places by much verbal felicity ; a
piece, in short, of richly modulated nonsense, and it
carried off the prize. " The Apostles " were not alone
in advertising its merits, although Milnes, with
charming audacity, wrote that " it is certainly equal
to most parts of Milton," and Frederick Maurice that
" it would have done honour to any man that ever
wrote."

Tennyson was certainly at this time fortunate in
the blind loyalty of his friends, and although it is
significant that he found himself too shy to declaim
his poem in the Senate House, he began, warmed by
the glow of friendly appreciation, to expand in private.
Already, when sufficiently pressed, he had been in the
habit of chanting the many old ballads he knew by
heart to select audiences in college rooms ; now, under
more urgent solicitation, he would intone also poems
of his own but recently composed, or actually in
process of completion, verses full of weird pictures,
mystical and undefined, as if his fancy was desperately
striving in them after powerful utterance, and simulating a vision which he did not possess. But the
conditions governing these recitations were peculiar.
The reverent listeners sat round the table by lamplight
while the poet crooned his mellifluous music ; but
while free to hear, they were forbidden to criticise.
They might express their approval ; they might even
loudly applaud. But of disapproval there must not
be a word. Silence, to so exquisite a sensitiveness,
was criticism enough.

3

Tennyson was now working continually at the poems
which were to be published in the following year.

The Cambridge country, with its wide horizons and

temperate colouring, was not unlike the marsh at Somersby. Walking along the curving road beneath tall trees to Trumpington, or through the fields by the willows and the river to Grantchester, Tennyson realised in Nature the same intimate calm, the same restfulness as he had learnt to love and depend upon at home; and from the sudden high ridge, before the road turned and dipped to Madingley, he experienced something of the gracious sublimity he associated with the wolds. There below him stretched a broad plain, rising in one direction to the Gog Magog Hills, but elsewhere a limitless prospect, folding about quiet villages, and finally stealing out of sight beneath a steep, cloud-serried sky. In early summer the fields glimmered through the haze of heat like a patchwork dwindling into the distance; the colours were of that heavenly transparency which Botticelli understood how to recapture. Faint blues and greens predominated, save where the poppies ran scarlet across a field of ripening corn. But in the middle distance, like an island lost in foliage, lay Cambridge. The pinnacles of King's Chapel tapered through the trees, and the sun cast gleam and shadow on the massive tower of St. John's.

It was, indeed, a prospect meet to soothe all fever, to which any wounded Arthur might come, and looking on this earth—

" Deep-meadow'd, happy fair with orchard-lawns
And bowery hollows crown'd with summer sea "

heal him of his grievous wound. And no less in the narrow streets of the town did the atmosphere conduce to a melting calm and a forgetfulness of purpose. On every side pressed memories of days long past. The mellow beauty of mediævalism glanced down upon him from building after building, and all its bigotry and squalor were effaced by kindly time. The past went with him as he walked along Trinity Street to dine in hall, or down the lime avenue to the Backs in summer twilight, or in King's Chapel saw the riches of the high windows blurring the stonework, or on a winter evening listened to the priest intoning remotely in the shut choir behind the crimson curtain, or heard the great voice of the organ linger down that roof. In these solitary moments of quiescence and sensuous absorption he found himself once again at peace with life. Inevitably, as it seemed, the music of sweetly modulated words awoke upon his lips. The world's discord fell dumb, and life again became the decorative tapestry which his fancy loved to trace. Certainly he still felt the sadness and transiency of things, but with a secret pleasure, of which was born a consoling song :

> " Where Claribel low-lieth
> The breezes pause and die,
> Letting the rose-leaves fall :
> But the solemn oak-tree sigheth
> Thick-leaved, ambrosial,
> With an ancient melody
> Of an inward agony,
> Where Claribel low-lieth."

To write such verses gave him exquisite satisfaction. His mind floated idly on the music, his feelings swooned in a golden languor, and he lived once again with " The Good Haroun Al-Raschid " in his prime.

Yet he was not always weary. In " Mariana " he had snared the essence of dreary lassitude, in "Oriana" of wild pathos and desperate woe. To other unearthly maidens, picturesquely named, he assigned the music of his lighter moods. There was " airy, fairy Lilian " with her arch daintiness, " Madeline " with her variety of " delicious spites and darling angers," and " Adeline " with her enigmatic smile ; pale, pensive

" Margaret," too, the bright-eyed frolic " Rosalind,"
imperial " Eleänore," and haughty, black-browed
" Kate." In such a collection of feminine minia-
tures, delicate in technique and colouring, but void
of all reality or characterisation, he exercised a gift
for melodious writing, and indulged a gentle sensuousness. He chose, in fact, these phantom ladies,
beautiful, but inhuman like faces seen in a dream,
as the earliest medium for the expression of that
romantic sentiment which was to obsess him all his
life. For he was always to prove most at home
with the unreal. Both the real and the ideal
disquieted him. Yet there were periods when the
fanciful cloyed, and he felt sated even by his own
seductive music, and by Nature, such as he now drew
her with a tender accuracy, in his pictures of " The
Dying Swan " and of yellowing autumn, or as a background for his moody maidens. It was then that the
spirit of the Apostles rose up in judgment against him.
Here were men braving the mystery of life, while he
played with its echoes. So the indictment, we fancy,
shaped itself, and he would turn with angry effort and
seek to acquit himself by more manly, serious verse.
The title he chose for his first attempt in this kind was
wonderfully appropriate. It ran " Supposed Confes-
sions of a Second-rate Sensitive Mind not in Unity
with Itself."

The discord within him was, in truth, severe. It
threatened to disintegrate not only his poetic powers,
but also his religious belief. As a poet, one who
surrendered to sensuous pleasure and cultivated
romantic fiction, he was assailed by a disagreeable
consciousness that truth demanded a more active
and creative vision ; yet such a vision he found it
well-nigh impossible to compass. On the other
hand, as a Christian, brought up in the habit of

unquestioning loyalty to revealed religion, he was startled and disgusted to find himself dislocated by doubts; yet he neither dared nor had the intellectual ability to use these doubts as the basis of a thorough rational examination of the tenets of his faith. He clung desperately to the comfort of faith; nevertheless his doubts, which could neither be silenced nor removed, made him feel a craven. Between faith, therefore, and doubt he vacillated according to his mood, now crying pathetically :

> " Oh ! wherefore do we grow awry
> From roots which strike so deep ? "

accusing himself of human pride and praying heaven for chastisement, now reclining upon the question :

> " Why not believe then ?   Why not yet
> Anchor thy frailty there, where man
> Hath moor'd and rested ? "

Yet rest he could not; for was it not " man's privilege to doubt " ?—" to look into the laws of life and death, and things that seem, and things that be, and analyse our double nature, and compare all creeds till we have found the one, if one there be ? " But though the will to analyse was there, the power was lacking. His search led nowhere, except to the lament :

> " O weary life !   O weary death !
> O spirit and heart made desolate !
> O damnéd vacillating state ! "

Tennyson was among the first to see the need of loosening " the knots that tangle human creeds." Every sensitive mind of his generation was to be occupied in the attempt to untie these knots while preserving the creed. To loose them, however, required not only humble patience, but also a fearless critical examination of life, which Tennyson refused.

He thought to cut them merely by the exercise of a vague and lofty tolerance. In this he failed, but he did not then renew the struggle with added concentration. Rather he spent his life in culling the flowers of Nature and of fancy, and embroidering with moral sentiments some of the facts concerning the physical universe which scientists had in process of annotation.

Strangely enough many of his contemporaries, who would not compromise either with faith or with doubt, and so could not escape so considerably as he this ordeal of faith come to judgment, were to credit him with an integrity in facing and even solving the problem such as he never possessed. Yet we believe that at this time he was more honest in self-criticism than ever again, that he even scorned himself in his sincerer moments for cherishing the dream that poets are born in a " Golden Clime " above the dust of the earth, or that there is any virtue in an exclusiveness which forbids association with a gross world.

And in a poem entitled " The Character " he drew, we can fancy, as in a glass darkly, the weaker side of his own nature, which none but he detected, speaking of one who " most delicately hour by hour canvass'd human mysteries, and trod on silk," of one who

" Stood aloof from other minds
In impotence of fancied power."

In his heart of hearts he realised that he was not one of those powerful spirits who, by the divine ardour of genius, pierce to the core of things and fashion it anew ; yet in one other poem in this year he attacked boldly the obscured front of life, the mystery which for him was to remain insoluble. " The Mystic " is not a great poem technically, and he erased it therefore from his later works ; perhaps, however, the hours of querulous agitation it embodies are more to be valued, in the ultimate judgment of truth, than a lifetime of sentimental pleasure or serene melancholy. It images a struggle for the assurance of belief in God, a facing of the possibility of that individual extinction at which so tenacious an egoist as he could only shudder. The struggle is scarcely victorious; he ends much as he began, with the pathetic wish fathering a quaking hope. But he came nearer, we believe, in this poem to an absolute standpoint than ever he had the courage to do again, even though he heard, with a cold prescience of corruption,

> "Time flowing in the middle of the night,
> And all things creeping to a day of doom."

The poems thus pondered, together with his musical variations on the theme of ladies' names, were issued in the following year under the title " Poems, chiefly Lyrical," and were greeted by the Apostles and by Cambridge generally with a chorus of praise. Sir John Bowring, in the *Westminster*, and Leigh Hunt, in the *Tatler*, both wrote favourably of the volume and hopefully of the poet's future. But as an example of praise, enthusiastic to the point of folly, Arthur Hallam's review in the *Englishman's Magazine* can seldom have been bettered. Not content with discovering one excellency, he enumerated five:

" First, his luxuriance of imagination, and at the same time his control over it. Secondly, his power of embodying himself in ideal characters, or rather moods of character, with such accuracy of adjustment that the circumstances of the narrative seem to have a natural correspondence with the predominant feeling and, as it were, to be evolved from it by assimilative force. Thirdly, his vivid, picturesque delineation of objects, and the peculiar skill with which he holds all of them fused, to borrow a metaphor from science, in

a medium of strong emotion. Fourthly, the variety
of his lyrical measures and the exquisite modulation
of harmonious words and cadences to the swell and
fall of the feelings expressed. Fifthly, the elevated
habits of thought implied in these compositions, and
imparting a mellow soberness of tone, more impressive
to our minds than if the author had drawn up a set
of opinions in verse, and sought to instruct the understanding rather than to communicate the love of
beauty to the heart."

Few authors could survive the burden of such
praise, so lavish, so careless of temporisation. Nemesis
lurked at hand and decisively she struck. Professor
Wilson, writing under the pseudonym of " Christopher
North," was the last of the line of Dryden and Johnson,
of the virile critical minds of the eighteenth century,
with their honest, if limited, common sense and hatred
of cant, even as Leigh Hunt was the father of tender
efflorescent Victorianism. The insight with which
North detected flabbiness or affectation in a writer
was often as remarkable as his belabouring of it was
crude. It is the brutality, and not the truth, of his
criticism of Keats that has been called in question.
He cherished a sure and healthy detestation of exoti-
cism or weakly self-indulgence in literature, which he
only spoiled by over-statement. Soon after the
publication of the poems he had written of Tennyson
in *Blackwood:* " He has a fine ear for melody, and
harmony too, and rare and rich glimpses of imagination ; he has genius. I admire Alfred, and hope, nay
trust, that one day he will prove himself a poet. If
he do not, then I am no prophet." The hyperbole,
however, of Arthur Hallam's article seems to have
incited him to further criticism, and subsequently he
wrote :

" One of the saddest misfortunes that can befall a

young poet is to be the Pet of a Coterie ; and the very saddest of all, if in Cockneydom. Such has been the unlucky lot of Alfred Tennyson. He has been elevated to the throne of Little Britain. . . . The besetting sin of all periodical criticism, and nowadays there is no other, is boundless extravagance of praise ; but none splash it on like the trowel-men who have been bedaubing Mr. Tennyson. The worst of it is that they make the Bespattered not only feel, but look, ridiculous ; he seems as absurd as an Image in a tea-garden bedizened with faded and fantastic garlands. . . . The essay (Hallam's) ' On the Genius of Alfred Tennyson,' awoke a general guffaw. . . . But we must see justice done to the ingenious lad, and save him from his worst enemies, his friends. Were we not afraid that our style might be thought to wax too figurative, we should say that Alfred is a promising plant ; and that the day may come when, beneath sun and shower, his genius may grow up and expand into a stately tree. . . . But that day will never come if he hearken not to our advice, and, as far as his own nature will permit, regulate by it the movements of his genius. *At present he has small power over the common feelings and thoughts of men. His feebleness is distressing at all times when he makes an appeal to their ordinary sympathies. And the reason is, that he fears to look such sympathies boldly in the face.*"

There follows some detailed and rather clumsy raillery levelled at the preciosity of the weaker poems, and some judicious praise of the finer, concluding with the sentence : " We feel assured that we have done no more than justice to his fine faculties—and that the millions who delight in Maga will, with one voice, confirm our judgment—that Alfred Tennyson is a poet."

It was a just, sometimes ribald, but in the main

salutary piece of criticism, one, too, which any poet unblinded by egotism might have been content to have evoked. Praise there was in plenty, and the blame was of a breezy, bluff sincerity, laughter-giving and clean. But in Tennyson and his friends it created consternation. Words failed them to express their disgust at its violence, falsehood, and lack of nice feeling. For they were attacked even more directly than he, and thus in clinging the more loyally and reverently to him, they preserved also their own self-respect, so rudely assailed.

Tennyson himself shrank from the thought of it as from a grievous blow; his sensibility was sorely wounded, but beyond that he realised that he had been found out. An honest man had learnt the secret which was hid from his friends. In public he accepted his friends' sympathy and echoed their scorn of the article, but secretly he knew that the man was right, and swore never to republish any of the condemned poems. He kept his oath.

Yet the effect of North's criticism was not to rouse Tennyson to action, but only to make him more secretive. He must learn, he realised, to conceal his limited sympathies more effectively by a wider range of subject and a greater mastery of style. A healthy breeze had blown in upon him from the unceremonious world, bidding him out into the wide earth to take his chance with others. But he turned away from it, to hide in the retreat of a sensitive pleasure-seeking temperament, barricaded from rude gusts by adoring friends, nor ever exposed to the realities of poverty and neglect. With ordinary sympathies they were no more at ease than he. The passions were their bane; they sought the idyllic in their terror of the vulgar, the moral in their fear of the true. With beautiful sentiments, however, they were all familiar, and to cultivate these, it seemed to Tennyson, was, at any rate, a fair alternative to looking the common feelings and thoughts of men boldly in the face. In truth he was too uncommon a type to hope to do the latter with success, and so Christopher North's advice, the last expostulation, as we see it, of honest, open-minded manhood before the nineteenth century closed its doors on reality, fell on barren ground.

Tennyson and his company of Apostles retired to their dainty garden of Hesperidean fancy to worship graven images and the featureless wraith of "progress." And thither many followed them in meek submission for fifty years.

4

In the spring of 1830, when Arthur Hallam was staying with the Tennysons at Somersby Rectory, a family named Sellwood drove over from Horncastle to call. One of the daughters, Emily, took a walk with Hallam in the Fairy Wood, and at a turn of the path the two of them came upon Tennyson. The girl was just seventeen, graceful and slender, and in her simple grey dress seemed to him to move like a sun-shaft across the woodland rides, so that, emboldened by the felicity of his impression, he asked whether she was a Dryad or an Oread, that wandered there. For in her gentle delicacy she appeared rather sister to one of the remote maidens of his fancy than a human being real and provocative. Twenty years were to pass before he exchanged this illusive picture for the more homely treasure of a wife.

During the summer of the same year, Tennyson, inspired by Hallam, embarked on the one romantic adventure of his life. The revolution which Torrijos had headed against the tyranny of Ferdinand of Spain, and which, after issuing its brief challenge to a sovereign inquisition, was destined to splutter out in sparks of glory, was then in progress. Its leader was a rugged man, no mean adventurer scheming for paltry gain, but an idealist, ardent and accomplished, enthusiastic for freedom's sake, and careless of peril; one, too, who had lived hard and suffered for his dreams. A star of chivalry defying the vapours of oppression he seemed to more than one generous youth in England. To Sterling, the father of the Apostles, and to many of its members, this struggle by a few gallant Spaniards, " stately, tragic," threadbare figures, against hopeless odds, made a strong appeal. That two Apostles could intervene with profit in the broils of a foreign nation was in truth a fantastic notion—yet Hallam and Tennyson set forth to their relief with a small sum of money and letters written in invisible ink. The game of conspiracy proved a not unpleasant one to play, and if the rugged rebels fighting for life in strait places gained little by so theatrical an act of sympathy, the two Englishmen ran no serious risks from what Hallam described as " the wild bustling time they had of it." Indeed, Tennyson did not neglect his opportunities, but in the valley of Cauteretz possessed his memory of some scenic effects, which later, in " Œnone " and elsewhere, he turned to good poetical use. By that time, however, the true conspirators had paid an abrupt penalty for their idealism on the Esplanade of Malaga !

Tennyson returned to England refreshed in body and mind. His residence at Cambridge was now soon to be cut short, as his father's failing health called him home early in the following year. He left Cambridge without either a regret or a degree, dancing with his friends a farewell quadrille in his rooms, before driving away down Trumpington Street in the chilly dark of a

February evening. He took away with him little learning, but many dreams and memories to cheer dark days to come. " How many puns have we made together ! how many walks have we taken arm-in-arm in the dark streets of the old University and on the Trumpington Road ? and how you used to scepticise till we both ran away ! " So he wrote to his friend Tennant in the days of his sorrow, and such recollections are the chief, and often the only, treasure carried away from Cambridge by the sensitive undergraduate, exiled from that haunt of ardent friendship and wizened pedantry in a labouring world. The University had contributed little to his development. His temperament, moody, indolent and absorptive, was the fruit of Somersby, and so it remained. Something spacious and symmetrical in the architecture of Cambridge doubtless helped to chasten by its unconscious influence his luxuriousness, and to confirm his sense of form, while " The Apostles " quickened and emphasised the deepening seriousness of early manhood. But if he thought more about problems of the day, the electoral franchise, reform, or religious doubt, for example, this speculation did not affect his feeling for life, which remained, therefore, fundamentally the same as when he drove across the marsh to Mablethorpe.

This failure to purge and widen his conception of life by knowledge and thought as they came to him, was to remain typical of his whole career. Opinions crowded on him, and he would choose what seemed to him the wisest, but rather as a connoisseur than as a man who wished to think out life for himself, to apprehend by his own passionate effort the meaning of life and of death. And so, although his knowledge of the world and of varying schools of thought increased, he remained essentially the poet of delicate, sometimes mystical sensuousness, expending his emotions on the decorative music of words, or on the external adornment or illustration of opinions, which in his verses continued to be opinions, and were rarely transmuted by conquering emotion into convictions. In brief, his emotions and his thoughts were never reconciled in passionate imagination, because the former were too indolent and the latter too superficial.

Safe once more in Somersby, he felt poetically at home. Here for the moment there was nothing to accuse the abstraction of his mood or shatter the dream of life he cherished. Scarcely a month, however, after his return, his father was found dead in his study chair. The dread and lofty countenance of death, no less than the real poignancy of his loss, made deep impression on Tennyson. He hated the " strong troubles " of life and its " bitter fancies," and at this time, as one of his poems shows, he was not averse from playing with the idea of death as being a kind narcotic. Within a week of his father's death he slept in the dead man's bed, " earnestly desiring to see the ghost, but no ghost came." For death is as uncommunicative to sentimentalists as is life.

Fortunately the Tennyson family was able to continue in residence at the Rectory until 1837, and here, in the retreat of the countryside, the poet found time for leisurely elaborating his dreams, refining his fancies, or constructing his idylls, now going on a brief visit to a friend or to his old counsellor the sea at Mablethorpe, and now entertaining, with simple affectionate hospitality, one or other of his Cambridge associates. Hither particularly often came Hallam, long attached, and now betrothed to Tennyson's sister Emily, dark-eyed and Italian-featured, charming all to gladness and irresponsibility by his " bright,

angelic spirit and his gentle, chivalrous manner."
Here in the early summer mornings he and Tennyson
would wander talking and musing together about the
lawn, shadowed with elm and sycamore, and after a
studious hour or two, would go off for a long tramp
over the wold by the white road that climbs northward
to Tetford, or along the eastern ridge to Alford ; or,
if the day were hot, they would stroll idly to the
picturesque little village of Bag-Enderby near at hand,
or follow the Somersby brook to Stockworth Mill.

Yet even in such familiar surroundings, amid
friends and relations, Tennyson seemed often to be
lost to their concerns and entangled in the meshes of
his dreams ; so that they accepted him quite unques-
tionably as " a mysterious being, seemingly lifted high
above mortals, and having a power of intercourse with
the spirit-world not granted to others." " O my
beloved," his sister Mary wrote to a friend, " what
creatures men are ! My brothers are the exception to
this general rule ! " and again, " Alfred is one of the
noblest of his kind." So unique a reputation, gratifying as it was, must at times have proved exceedingly
difficult to sustain !

Towards his mother he was always tender and
considerate, deferring in his judgments and opinions
to her, and often to be found reading poetry to her
in her room. The sisters were very musical, and on
many evenings as he sat smoking in his attic den,
as was his wont after supper, the sound of singing and
harp playing must have floated up to him, mingled
with the music of laughing voices. He himself cared
chiefly, in music, for the lucid elegance of Scarlatti
and Corelli, with their complicated transparency of
themes, which suggested to him very cultivated
" echoes of winds and waves." The dark and passionate introspection of Beethoven, the intellectual

concentration of Bach, did not so much appeal to him, but he loved Mozart's affectionate joyousness and wayward sentiment ; many national airs and ballads, too, which he himself would finger out on the flute.

Sometimes the music would draw him down from his attic, and he would sit and smoke with senses soothed to dreamy satisfaction in that circle of loving-kindness ; sometimes the lingering twilight would hold them entranced upon the lawn watching the shadows deepen in the trees, until Hallam could no longer read the " Tuscan Poets " and the stars caused tongues to be silent. A light mist trailed along the garden edge, an emanation of the murmuring brook, bats flitted through the sycamores, and the scent of lilies and roses floated across to them from the darkening flower border. Already the golden afternoon, with its hours of talk and laughter, had become a memory, breathing its benediction over all, while they shared the unspoken, unformulated longing that such days as these should stay for ever, safe withdrawn from the fever and the rout of life.

And then the moon would rise red over the wolds, and Emily would fetch her harp and fling " a ballad to the brightening moon." Under the soft enchantment of the hour the singer was lost in the voice, and the voice in the folds of the summer night. Little wonder was there that Hallam sat enraptured. As the moon brightened tongues once more were loosened ; the girls flitted off to bed and " in the house light after light went out." But still the men sat talking low and spasmodically of the beauty and wonder and sweetness of life, till, startled by a shiver of grey in the sky, they knew the dawn at hand and sallied forth, sleepy-eyed, to hail the sunrise from the hill, " broadening into boundless day."

These indeed were days such as life can give but once, days when youth, with all its clean and generous impulse, its will to love, its surprised affection and delight, its hunger for pure undying beauty and for romance the golden-tongued, was set in a paradise as yet unimperilled by pain or grief.

Ardent, sensitive natures, of an instinctive nobility, they gathered together here for a moment in the morning of their days; they shared a fellowship of rare emotion, of pleasures courteous and refined. But beyond the garden of Somersby the rude world went upon its way, spurning fine sentiment and crushing the delicate under its foot. For one of them this was but a day's sunny pause before the night of death; for all it was to be a time of pure gladness never regained. Later in life Tennyson knew many perfect hours, but none approached these summer days and nights in vivid peace and consolation of utter happiness. Yet their serenity only made more terribly poignant the hunger that was to haunt the coming years, the cry of a bereft spirit " for the touch of a vanished hand, and the sound of a voice that is still."

5

These three years of quiet study and occasional diversion proved very propitious to the culture of poetry. Despite Christopher North's raillery, the lyrical poems already published had served to make Tennyson the centre of a small but intent group of admiring friends, reaching even beyond the boundaries of Cambridge, while the poems which he circulated in manuscript brought back to his retreat from the outer world such rhapsodies of praise as would have heartened the most diffident of writers. Hallam wrote, for example, " Thanks for your batch of MSS.

The lines to J. S. are perfect. . . . ' The Old Year ' is excellent. . . . Moxon is in ecstasies with the ' May Queen.' " Or again, " The ballad of ' The Sisters ' was very popular at Cambridge. Indeed it is very perfect. . . . All were anxious for the ' Palace of Art,' and fierce with me for not bringing more." Charles Merivale wrote in the same spirit to Thompson that " a daily divan continued to sit throughout the term," and that " the ' Palace of Art ' was read successively to each man as he came up from the vacation." Hallam was of opinion that " The Dream of Fair Women " should be published immediately, as certain to establish everywhere the poet's reputation. Fanny Kemble, whom Tennyson met in London, divided an engaging enthusiasm between " the grandest head of any man, whom she has clapt eyes on " and the poems which made her sister " rave at intervals in the most Siddonian tone." Contributions, too, were solicited by the editors of various periodicals, and to *The Gem* Tennyson sent three short poems, of which one was an attenuated sigh of his seventeenth year, with its touching refrain, " Oh sad No More ! Oh sweet No More ! Oh strange No More ! "

It was significant of Tennyson throughout life that he could publish among poems newly written others dating from years back, without any contrast between the two being obvious. Most authors have outgrown the verse of their seventeenth year at twenty, and of their twentieth year at thirty. With him no such dynamic process was ever noticeable ; some poems in his last volume might well have appeared in his first. He never climbed Parnassus, striving year by year to approach the summit. Rather he sat musingly on one of its pleasant middle ridges where destiny and temperament had planted him. Thus at twenty-three he had not outgrown the musical morbidity of his

seventeenth year. Life still disposed him towards
a pleasing melancholy.

The unsettled condition of the country, the righteous
cry of the poor and exploited for reform, depressed
him superficially from time to time. Yet how was
he, who hated all sordid things, loving the elegant,
chaste and precious, whose whole aim was, in fact,
to escape at any cost from ugliness into beauty, how
was he to deal even mentally with such problems of
squalor, starvation and sweated labour as in town and
country alike started up for solution ? He felt himself
quite inadequate even to suggest a practical remedy
for such evils, and yet they cast upon his serenity the
shadow of pensive sorrow. He could proclaim that
they were wrong, he could pray for bettered conditions.
But he was no Hood. The voices of the poor and the
down-trodden did not tear at his heart. Such things
were, indeed, stains upon the shield of chivalry he bore.
And when Hallam came down from Cambridge and
lived for a time in his father's house in Wimpole Street,
studying law, the two would perhaps discuss in
Hallam's untidy room at the top of the house this
problem of the poorer classes, this blot on the fair
scutcheon of life, which did, in fact, dishonour even a
perfect culture, and must trouble a virtuous conscience.
Hallam would urge, above all, an honest examination
of things as they were ; he would beg his friend not to
flee the Real in his love of the Ideal, but to try
to reconcile the two ; and he would argue that
" where the ideas of time and sorrow are not, and sway
not the soul with power, there is no true knowledge in
Poetry or Philosophy."

Tennyson would hasten to agree, and yet deep
down his ideals of art and of life remained stub-
bornly irreconcileable. Art ideally, he felt, was an
exquisite palace, into which realism had no right to

enter, catering rather in every way for the lordly indulgence of the senses. Life, on the other hand, was like a moral parlour where a good man discussed his duties to his less fortunate brethren, or it was an ill-organised edifice, in which the misery of the many compelled the favoured few to justify their privileged position by high philosophical and moral arguments, and a serious pursuit of virtue. As the poet of what he imperfectly considered the ideal, he discovered for himself an exquisite pleasure. He became a voice rather than a man—a phantom melting, romantic or a little wistful, dreaming of chivalry by far-off shores and haunted forests, daring moated granges, or turning to the countryside to court with perfect elegance a miller's or a gardener's pretty daughter, both queens "of curds and cream." It was a sumptuous experience to write such poetry as this ; and only in such moods, when the charm of words and of rhythm put his mind to sleep and he floated on a stream of delicate sensation, as did his Lady of Shalott down the winding river to Camelot, was he really at ease, the master of his craft and

> " likest Gods, who have attain'd
> Rest in a happy place and quiet seats
> Above the thunder, with undying bliss
> In knowledge of their own supremacy."

Yet his friends, and Hallam in particular, still blind to this overpowering indolence that obsessed him, would urge on him the necessity of finding truth " that bears relation to the mind," or unconsciously taunt his tender artificiality with the thrust, " Fare thee well, old trump ; poems are good things, but flesh and blood is better." They would not allow his conscience to slumber, and outwardly at least he was forced to respond, to claim that it was his desire " to war with

falsehood to the knife," even if he added the protective
rider, " And not to lose the good of life."

Only he knew how hard a task it was for such a
nature as his " to pluck resolve." To Hallam disinterested mental effort was a joy, to him it was a labour
almost unendurable. Hallam seems to have had
glimmerings of the truth. It is a significant fact,
which has generally escaped notice, that he abandoned
the idea of publicly collaborating with his friend in a
volume of verse, as did Wordsworth and Coleridge,
only after such a volume had actually been put into
type. A copy of it exists to-day to attest the reality of
this withdrawal, and it is questionable whether the
modesty of one conscious of inferior powers was the
only motive for it. In a letter to a friend discussing
the poem " Mariana in the South," he wrote : " an
artist, as Alfred is wont to say, ought to be lord of the
five senses, but if he lacks the inward sense which
reveals to him what is inward in the heart, he has left
out the part of Hamlet in the play." At another
time, outlining the differences of their two natures,
he was more apologetic. " What with you," he
wrote, " is universal and all-powerful, absorbing your
whole existence, communicating to you that energy
which is so glorious, in me is checked and counteracted
by many other impulses, tending to deaden the influence of the senses, I mean those employed in the
processes of imagination, viz., sight and hearing.
You say pathetically : ' Alas for me ! I have more of
the Beautiful than the Good !' Remember to your
comfort that God has given you to see the difference.
Many a poet has gone on.blindly in his artist pride."

Hallam's uncritical admiration led him to exaggerate
the energy and vivacity of his friend's genius no less
than his imaginative power, but his diagnosis of
sensuous absorption was correct. The pity was that

he urged on Tennyson not artistic humility, a widening and deepening of human sympathy, a more
manly pursuit of the beautiful, but rather the cultivating of a moralistic intention.   And the poetry
which Tennyson was composing at this time, which
was published in the following year, proves that
he laid his friend's advice to heart.   It was a
significant trait in him that, proud and exclusive
though he was in taste and temperament, he was
extraordinarily humble in his acceptance of advice,
even from hostile critics, whether technical or sententious.   It revealed a diffidence and self-distrust
common in men of talent, but opposed to the innate
spirit of genius.

The hidden struggle, therefore, between the two
sides of his nature—the pleasure-loving and the duty-
seeking—which the spirit of the Apostles had called
into being, became the more intense during these years
of silent self-examination at Somersby, when Hallam's
character dominated his mind and challenged his
uneasy conscience.   Yet if it led him to chasten
the luxuriance of his style and to arraign continually
what he considered his weaker self in second-rate
stanzas, it did not, in truth, quicken his imagination
to a more vital comprehension of life.   The change
was not in a deepening and purging of emotion by
passionate thought, but only in an increase of moral
and sentimental seriousness.   His emotion expended
itself less on irrelevant adornment and more on the
decoration of moral maxims or religious disputations.
His style, therefore, improved, but his matter, so
far as we estimate its poetical expressiveness, actually
deteriorated.   What he had done well before, his
exact transcripts of Nature, his capture in words of
relaxed moods, he did better now.   In this kind
"The Lady of Shalott," "The Palace of Art," "The

Lotos Eaters," "A Dream of Fair Women," are often magical, word melting into word, line sliding into line, sound and cadence near unimpeachable. He had made sultry summer his own, with her languid noon, her fainting scents and stifled quietude. In the dainty cultivated lyric, too, he was a proved performer. But in the only province about which a poet should cherish a deep concern he had made no advance whatever. He was no nearer reality than before, and he knew it; by varied but vain effort he tried to escape the sweet shadows which haunted and allured him, but of which he grew at times to be " half-sick."

At one time it had been the religious problem of faith and scepticism which troubled him most. He had now put that unsolved behind him, retaining for himself the sentimental consolations of orthodoxy and preaching vaguely the liberal doctrines both of progress and of fidelity to truth. But now the personal artistic problem had only become more acute. Though it was the shock of a poignant sorrow still to come that later dictated the words, he saw even then in Hallam and others of his friends

> " men, thro' novel spheres of thought
> Still moving after truth long sought,"

and he longed to go with them,

> " not rotting like a weed,
> But having sown some generous seed,
> Fruitful of further thought and deed,
>
> To pass, when Life her light withdraws,
> Not void of righteous self-applause,
> Nor in a merely selfish cause—
>
> In some good cause, not in mine own,
> To perish, wept for, honour'd, known,
> And like a warrior overthrown : "

His higher impulse, we must admit, was not here a disinterested desire for truth, not in any sense a selfless creative passion. Of that he was incapable. He wished rather to prove himself, as a poet, the somewhat theatrical benefactor of mankind, and earn by his knightly prowess in the field of instructive virtue the gratitude of a bettered world. Yet even this imperfect revolt from vague sensationalism to vague philanthropy indicated progress, if he could have continued in it. That, however, was to prove beyond his powers, as circumstances decreed. The palling of pleasure, the fading of his earliest dreams, was to suggest to him not an assault on truth to discover delights more lasting, but a surrender to death. He played pleasantly with the idea of suicide, because

> " I toil beneath the curse,
> And, knowing not the universe,
> I fear to slide from bad to worse."

He feared, in fact, the risks and the sacrifice of ease inevitable to an honest attempt to know the universe. Though of some pleasure he sickened, he was at heart too wedded to it to dare the unknown on the chance of distant victory :

> " He knows a baseness in his blood
> At such strange war with something good,
> He may not do the thing he would."

And so, instead of learning bravely at life's hands and letting his experiences mould his verse because they must, he eased his conscience, when it cried too loudly against the sloth of lotos eaters, by poetising the principles of progress and political science, versifying his own timid introspection, and giving lyrical advice to Lady Clara Vere de Vere on proper conduct towards her tenantry and the poor of her parish.

The revolt, however, of conscience against hedonism took other directions than didactic verse. Sometimes he would lash himself despairingly into passion, as in " Fatima " ; but the note was thin and forced. Love that was never a pure fire to him he could only simulate as an angry fever, or affect its manner in such a ballad echo as " The Sisters." But the rustic peace of Somersby suggested to him another way of escape from that palace of art where, as he reasonably conjectured, Dante " somewhat grimly smiled." " Make me a cottage in the vale, where I may mourn and pray." The simple sentiments of country life, the loves and hates and sorrows of the people, were about him on every side. He could forget himself and the gilded munificence of his dreams in telling, more mellifluously and with a lighter touch than Wordsworth, stories of rural kindliness and pathos. He would paint these labouring folk, not in their rather depressing work-a-day garb, with the loam upon their hands, but as actors in Pan's flowery festival, or in gracious May day revelries ; in short, as beings, like himself, attuned to the beauty and pity of earth. These idyllic narratives, with their fresh pastoral scenery and ingenuous sentiment, relieved and enlivened his senses when they experienced satiety. And when the two voices of hope and despondency within him were in bitter conflict, as frequently they were, the sound of " the sweet church bells " and the sight of a guileless family dressed in their Sunday clothes and walking, " with measured footfall firm and mild," to service was enough to win the day for hope.

His familiarity with classical literature suggested another medium sufficiently removed from the realities of life for his technical powers to develop. Into the retelling of classical myths he could insinuate his own troubles no less than his own mastery of beautiful Virgilian language. So on the lips of Œnone he put the words of his own dilemma at this time, " And I am all aweary of my life," while Pallas could by her sculptured dignity lend the charm of poetry to earnest preaching, declaiming :

> " Self-reverence, self-knowledge, self-control,
>   These three alone lead life to sovereign power."

Lastly, the possibilities of gentle elegy could not fail to present themselves to one so often under the influence of " mild-minded melancholy " and already so tantalised by the mystery of death. The autumnal in Nature, the falling leaf and the fading colour, had before this inspired many pictorial verses, but now more and more he tended to make mournful Nature voice his own uneasy resignation as he scanned the perishable, his own sense of the vanity of fair things and his own wish for solace in the face of decay. In his lines of sympathy to Spedding on the loss of his brother he discovered that vein of soothing argumentative regret for which fate was even then preparing a grievous stimulus.

6

These, then, were the moods, as we gather from his verse, through which Tennyson was passing in the haven of Somersby or on the high seas of Hallam's conversation. " Alfred," Spedding wrote, " continued writing like a crocodile, sideways and onwards," and the vacillation, we fancy, was more obvious than the advance.

In the summer of 1832 Hallam and he went for a tour on the Rhine, and found Cologne " a paradise of painted glass," and the Gothic grandeur of the cathedral very impressive. Tennyson was in raptures with it, but could not bring himself quite to share Hallam's enthusiasm for mellow old German pictures, preferring the more regal masterpieces of Titian or Raffaelle. Above Bonn they " took a luxurious climb up the Drachenfels," and " ate cherries under the old castle wall at the top of the crag." It proved to Tennyson a very gratifying mediæval experience, relieved of all the inconveniences of mediæval life. On his return he settled down once more to the quiet round of Somersby. Proofs of the new volume of verse were seen through the press, and late in 1832 made their appearance, under the simple title of " Poems...1833."

Their reception was by no means inauspicious. Rogers, now an old man, welcomed Tennyson openly as the most promising genius of the time, and the Cambridge Union debated the question whether he or Milton was the greater poet. The volume found many admirers, who were quick to express their enthusiasm in public and in private; and even if professional critics had the effrontery here and there to be critical, they honoured the book with elaborate attention. But, as in the reception of the other volume, there was one article which nullified for Tennyson every word of praise voiced, however fervently, elsewhere. So did it sour his disposition that he half resolved to live in Jersey, the South of France, or Italy, beyond the boundaries of an England so unsympathetic to his genius that it could nourish one reviewer brutally hostile to his poetry. For this one article convinced him that Englishmen would never care for his poetry, and had it not been for the intervention of enthusiastic friends, it is not unlikely that he would have ceased altogether to write.

The *Quarterly Review* was, on this occasion, an offender, infamous even beyond *Blackwood* in its imputation of " infantile vanity," because, like

Christopher North, the critic seasoned his judgment with ridicule. Above all things, Tennyson could not bear to be laughed at. Though he could write later, " I dare not tell how high I rate humour, which is generally most fruitful in the highest and most solemn human spirits," it was humour in the grand style, large and impressive, to which he referred. Criticism cutting its comic capers, hunting down affectation with shrewd mockery he professed to scorn, because at heart he feared its searching eyes. He had never, even from childhood days (to his loss !) had to endure in his person a breath of honest ridicule. He had always been accepted seriously and, even reverenced as a prodigy. His dignity had never been assailed ; and yet the heartless *Quarterly* reviewer first quoted the following lines from his volume :

> " O darling room, my heart's delight,
> Dear room, the apple of my sight ;
> With thy two couches, soft and white,
> There is no room so exquisite ;
> No little room so warm and bright,
> Wherein to read, wherein to write."

and, added the note, " we entreat our readers to note how, even in this little trifle, the singular taste and genius of Mr. Tennyson break forth. In such a dear little room a narrow-minded scribbler would have been content with one sofa, and that one he would probably have covered with black mohair or red cloth, or a good striped chintz ; how infinitely more characteristic is white dimity !—'tis, as it were, a type of the purity of the poet's mind."

The gibe was unnecessarily barbed, but it was not without justification. For this cosy little poem, with its *dilettante* upholstery, was not a mere lapse of youth into foolishness ; it revealed more nakedly than elsewhere the relaxed fastidiousness which continually sapped Tennyson's energy, as, for example, in the earlier " Lotos Eaters " :

> " This is lovelier and sweeter,
> Men of Ithaca, this is meeter,
> In the hollow rosy vale to tarry
> Like a dreamy Lotos-eater—a delicious Lotos-eater."

The ambling protestation of the sonnets, too, must have convinced a candid critic of the lack in their author of creative necessity or ruling thought, of, in fact, " the strength of spirit fierce and free," which in one of them he invoked.

Such open ridicule certainly taught Tennyson the wisdom of concealing intellectual emptiness and listless feeling under a more closely woven fabric of style, but the *Quarterly* reviewer laid a finger with rare exactness on his fundamental weakness, while Tennyson himself was glad to profit by the critic's verdict on particular lines and passages in later emendations.   Equally correct were the reviewer's comparison of Tennyson's sickly sensuousness with that of Keats, and his claim that Tennyson's attitude to Nature was false.

Tennyson's sensuousness was not as deep, avid or vulgar as that of the young Keats often was.   It was more decorous and less true.   Yet not only in his voluptuous abandonment, his " resting of weary limbs on beds of asphodel," but also in his sentimental colouring of mediævalism and classical myths, and his overtrailing of life with profuse flowers, he bore an imperfect resemblance to Keats.   But while Keats' sensuousness was vital enough to portend the birth of a powerful, penetrating genius, Tennyson's was too cultured and superficial to promise a like harvest.   The reviewer was correct in stating that he caressed all things too carefully, revelling in the far-fetched and euphemistic, in tasteful adornments,

polished rustic scenes, languid memories, the moral
and the idyllic. And this exclusive artificiality prejudiced his approach both to Nature and to humanity.
He observed the facts of Nature with marvellous
patience and recorded them with lavish exactitude.
The scenery of Provence, which he had studied
closely on a tour, was embodied realistically in
" Mariana in the South," the landscape of the Pyrenees
was borrowed for " Œnone." But he imitated her at
the cost of her inspiration. Painstakingly he possessed
himself of her riches, and she refused him her intimacy ;
greedily he took her body, she withheld her soul. He
even stooped to emotionalise natural science, to
poetise the problematic moon of astrologers, rather
than paint her as he saw and felt her. The poets who
created out of their own moon-worship the myths of
Cynthia or Diana knew better than to borrow from
astrologers, knew that the image of reality would flee
before the knowledge of the telescope.

Only the sea was too vast and volatile to yield to his
scrutiny. She alone of Nature's elements gave him
ungrudgingly her spirit.

His attitude towards human beings was the same.
He studied them as a problem or used them as actors
in an idyll of his own invention ; he did not yield himself to their experience, absorbing their passions, hopes
and fears, and sharing alike in the comedy and tragedy
of life. Instead of voicing the religion of life, he
versified his own religious formulas or pseudo-meta-
physical analyses, or his friends' views of reform, or he
sentimentalised country bumpkins and dairymaids
that they might take their part with refinement in
a love-tale manufactured by himself.

The *Quarterly* reviewer realised with prophetic
insight these elements of affectation from which
Tennyson was never to escape. And considering the

number of weak lines, later amended, which even such a poem as the " Lotos Eaters," as it appeared in this issue, contained, both his criticism and his appreciation were just. Only blind loyalty and the felicity of particular lines could have persuaded Tennyson's friends that, for example, in " The Palace of Art," not only a great poet, but a great thinker, was expressing himself. Yet so they claimed, failing in their own reforming zeal to see that the limited genius of their friend only truly discovered itself in such a poem as " The Lotos Eaters," where thought scarcely existed amid the suffusion of pleasure. Indeed, all Tennyson's best moments were to prove returns to some such mood of sweet surrender as this, while all his worst signalled an abandonment of pleasure to capture, not truth, but sententious conversation in rhyme, generalised argument and mild speculation, earnest soliloquy and moral interrogation.

The review, however, perhaps because he recognised its basic justice, though asserting publicly that it was without " a spark of genius or a single touch of true humour or good feeling," embittered Tennyson sorely. He recalled a poem entitled " The Lover's Tale," at that time in the press, a narrative of amorous complication much after the manner of Shelley, though lacking the pure passion which informs all Shelley's writing, and withdrew even further behind the veil of an outraged nervous sensibility.

Meanwhile, in England at large, revolution had ceased to be the creed of a few fanatics, and was beginning to find practical, if timid, expression in political reform and religious dissent. With such movements Tennyson professed a general but cautious sympathy, and when the news of the passing of the Reform Bill reached Somersby at dead of night the Tennyson family, to the consternation of a Toryminded rector, braved the dark and rang the church bells with a vigour worthy of the arrival of the Millennium itself. With Hallam, too, Tennyson discussed the tenets of a sect named St. Simonians, whose ideals of Shelleyean socialism and transcendentalism were causing some stir at the time, and making a few converts. In conversation he assumed towards these enthusiasts an air of lofty tolerance, but his private opinion was less gracious. He wrote at this time to his aunt, Mrs. Russell :

" What think you of the state of affairs in Europe ? Burking and cholera have ceased to create much alarm. They are the least evils, but reform and St. Simonism are, and will continue to be, subjects of the highest interest. The future is so dark. . . . Reform (not the measure, but the instigating spirit of reform, which is likely to subsist among the people long after the measure has passed into a law) will bring on the confiscation of Church property, and maybe the downfall of the Church altogether ; but the existence of the sect of the St. Simonists is at once a proof of the immense mass of evil that is extant in the nineteenth century, and a focus which gathers all its rays. . . . But I hope and trust that there are hearts as true and pure as steel in Old England, that will never brook the sight of Baal in the sanctuary and St. Simon in the Church of Christ."

His own religious questioning seems not to have survived the necessity of purifying and bracing his heart to resist the mildly revolutionary inroads of Saint-Simonism. It was better and safer, and, incidentally, demanded less energy for everyone to preserve their

> " faith and trust,
> And solid hope of better things."

Tennyson's zeal for a better world was so little passionate that a faint threat of social upheaval

quickly quenched it. The doctrine of holding to the
solid gains of life, and piously praying that some day
more would be allowed to share them, as reform in
some mystical way begot itself, appealed to him most.
Any other course endangered too much his dignity
and the peace he needed for exercising at their best
his talents.

Yet strangely enough he was not happy. " For
myself," he wrote at this time, " I drag on somewhat
heavily thro' the ruts of life, sometimes moping to
myself like an owl in an ivy-bush, or that one sparrow
which the Hebrew mentioneth as sitting on the house-
top (a passage which used always to make me uncom-
fortable), and sometimes smoking a pipe with a
neighbouring parson and cursing O'Connell for as
double-dyed a rascal as ever was dipped in the Styx
of political villainy."

A curious stranger would possibly have searched
in vain for any obvious ruts to bruise the feet of
Alfred Tennyson at this time—the feet, too, of a
pilgrim of such outstanding physique that one of his
deeds of local prowess had won from a friend the
remark " It is not fair, Alfred, that you should be
Hercules as well as Apollo." Indeed, it would have
been noticed how extraordinarily privileged was the
life he led, praised, petted and revered by family and
friends, consoled by a gentle household in a lovely
countryside, or diverted by visits to and from his
acquaintances. His life seemed one of cultured
austerity, but rarely troubled even by the distant
rumour of the labouring world. Surely he had " fed
on the roses and lain in the lilies of life." The ruts
were of his own fanciful making. Yet we can believe
that they were real enough. He suffered from the
nostalgia that dogs an over-intensive culture. This
solitary meandering melancholy, this moping dislike

of power and enterprise, whether revealed by St.
Simonians or O'Connells, this gloomy unease at any
sign of venturesome idealism, coupled with a " solid "
but passive " hope of better things," was the necessary
consequence of a too guarded and self-centred life.
Over one idling in the house of art, among the
accumulated impressions of a favoured existence,
moods of pessimism were bound to drift, during
which the world of activity seemed coarse and
menacing and even poetry false and vain. He had
" built his soul a lordly pleasure-house, wherein at
ease for aye to dwell," and all was not well. He had
found that to contemplate the world vaguely in
God-like isolation induced a melancholy which not
even the incense of pleasure could alleviate. Nor
had the solution which he had propounded, that

> " Beauty, Good, and Knowledge are three sisters . . .
>   That never can be sunder'd without tears,"

proved effective. Not acquired knowledge, nor good
intentions, nor the beauties of cultivated art seemed
to give him health, for reality was not necessarily in
any one of them. Truth, he knew, could only be
followed up " in the teeth of clench'd antagonisms."
But he drew back fastidiously from so reckless an
assault.

Incidents, however, were not lacking to divert his
thoughts from overbrooding. In March of the year
1833 Tennyson, Mary, and Hallam shared some sight-
seeing in London, visiting the Elgin Marbles, the
Tower, and the Zoological Gardens. Together they
looked through microscopes at " moths' wings, gnats'
heads, and at all the lions and tigers which lie perdus
in a drop of spring water." It was very edifying.
Hallam again visited Somersby a month or so later,
but Tennyson was then away from home.

Late in the following July Hallam wrote as follows :

" I feel to-night what I own has been too uncommon with me of late, a strong desire to write to you. I do own I feel the want of you at some times more than at others ; a sort of yearning for dear old Alfred comes upon me ; and that without any particularly apparent reason. . . . I should like much to hear your adventures, but I daresay it will be difficult to persuade you to write to Vienna, whither I am going on Saturday with tolerable speed."

Hallam's health had recently caused some uneasiness. He had recovered but slowly from an attack of influenza in the spring, and his father, the historian, had planned to take him for a brief holiday from legal study to the Tyrol, Salzburg, and Vienna. Tennyson and Tennant journeyed to London to bid the travellers farewell. They devoted some of the day to a visit to Rogers' gallery of paintings, admiring particularly a superb Titian, and at night they supped with Moxon, the publisher, and Leigh Hunt, when Tennyson was prevailed upon to repeat some " glorious fragments " of " The Gardener's Daughter " with proper effect ; nor did they part till half-past four in the morning.

Hallam wrote enthusiastically from abroad. Never had mountains seemed to him more sublime. He rhapsodised over the picture gallery at Vienna : " The gallery is grand, and I longed for you : two rooms full of Venetian pictures only ; such Giorgiones, Palmas, Bordones, Paul Veroneses ! and oh, Alfred, such Titians ! by Heaven, that man could paint ! I wish you could see his Danaë. Do you just write as perfect a Danaë ! Also there are two fine rooms of Rubens, but I know you are an exclusive, and care little for Rubens, in which you are wrong ; although no doubt Titian's imagination and style are more analogous to your own than those of Rubens or of any other school."

How stimulating was the enthusiasm of such a friend to Tennyson in his sultry moods of depression can only be imagined.

Yet, if we are to believe a few brief lines of verse left by him at this time, Hallam, too, was struggling forward through darkness to a truth at which he could only guess. But his was a brave and buoyant soul, ever battling, as he wrote,

> " Through the impenetrable gloom to fix
> That master light, the secret truth of things,
> Which is the body of the infinite God."

The knowledge that earth harboured so eager and generous a spirit was to Tennyson both a comfort and a challenge. It confirmed his faith in all things good and stimulated, if sometimes in wrong directions, his slumbering activity.

But in Vienna, only one week after this letter was written, life was staging a tragedy which, in itself pitiable, was to stun Tennyson with all the excess of cruelty that unexpectedness could contrive. On September 15th Mr. Hallam, returning from his daily walk, saw his son, as he supposed, asleep upon the couch in his room. He sat down at his desk to work, and then something tense and breathless in the atmosphere struck him. Startled, he turned and looked at his son, leapt up, and touched him. In a moment a ghastly realisation broke upon him. The silence was not of sleep, but of death.

Two weeks later, as an unsuspecting Tennyson was seated at dinner, his sister returned from a dancing lesson at Spilsby with a letter bearing the postmark of Clevedon. It was from Henry Elton, Hallam's uncle, and opening it, he read the words : " At the desire of a most afflicted family I write to you because they are unequal from the grief into which they have fallen to do it themselves. Your friend, sir, and my

much-loved nephew, Arthur Hallam, is no more."
He read no further, but rose with tears blinding his
eyes and left the table.   Later Emily was summoned to
him, and in broken words he told her the terrible news.

His whole being reeled before the blow.   It was
incredible that so keen and sparkling an intellect, so
young and pure a heart, should thus in a moment be
annihilated.   His life and faith were wrapped up in
Hallam, the memory on which he loved to draw, the
hope by which he dared to venture forward.   " God's
finger touched him and he slept " ;   in some such
words, perhaps, he framed his friend's death to himself
when the first shock had passed and his dazed senses
had recovered a whisper of articulation.   Yet could
God act so wantonly ?   Was it not more like devil's
work to choose for sacrifice, out of a crowded world,
just him who was " as near perfection as a mortal can
be " ?   Anguish launched strange arguments upon
the deeps of his desolation.

Emily was ill for many months, struck down in
body and soul, and eventually returning to a clouded
life the shadow of herself.   On Tennyson there settled
at first a grey, all-pervading despair ; for he had lost
not only the voice he loved, the hand he once would
clasp, the eager, sensitive face, quick-smiling, now
pensive, now radiant.   Of that, it is true, he could
only think at first, as Emily did ; but when Hallam,
in the kindness of time, had become for her a proud
and healing memory, treasured safe in death's good
keeping from change or decay, the knowledge of a
subtler, more irremediable loss than that which
centred upon the physical came to oppress her brother
and inhibit his powers.   For with Hallam had perished
the voice of his conscience, the spur to a more virile
imagination, the inspiration which might have enabled
him to triumph over his weaker nature in the end.

He was left alone to seek with pathetic loyalty that upward path to which Hallam had pointed him. For twenty years he was to lament the unreason of fate, to puzzle over the meaning of death, and try to recall the onward spirit of his friend, that " noble being full of clearest insight."

And then the flame was to die down and smoulder impressively in the ashes.

PART II
APPLICATION

APPLICATION

I

ENGLISH poetry in 1830 had sunk to a prosaic level. Both the high idealism and the violent sentimentalism of the romantic poets had failed. Keats, Byron and Shelley were dead; Scott had deserted poetry, Moore had plucked all the strings of his gilded lyre, Wordsworth was moralising, Coleridge lay a derelict at Highgate, Crabbe had but two years to live. The educated public mind was tired of prodigies and revolutions, of men who shot at the moon and slipped in the mire, of passion and all its pains. They had had enough of poetry battling in the open seas, and would stay henceforth in harbour. The future that dimly they promised themselves was a life of industry relieved by moments of pleasure and edification; their fathers had lived through a stormy period of ecstatic adventure and troubled melancholy. Poetry should no longer seek to free men, but to entertain and sanctify their leisure; science and commercialism were to occupy their business hours. Thus did the young Victorian age, in its revolt from license, sketch a programme of orderly purpose. The new wine of the century, which had gone to young heads, was to be discreetly watered. The idyllic spirit of Wordsworth, the dramatic of Byron, the luxurious of Keats, the transcendental of Shelley, all tempered to comply with the decent regulations of society, were to be

mixed together to form a poetical beverage very
gratifying alike to religious, sensuous and romantic
tastes.

For the moment, however, all was dullness. Southey
still beamed, a faint luminary in a world of prose ;
upon Crabbe, Milman, Rogers, Campbell and Bowles
a dejected silence had settled. Mrs. Hemans had yet
five years before her, and Mrs. Norton was considered
" likely to attain an elevated place in poetry." A
poem entitled " Pauline," by a young man named
Robert Browning, when it appeared three years later,
was neither welcomed as a masterpiece nor remarked
as a portent.

Nor is this to be wondered at when we remember the
general outlook of the day. A prominent reviewer,
writing in 1831, said, " We regard poetry not as our
daily mental food, but as a sweet and costly fruit of
which, though we derive from it greater pleasure, we
partake more sparingly and less often than of the
homely prose which contributes the staple aliment of
our minds."

Again, " The public taste seems also to have decided
that a poem should not be long. The pleasurable
excitement which ought to arise from the perusal of
poetry is, like that produced by music or painting,
necessarily of short duration."

The times, in brief, were drab ; and one part of the
public looked to poets to relieve their *ennui* with
tasteful confectionery. But there were others more
serious-minded, who watched with reverence and
anxiety the dominion man was beginning to assert over
the elements, the new strides of commerce and com-
munication, the wonder of machinery, with all it
seemed to imply of enlarged power and richer opportunities, the advance of science, which as yet in the
general mind tended all to the glory of God, and not,

as but a few years later, to the very grave discredit of the devil.

These were topics to which many minds in a vague way responded. And although one writer at least had the wisdom to conjecture that " The star of the engineer must be on the decline before that of the poet can culminate again," yet, so far as the great majority of men were concerned, a popular welcome awaited the poet who could assimilate the mechanical temperament of his age to his genius.

Tennyson's genius was pictorial, musical and fanciful. It was neither creative nor imaginative. Far more than has been generally recognised it was, in early years at least, imitative. Byron's erotic melodrama without his virile energy, Wordsworth's pastoral tone without his profound and pene-trating humanity, Coleridge's mysticism without his supernatural vision, Shelley's aerial music without his idealism, Keats's luxury without his intellect—all these voices can be traced in one or other of the poems published in Tennyson's first two volumes. Bulwer Lytton's satirical lines, fifteen years later, contained a modicum of truth. He wrote :

> " Of borrowed notes, the mock-bird's modish tune,
> The jingling medley of purloined conceits,
> Out-babying Wordsworth and out-glittering Keats ;
> Where all the airs of patchwork pastoral chime
> To drown the ears in Tennysonian rhyme ! "

and later spoke of the poet as chanting

> " ' I'm aweary ' in infectious strain."

For the question inevitably arose—behind all the fine tissue of this verse, woven often with such felicity of colour and delicacy of thread—what reality was there ? What truth for mind and heart to feed upon ? The question troubled Tennyson constantly ; it found

voice in one of his critics. " Early youth appears," he
wrote, " to take peculiar pleasure in seeing language
float along like an exhalation. . . . Mr. Tennyson
must not set it down to acidity and moroseness if
persons of riper years have regretted that his style was
not sufficiently impregnated with thought ; that more
mind was not apparent behind his words." It was
a consummation Tennyson devoutly desired. For
neither he nor the best of his contemporaries acquiesced
completely in the public taste for sugared sweetness.
They could not help their cloistered upbringing and its
softening influence. They belonged to a leisured
middle-class, cultured, respectable, and reacting from
the ardours and excesses of revolution, now overpast
like a bad dream, towards the stability and decency
of home comforts at any cost. They had been born
too late even to share with the later Romantics the
privilege and discipline of disillusionment. They were
the heirs of liberty's failure, and their creed was
inevitably one of tame progress and condescending
humanitarianism. In this they were serious enough,
but because their aim was a compromise their seriousness was solemn and sententious instead of vital and
real ; and their attitude to poetry was coloured by a
timid feeling that life should be safe and decorous ;
that to live perilously was a disproved ideal, and that

> " Gently comes the world to those
> That are cast in gentle mould."

They desired, therefore, sincerely to create a beauty
that was at the same time exquisite, sumptuous and
human, that certainly answered men's needs, but
mirrored also a delicacy of instinct above the brutal
and the vulgar. They erred, however, in believing
that beauty, however refined and condescendingly
human, could also be true, unless they gave themselves fearlessly to life. In the pursuit of reality

man must take risks ; the soul finds itself in danger, in humility, in nakedness and in the ambushes of pain ; and only the fineness which has attested its purity in muddy places can stand the verdict of time.

And so, discontented though Tennyson increasingly was with a poetry of melodious fancy, his attempts to deepen and humanise his content only rarely met with success ; for he did not look life nakedly in the face, stripping off the veil of selfish illusions, he did not dare to think without traditional qualifications, and so he mirrored life as he and his class persisted in liking to think it was, fearing to test their dreams and dogmas, and so discover that their conception was superficial and blurred.

To assimilate the mechanical knowledge, the scientific and religious half-truths which he borrowed from his age, being not so much part of his own self-striving experience as of the current information of the day, was an easy matter. And his talent for precise, lucid and musical words was perfectly suited to summarise attractively the transient drift of contemporary opinion.

Yet there was one emotion, one dread, one anguish, which was real enough to be individual, to bring him trembling to the judgment seat of life and force him in desperation to close with death. It was the loss of Hallam, the severing of his soul from one he knew to be more than his brother, his spiritual complement. It is easy but foolish for a generation inured to the loss of friend and brother in the brawls of nations, familiarised, too, with the scepticism of science and pessimistic philosophies, to think Tennyson's longing for an assurance beyond doubt of individual survival significant of morbidity or moral cowardice. For us in this disintegrated age such a wild longing may be so—yet how many of us in our hearts cherish it in hope

or in fear? But in 1830, naked disaster had not yet
shaken men's faith in life, and religion had preserved
their faith in death. Even to question immortality,
to face shrinkingly in the dark the new horror of
nothingness, was mark enough then of a brave, truth-
honouring man. To accept doubt as the only tenable
position without a paling countenance was beyond
the powers of any.

Tennyson had also to endure the first assaults of
science on spiritual conviction. These seemed then
far more threatening than does the history of that
materialistic siege viewed in retrospect by a generation
which has had time to learn how secure is the citadel
of the soul from the tunnelling of analysis. Quite
unnecessarily man's imaginations were humbled before
the new discoveries of Nature's antiquity, and the
slow but sure grinding of her mills. The monotonous
"lapsing of the Ages" seemed at that time to render
all human endeavour petty and futile, and invited an
Epicurean resignation to a process which man's
individual will could do little to control or direct, and
which so soon would wipe him from the scroll of life.

Fitzgerald's words to a friend some fifteen years
later well typify the temporary cloud which science
cast over sensitive spirits at this time. "Yet as I
often think it is not the poetical imagination, but bare
Science that every day more and more unrolls a greater
Epic than the 'Iliad'; the history of the world, the
great infinitudes of Space and Time! I never take up
a book of Geology or Astronomy but this strikes me.
And when we think that Man must go on in the same
plodding way, one fancies that the Poet of to-day may
as well fold his hands, or turn to dig and delve, considering how soon the march of discovery will distance
all his imaginations and dissolve the language in which
they are uttered."

Such words are proof enough of the spiritual back-water in which Victorian minds unconsciously lay. The province of science seemed, to the parish of fanciful art and sentimental religion, a limitless universe. The knowledge of it overwhelmed and dwarfed their insight. It made man insignificant and robbed him of his dignity. Yet to the vision of time-less imagination, the æons of physical growth which science has discovered are nought save in so far as they declare the upward trend of matter towards that spirit which it is poetry's office to interpret.

For we know now that the spiritual and the scientific categories are distinct. Modern psychology, it is true, is attempting to throw across a bridge between science and poetry, matter and spirit, but the gulf has not yet been crossed. We now admit that science may purify faith, but cannot overthrow it, while, without the complement of spirit, science is no more than know-ledge of the brute world's mechanism.

But this Tennyson had to discover for himself, in an age scared by the first symptoms of the disease of doubt, and when bowed beneath a load of poignant grief. That he solved the problem satisfactorily, or opposed a candid intellect to the cravings of faith, few will assert. He had neither the power to do that, nor the data. The important thing is that the problem of death was for a time burningly his own ; incidentally it became that of his age, but poetically this is irre-levant. He dealt with it not as a topic of the day to be versified elegantly, but as a personal obsession, inviting now to wasting melancholy, now to dread, now to rapturous hope, or sad serenity. And so, poetically, it was real.

At other times he was the poet of his age, hymning the achievements of science and reconciling them with the onward march of a facile faith. As the near memory of his loss receded, and time healed his wound, he became more and more this alone ; and the public took their image to themselves. Yet to the end of his life the memory of Hallam, taken from him in all that gallant purity of purpose, would hover momentarily amid new associations, and recall the note of passion to his verse. It was the " Gleam " he followed because the Master whispered.

In the ten years which followed Hallam's death it inspired all the truest and deepest poetry that he ever wrote.

2

For a time Hallam's death blotted all joy from his life, and Emily's grief could only enhance his peculiar pain by the calls it made upon his sympathy. Yet his creative powers were stimulated rather than depressed ; his sorrow awoke emotions which craved expression with a peremptoriness such as he had never yet experienced. Lines that were later to figure in " In Memoriam " came unbidden into his mind, while, in a manner typical of his temperament, he comforted his own heart and honoured the memory of an ideal friend by embodying the mystery and severance of death in a poem mournful but majestic, the " Morte d'Arthur."

Grievous though his sorrow was, the challenge of death not only roused his heart to life, but also lifted him at times to a level of reality, where the barbs of hostile criticism could no longer wound him to the quick. He was at battle with greater matters than *Quarterly* reviewers. He forgot that " barbarous people," who

> " Blind to the magic,
> And deaf to the melody,
> Snarl'd at and curs'd me."

They had dwindled momentarily into insignificance.

This was fortunate at the period when a strong current of depreciation actually was running in certain literary quarters. Mrs. Tennant wrote of him: "Alfred, although much broken in spirits, is yet able to divert his thoughts from gloomy brooding, and keep his mind in activity." And although at times he would even question the worth of life, and indeed argued in a poem the case of suicide, or would turn appealingly to Nature with the pathetic cry:

> "O leave not thou thy son forlorn;
> Teach me, great Nature; make me live,"

yet he loved life with too fond a dependence to be long disloyal to her, while he ceased to question the worth of his poetry.

Sympathy, too, led his friends to redouble their encouragement. Critics such as Venables wrote that his poems "were too much concentrated power and thought, too imaginative, and too largely imbued with the 'innermost magic' easily to excite popular interest," and Kemble, that "in Alfred's mind the materials of the greatest works are heaped in an abundance which is almost confusion." And while Tennyson's own instinct was to brood upon his loss, and shape out of it something of consolation and truth, his friends, doubtless wishing to divert his melancholy, urged him to discover modern subjects for poetical treatment. "If," wrote Venables, "an artist could only now find out what such popular subjects were, and work on them, he would be the artist of modern times"; and he thought that in "the convergent tendencies of many opinions" on religion, art and Nature lay the popular subject of which Tennyson, "with his commanding intellect and conspicuous moral courage," ought to be the artistic exponent and unifier.

It was an alluring suggestion ; and when Tennyson's despondency became intolerable and the new purpose which Hallam's death had graven on his heart seemed beyond his reach, he turned not so often as before to the consolations of fancy and the blandishments of the senses, not indeed to life nor universal humanity (for that was as painful to him as death), but to these interests and requirements of the age which his friends perpetually brought to his notice.

Meanwhile, in such silence and seclusion as friends would allow, he continued for seven years to live with his family at Somersby, reciting his vows in a solitary shrine and preparing himself for a battle that was to come. Industry and application was not only a wise policy, but a necessity in the presence of ever-wakeful remorse. " It is only the concise and perfect work that will last," he wrote, and " perpetual idleness must be one of the punishments of Hell." He drew up a weekly programme of work, which included History, German, Chemistry, Botany, Electricity, Animal Physiology, Mechanics, Theology, Italian, Greek, and Poetry.

He had determined to refine the best of his published poems, and, binding them with such new ones as Hallam's memory and his own attempt to attain a more human content had inspired, to capture the public favour. Until then he was glad to court obscurity, and deprecated all haste and all references to his early poetry, even so complimentary a notice as J. S. Mill penned in July, 1835. " John Heath writes me word that Mill is going to review me. . . . I do not wish to be dragged forward again in any shape before the reading public at present." Seated meditative before the fire in his attic, he confessed that he would blow hundreds of lines up the chimney with his pipe smoke, or he would jot them down only to throw them away later as not being perfect enough for preservation.

At intervals during these years he would go to London or visit his friends in their homes ; otherwise it was only through letters that he kept in touch with poetical or political topics. But Spedding, Spring Rice, Brookfield and J. M. Kemble, to name but four, were enthusiastic correspondents, content with a very meagre return. Tennant wrote to him : " May your success in rhyming vary inversely as the number of letters you write ! "

Tennyson, though himself no letter writer, did not expect that fact to damp the ardour of his friends. To Spedding, early in 1833, he complains : " You should not have written to me without telling me somewhat that was interesting to myself (always the first consideration !) or that bore some reference to you and yours (always the second !), or, lastly, without giving me some news of the great world, for know you not I live so far apart from the bustle of life that news becomes interesting to me ? . . . Write to me now and then lest I perish."

Later in the year, in reference to the poem already known in MS. to a small circle, Kemble wrote jestingly : " We are all pretty well, and, looking out for more sprigs of the garden (or the gardener's daughter, for I suppose she was not so imperfect a woman as not to be wife as well as maid and married ?). Is there no gardener's granddaughter ? " And from an Apostles' dinner held in Cambridge Milnes sent the following bulletin : " I suppose nobody writes to you because you never write to nobody. John Heath and many others were full to the brim of enquiries after you, and if you had heard the cheer that followed the health of A. T., the Poet of the Apostles, at our dinner, if you had ! "

Poems were steadily taking shape. " Morte d'Arthur," " Ulysses," " St. Simeon Stylites," " Thoughts of a Suicide," were conceived, if only tentatively written, in this year. As early as January, 1834, Trench wrote to Donne : " Alfred Tennyson has so far recovered from the catastrophe in which his sister was involved as to have written some new poems, and, they say, fine ones." About the same time Spedding told Thompson that Wordsworth " doubts not that Alfred's style has its own beauty, though he wants the faculty to enter fully into it." Hartley Coleridge, however, proved eloquently appreciative, and a favourable review from far-off Calcutta came to cheer Tennyson in his solitary work.

In the summer, when he visited John Heath at Kitlands, near Dorking, they journeyed on to Worthing, where they arrived on " a beautiful still night with the sea calm and golden, and boys bathing in a glowing sunset and gray fishing boats in the distance." He would not be persuaded to go on to Brighton, but returned to Kitlands to take " lonely walks in dark valleys," and by the side of streams that rise in Leith Hill.

But since his father's death, his brother Frederick's departure to a villa near Florence, and Charles's ordination, the cares of the family devolved almost wholly upon him, and as both his mother and Emily were troubled with nervous ailments, his absences from home were brief and occasionally anxious. In his short absence at Kitlands Emily wrote lugubriously enough : " You will be sorry to hear that I have been considerably worse in health since your departure. . . . And once or twice indeed I thought that the chilly hand of death was upon me." Such news was not of a nature to increase the happiness on holiday of one devoted to his family, despite the suggestion his mother could make in a postscript that Emily's illness was " a fanciful lassitude which made her feel unequal for exertion." Yet Mrs. Tennyson herself would grovel on the floor in a thunderstorm, and could not be left by her son, even for a short time, with an easy mind.

For in his sympathetic management of his family Tennyson showed real practical ability, manfully shouldering domestic responsibilities in spite of the indifferent health and variable spirits from which he had suffered since Hallam's death, while his chief diversion was to drive over to Tealby to renew acquaintance with the patient spirit of his brother Charles.

In October Spedding wrote : " I received by Douglas and John Heath divers of your compositions, albeit too few for my appetite : to wit, ' Sir Galahad,' which enjoys my unlimited admiration. The virgin knight is as beautiful a spirit as Don Quixote in a more beautiful kind, if that could be. Also " Nature, so far as in her lies," one of those pieces which nobody except yourself can write, and, I think, the most exquisite of an exquisite race. Of the rest I cannot find words to express what and how great is the glory. . . . Last and greatest (tho' not most perfect in its kind) I have received " The Thoughts of a Suicide " ; the design is so grand, and the moral, if there is one, so important that I trust you will not spare any elaboration of execution."

Such admiration was not the fruit of loyal friendship alone. It also showed that Tennyson's range of mood and sentiment found a quite immediate and general response in others of his own class and generation, and that it only needed widening in other less esoteric directions to capture the whole of earnest middle-class opinion. In his reply to the above letter Tennyson wrote: " I have written several things since I saw you, some emulative of the ' ἡδὺ καὶ βραχὺ καὶ μεγαλοπρεπὲς ' of Alcæus, others of the ' ἐκλογὴ τῶν ὀνοματων καὶ τῆς σονθέσεως ἀκρίβεια ' of Simonides." He remarked, too, *apropos* of a criticism of Byron and Shelley, " However mistaken they may be, they did yet give the world another heart and new pulses, and so are we kept going. Blessed be those that grease the wheels of the old world, in so much as to move on is better than to stand still." He himself was even then discovering shrewdly the uses both of the old world and the new, and was to wed the style of many a classical author to the vague sentiments of orderly progress with singular success. At the same time that sturdy nationalism which saw in England the world's appropriate schoolmaster, and was ready to mete out a dignified chastisement to all recalcitrant pupils, found its earliest expression in the lines :

> " Grave mother of majestic works,
>   From her isle-altar gazing down,
> Who, God-like, grasps the triple forks,
>   And, King-like, wears the crown :
>
> Her open eyes desire the truth,
>   The wisdom of a thousand years
> Is in them.   May perpetual youth
>   Keep dry their light from tears ! "

It was a string which in future Tennyson was to pluck ever more vigorously as his belief in the implicit wisdom of every Englishman and the " blind hysterics " or shifty casuistry of every foreigner increased. The music grew thin and noisy in the middle years, but it evoked redundant applause, until the crowd found its perfect war song in the lines :

> " Who fears to die, who fears to die ?
> Is there any here who fears to die ?
> Chorus : ' Shout for England !
> Ho for England ! ' "

To shout, Tennyson discovered, with so many of his generation, was the best way to silence both fear and reason, and it might now appear that in the distraction of his personal trouble he turned to his country, crying, " Love thou thy land with love far brought," as to an emotion large and solid.

But already his early Liberalism, which had never been more than an affectation of superior social service and of progressive fervour, caught from enthusiastic friends, had cooled. Burning stacks, Chartist riots, " the red fool-fury of the Seine," the folly of ignorant men, his own need of comfortable security, and the reaction from idealistic hope into which he and his generation were caught, all combined to suggest a Conservative attitude under the veil of Liberal sympathy. While his love for his country as a vague entity standing for general decency and government increased, his compassion for the intolerable state of the downtrodden classes declined. The Imperialist waxed as the reformer waned; Law and Discipline became the catchwords of his creed, in the place of Love and Progress. At the end of his life he was to denounce with a defiant and sardonic gesture the generous fashion of his youth :

> " ' Forward ' rang the voices then, and of the many mine was one,
> Let us hush this cry of ' Forward ' till ten thousand years have
> gone."

In the spring of 1835 a new friend was added to the faithful, and one who, standing outside the impressionable Apostolic circle, was able to preserve a measure of criticism amid the fullness of his appreciation.

This was Edward Fitzgerald, who met Tennyson at a visit to the Speddings' house by Bassenthwaite Lake. With a shrewdness which was afterwards to reveal itself in singular and candid indifference to some of Tennyson's most applauded work, Fitzgerald was more deeply impressed by the man than by the poet. "The more I have seen of him," he wrote, " the more cause I have to think him great."

Once again the regal presence, from which not even " little humours and grumpinesses " could detract, exercised its physical dominion over a keener but less magisterial mind than its own. Fitzgerald, in the first rapture of friendship, spoke of occasional feelings of depression " from the overshadowing of a so much more lofty intellect " ; and he felt that Tennyson, " by raising and filling the brain with noble images and thoughts . . . prepared and fitted us for the reception of the higher philosophy." Perhaps, in ways other than Fitzgerald supposed, Tennyson did ; but the higher philosophy was left for other minds than his to formulate.

Earlier in the year he had been pondering the first stanzas of " In Memoriam," but he had with him on this visit a number of miscellaneous poems, among them the " Morte d'Arthur," " The Day Dream," " The Lord of Burleigh," " Dora," and " The Gardener's Daughter " ; and of an evening, while Fitzgerald was playing chess with Spedding's mother, or late at night, " when all the house was mute " and the friends were free from disturbance, Tennyson would chant them aloud, " between growling and smoking," in a deep, impressive monotone, emphasising the rhythm and the vowel music, but nervously slurring the articulation, as if anxious to overwhelm the sense, of which he was perhaps a trifle doubtful, in a volume of sound. This was ever his practice in reading ; it

EDWARD FITZGERALD

From a photograph, by kind permission of Mr. Clement Shorter

[To face p. 84

made his poetry sound akin to moving water—the element which best he loved.

Despite the suspicions of Spedding's father, who was so practical-minded as to consider association with poets and poetry likely to corrupt his son's character, the days at Bassenthwaite passed happily. Wordsworth, " the dear old fellow," was read constantly, Keats " for the innermost soul of poetry he showed in almost everything he wrote," Milton's " Lycidas," in particular, the test piece of " poetic instinct," as Tennyson called it. There was argument over Shakespeare's sonnets, which Tennyson would have greater than his plays, and talks with the eccentric, lovable Hartley Coleridge, who inherited his father's gift of limitless monologue. But Tennyson could not yet be persuaded to meet the old seer at Rydal Mount, although Wordsworth was " hospitably minded towards him." It may be that he dreaded the penetration of those eyes which had for so long looked into the naked heart of man.

Nevertheless, Tennyson seems upon this visit to have reached a hitherto unknown level of confidence in his own powers and in what he had so far accomplished. Resting on his oars one calm May day on Windermere, he relaxed for a moment his usual taciturnity. Looking into the unruffled depths of the lake, he quoted :

> " Nine days she wrought it, sitting all alone
> Upon the hidden bases of the hills,"

and added : " Not bad that, Fitz, is it ? "

His patient industry was beginning to bring its reward. No longer did he shudder before every potential critic ; no longer strike the onlooker as " a nervous, morbidly-irritable man, down in the world, stark-spoiled with the staggers of a mismanaged imagination, and quite opprest by fortune and by the

reviews." Already visioning in the near future the
promise of a more general applause, he dared even
to relieve a friend of the now familiar privilege of
approving his genius!

Fitzgerald, with typical generosity, found other
means of heartening the poet. Writing two months
later, he said : " I have heard you sometimes say
that you are bound by the want of such and such a
sum, and I vow to the Lord that I could not have
a greater pleasure than transferring it to you on
such occasions ; I should not dare to say such a thing
to a small man ! but you are not a small man assuredly ;
and even if you do not make use of my offer you will
not be offended, but put it to the right account. It
is very difficult to persuade people in this world that
one can part with a banknote without a pang."
Tennyson was indeed happy in his friends !

A year later, on May 24, 1836, his brother Charles
married Louisa Sellwood at Horncastle, and among
the bridesmaids was her elder sister Emily, the
auburn-haired Dryad whom Tennyson had met with
Arthur Hallam six years before. It fell to him to take
her into church, and the surroundings suggested less of
fantasy than the Fairy Wood. For bending towards
the graceful, timid creature at his side, he whispered :
" O happy bridesmaid, make a happy bride ! "

> " And all at once a pleasant truth I learn'd,
> For, while the tender service made thee weep,
> I lov'd thee for the tear thou couldst not hide,
> And prest thy hand, and knew the press return'd."

3

Averse though Tennyson was at this time to
publicity, he allowed two poems to appear in
periodicals, the second, however, only after urgent and
injured solicitations from Milnes. To the *Keepsake*

he sent the chaste and marmoreal " St. Agnes," a
poem not unlike a piece of decorative sculpture in a
fashionable church, and " O ! that 'twere possible,"
the germ of the later " Maud," to the *Tribute*, a
charitable publication edited by Lord Northampton.

In the silence of his attic or the deep lanes of
Somersby work went steadily forward. But the
environment which had enfolded him for twenty-eight
years was at last to be abandoned. Early in 1837
Mrs. Tennyson decided no longer to stand in the way
of the new Somersby incumbent, but to vacate the
Rectory and live nearer London. It was Tennyson's
duty to find and furnish a new and congenial home.
The combined resources of the family justified the
choice of a comfortable mansion. He chanced upon
High Beech in Epping Forest, an agreeable, even
stately house standing in its own park, with a private
pond. This possibly commended it, for " an old
park," he would say, " is my delight and I could
tumble about it for ever." To take a fall on a rough
hillside, or romp in a meadow, lacked, it may be,
distinction ; but to tumble in a park, like the frolic
of the pagan gods, entailed no loss of dignity. The
environment condoned the impropriety !

This love of the lordly and the spacious reveals itself
more than once in his correspondence, as when he
wrote of Kenilworth : " We tumbled about the ruins
for three hours, but I was rather disappointed. I had
expected to find them larger and more august." And
years later he confided to a friend, " How I should love
to rove about that parklike scenery of which you give
such a fascinating account ! " Not the least of the
Victorian vices was a worship of size, of quantity and
of impressive forms for their own sake.

Nevertheless, the dignity of High Beech soon proved
a little dreary. It was pleasant in winter to sail about

the ice on the pond with his long blue cloak curving behind him; but, after only two years, he wrote: "I have been at this place all the year, with nothing but that muddy pond in prospect, and those two little sharp-barking dogs. Perhaps I am coming to the Lincolnshire coast, but I scarcely know. The journey is so expensive, and I am so poor."

He was homesick for the sea.

Yet for one who averred "I require quiet, and myself to myself, more than any man when I write," the large study over the dining-room with its bay windows, red curtains, and a Clytie on a pedestal in the corner, was all that could be desired. And his informal engagement to Emily Sellwood gave a new and romantic impulse to his concentration on a perfect volume of poetry.

Without popular success marriage was for him impossible. Between the sacrifice of his art and his lady he was singularly determined that there should be no compromise. The only hope, a distant one, of domestic happiness, therefore, was to sift and arrange the material, that the volume, when he gave it to the world, should be as perfect as he could make it. Its success or failure would then be a sure test of his right to hold his lady to her promise. Of one thing he was certain : " If I meant to make any mark at all, it must be by shortness, for the men before me had been so diffuse, and most of the big things except ' King Arthur ' had been done."

Thus another and more moving argument was added to that of his friends, who invited him to cater for the requirements of the public and to cease the ardent pursuit of true and personal experience which Hallam, alive and dead, encouraged. One who could not compromise his art by marriage was unconsciously willing to compromise his soul by policy.

The knowledge, however, of Emily Sellwood's pure and disinterested love now served to relieve his mind of any lingering melancholy. They corresponded regularly, exchanging sentiments and opinions in a tone almost religious. " A good woman," he wrote in 1837, " is a wondrous creature, cleaving to the right and the good in all change ; lovely in her youthful comeliness, lovely all her life long in comeliness of heart." In another letter come the sentences, " That world of perfect chrysolite, a pure and noble heart," and " There is the glory of being loved, for so have we laid great bases for Eternity." To her, too, far more intimately than to others, he revealed the haziness, the strange, even sickly miasma, which so often clouded his mental powers ; the vague provocation also of " far, far away," which from boyhood haunted his ears. " Annihilate within yourself these two dreams of Space and Time. To me often the far-off world seems nearer than the present, for in the present is always something unreal and indistinct, but the other seems a good solid planet, rolling round its green hills and paradises to the harmony of more steadfast laws. There stream up from about me mists of weakness, or sin, or despondency, and roll between me and the far planet, but it is there still." He confessed that " the far future has been my world always," and that he shared " dim mystic sympathies with tree and hill reaching far back into childhood," while with a grieved stoicism that scarcely rings true, he wrote : " We must bear or we must die. It is easier perhaps to die, but infinitely less noble." To him, if truth be told, it was neither easy nor noble. It was unthinkable.

Nor was the moralising note absent. " All life is a school," he wrote, " a preparation, a purpose ; nor can we pass current in a higher college, if we do not undergo the tedium of education in this lower one." The letters strike one as those of a grand preacher rather than a great poet ; of a guardian rather than a lover.

The monotony of High Beech was occasionally relieved by visits to Lincolnshire, also to London to foregather with old friends, although his mother's nervousness in his absence rarely allowed him to stay away for even one night.

Appreciations came to him about this time both from France and America, a French reviewer naming him, not very happily, "*jeune Enthousiaste de l'école gracieuse de Thomas Moore.*" Emerson suggested an American reprint of the two published volumes, and infected transcendental circles with his zeal, while in July Leigh Hunt showed his admiration by begging a contribution for a new magazine of which he had become editor, speaking " of a fair and no unworthy imitator of yours, a Miss Barrett, who really has sparks of the ' faculty divine.' " He wrote shortly afterwards of the three Tennyson brothers : " Here is a nest of nightingales for you ! . . . The materials of the noblest poetry are abundant in him (Alfred), and we trust will not find any too weak corner in the sensitiveness of his nature to oppress him with their very exuberance." The favour of the author of " Rimini " was perhaps an ambiguous testimonial, but any appreciation is balm to a struggling author. It arms him against that worst foe of the creative life, insidious diffidence, and self-criticism is a stern enough master to all writers worthy the name.

Steadily the toil went on and the fabric grew beneath his hands. There was method in his industry. Here memories of a Titian background served for a descriptive passage ; from such books as Pringle's " Travels " he stored his mind, with usable similes of landscape he would never see, and of lions he would never have to face, while in Lyell's " Geology " and kindred manuals he kept his mind abreast with the distressing but enthralling discoveries of natural science. Only beneath the surface of this very practical and purposeful activity the image of Hallam beckoned, and " In Memoriam " took shadowy shape.

In the autumn of this year he escaped again to the sea, not to the " grand sea " of Mablethorpe, but only to " the angry curt sea " at Torquay. The " loveliest village," which Torquay then was, and the inspiration of Abbey Park, proved very helpful to composition, and here " Audley Court " was written. Many an image, too, marketed in later years, may well have been garnered here, as he came down from the hill of an evening, and saw beneath him the little hushed town, " the glooming quay," and beyond the bay, glassy calm, with the harbour buoy set in the midst of it like a phosphorescent star, or again, on days of wind and rain, heard the shriek of recoiling pebbles on the shore, or felt the silence breathless after the long roll of a thundering wave. He discovered a new temper in that element which above all he loved.

His friends, however, began to show some anxiety at his continued retreat from society and the world. " Do not continue to be so careless of fame and of influence," one wrote, bidding him to go and live at Cambridge or at Prague, both places congenial to one with a " love of music and tobacco," where he " would receive new impressions and a new stimulus to the imagination." But he would not be moved. His aim was now defined, uncertainty had vanished, poetry was become a business in which he meant to succeed. The materials of his trade were accumulating, he had only to wait and the market was assured. Meanwhile brief excursions to friends' houses were change enough.

In 1840, High Beech, disliked for its want of birds

and men, was abandoned for Tunbridge Wells, but the new residence proved neither agreeable nor healthy, and after only one year the family migrated to Boxley, near Maidstone. Edmund Lushington, a distinguished Greek scholar, a nice critic and a great gentleman, married Tennyson's sister Cecilia shortly afterwards, and the two lived at Park House, close at hand. Lushington and Tennyson had become acquainted at Cambridge, and shared a deep mutual regard ; and at Park House met many old friends and new, and sometimes had " dance and song in the evening." More frequent now and prolonged were Tennyson's visits to London, where he would put up in lodgings off the Strand or at the Temple or in Lincoln's Inn Fields, and dine with friends at the " Cock," where he composed his " Lyrical Monologue," and at other taverns. Of one of these dinners given by Thackeray it is reported that " the largeness of Alfred's proportions, both physical and poetical, were universally the theme of admiration. Maclise admired him excessively, and quite fell in love with him." A beefsteak, a potato, a cut of cheese, a pint of port, and afterwards a pipe, was the customary fare, and doubtless the assembled company gave unanimous support to Tennyson's solemn contention that " All fine-natured men know what is good to eat," but although he would surrender himself to the hilarity of the hour, his laughter, we are told, was still often interrupted by fits of sadness.

After the hush of the countryside there was delight in the city's " central roar," and the " Sterling Club," of which he became a member, while providing very pleasantly a new meeting ground for the old Cambridge circle, introduced him also to other minds less provincial than they. Rogers, " Barry Cornwall," Dickens, Landor and Campbell were of their number, but chief among them was Carlyle.

That Tennyson's physical presence explains the uncritical reverence which his friends accorded to his genius is nowhere more strikingly proved than by Carlyle's immediate surrender, in his favour, of a deep-rooted antipathy to "poetising." The "Life-Guardsman," as Carlyle called him, was so impressive a spectacle that though Carlyle might protest laughing that he was "spoilt by making poetry," the poetry was allowed to partake of the dignity of the stature, and to escape all such caustic depreciation as would have fallen to the lot of a poet of identical attainment but measuring five feet two.

As it was, the "fine, large-featured, dim-eyed, bronze-coloured, shaggy-headed man," captured Carlyle's romantic imagination, and the contrast between his heroic build and his indolent muse, which so puzzled Fitzgerald, went for long unnoticed. "One of the finest-looking men in the world," he wrote of him, " I do not meet in these late decades such company over a pipe!" Mrs. Carlyle, conquered by Tennyson's gallant devotion of a whole evening to her company, echoed these sentiments in a lighter vein: "He is a very handsome man, and a noble-hearted one, with something of the gypsy in his appearance, which for me is perfectly charming. Babbie never saw him, unfortunately, or perhaps I should say, fortunately, for she must have fallen in love with him on the spot, unless she be made absolutely of ice; and then men of genius have never anything to keep wives upon."

In London Tennyson listened readily to the prevalent talk on politics, theology, scientific discoveries and mechanical inventions. It was his business as a poet of modern sympathy to keep up to date; and upon Chartist and Socialist agitations he would reflect deprecatingly, but with the large philanthropy, the high-minded detachment so fashionable then in

privileged circles. These were days when many
educated and sensitive minds proclaimed the need
of reform and condemned with sorrow the abuses
evident in social life. Those who so expressed themselves doubtless enjoyed a sense of altruism and
magnanimity, an easiness of mind in an uneasy world,
very soothing to the conscience, and making no
serious calls upon either purse or privilege.

The spirit of these discussions as it affected Tennyson
is well illustrated by quotations from " The Golden
Year," written some years later, in which the " tongue-
tied Poet in the feverous days " speaks of

> " the fair new forms
> That float about the threshold of an age,
> Like truths of science waiting to be caught,"

sketches the orderly evolution of democracy in the
lines :

> " And slow and sure comes up the golden year,
> When wealth no more shall rest in mounded heaps,
> But smit with freer light shall slowly melt
> In many streams to fatten lower lands,"

hails a heavenly journalism, a strenuous missionary
endeavour and a voluptuous free trade in the lines :

> " Fly, happy happy sails, and bear the Press ;
> Fly happy with the mission of the Cross ;
> Knit land to land, and blowing havenward
> With silks, and fruits, and spices, clear of toll,
> Enrich the markets of the golden year,"

deprecates any immediate effort towards the attainment of such an issue in the words :

> " Ah, folly ! for it lies so far away,
> Not in our time, nor in our children's time,
> 'Tis like the second world to us that live ; "

and ends by consoling himself with the industrious
thought, familiar to school-chapel pulpits, that

> " unto him who works, and feels he works,
> This same grand year is ever at the doors."

The spiritual antics of a number of saintly men in Oxford were causing orthodox Churchmen considerable anxiety at this time. The solid front of Anglican dogma was threatened, a situation the more embarrassing to Orthodoxy because the revolting party possessed by far the subtler dialecticians. Disputes on the degree of ritualism which constituted a lapse to the scarlet of Rome waxed rife, and few saw that the arguments advanced against ritual were in truth a ritual in themselves. It is fair, however, to say that the conflict was lifted on to a higher level than that of dogma or subjective casuistry by such Cambridge men as Kingsley and Maurice, who were honestly striving to bring into a narrow class-bound Church a wider spirit and a deeper brotherhood. Tennyson, for his part, took careful note of this various ferment, counselled moderation in all things, and retired to Boxley to put the last touches to the two volumes of poetry, which were now almost ready for publication.

Yet still he held back, waiting the psychological moment. He would take no chances, for enemies still lurked at every turning.

Early in 1842 he wrote to Edmund Lushington : " I have not yet taken my book to Moxon. Spedding's going to America has a little disheartened me, for some fop will get the start of him in the *Ed. Review* where he promised to put an article, and I have had abuse enough. . . . However, I intend to get it out shortly, but I cannot say I have been what you professors call ' working ' at it, that indeed is not my way. I take my pipe and the muse descends in the fume . . ."

Only a little longer did his shy and meditative muse shrink from common daylight. In two months hesitation was at an end, and " Poems by Alfred Tennyson " were public property.

4

Industry and moments of high inspiration, rarely
to be achieved in the years to come, had produced
a collection of poems worthy of the cultivated applause
they received.

The material was so variously characteristic. It
illustrated both the finest and the feeblest of Tennyson's qualities as a poet, both his slender range of pure
genius and his growing ability for polished commonplace. We may divide the poems into three classes.

Firstly, those which embody a deep and real
emotion, wonderfully expressed. These are few, but
they touch the highest point to which he ever attained.
They embrace the " Morte d'Arthur," " Ulysses," and
the two short lyrics, " A Farewell," and " Break, break,
break," written one early summer morning in a
Lincolnshire lane, to which we might add parts of
" Tithonus," composed but not published during
these years. These poems were born of Hallam's
death, they grew out of great personal suffering, they
speak the poignant truth of loss and the spirit of a
noble life attests their verity. The " Morte d'Arthur "
was nearly spoilt, and is, indeed, partly damaged by
a cross-purpose which degraded many poems in the
volume. In the Epilogue the poet says :

" Perhaps some modern touches here and there
Redeem'd it from the charge of nothingness—
Or else we loved the man, and prized his work."

Fortunately Tennyson's love of Hallam carried him,
absorbed by the grandeur of death's farewell, through
most of the poem, and the modern touches barely
survived, and were insignificant at that ; and so
King Arthur remains a man of poetry and nobility
compact, passing upon his way, and not

" a modern gentleman
Of stateliest port."

In " Ulysses " there is scarce a blemish. The spirits of Dante and of Hallam combine : " the great Achilles, whom we knew," has triumphed over " Lotos Eater," moralist and propagandist. The sword of the spirit rusts no longer unburnished, but " shines in use." In the two short lyrics, sadness and regret speak for once without a tremor of artifice. Feeling true and worthy dictated the lines, too often dulled by use,

> " But O for the touch of a vanish'd hand,
> And the sound of a voice that is still ! "

Of the second class are poems perfect in manner but of slender content. Among them are many of the early poems, purged of those weak lines upon which public criticism had fastened, and even reshaped—not only " The Lady of Shalott," peerless of its kind as anything Tennyson ever wrote, but also such poems as " The Day Dream " and " Sir Launcelot and Queen Guinevere." The art of these transcends the artifice.

In the remaining class are those poems, popular in their own day, which are too topical, or too pontifically trivial, to survive a change of fashion. Sometimes Tennyson embellishes sentimental love with high compliment, or colours it with gentle pathos ; or he pretends to rustic simplicity. Of such are " The Talking Oak," " Dora," " The Lord of Burleigh," " Lady Clare," " Audley Court," " Edwin Morris," " The Gardener's Daughter "—poems in which the lover in his most inspired moments will speak like this :

> " Ah, one rose,
> One rose, but one, by those fair fingers cull'd,
> Were worth a hundred kisses press'd on lips
> Less exquisite than thine,"

at which the maiden " look'd : but all suffused with blushes." In these poems the lover is generally a little patronising, lordly and dignified, and the maid

innocent, faultless and tearfully compliant : as he was
to word it later :

> " She dwells on him with faithful eyes,
>   ' I cannot understand : I love.' "

And if his ways should prove harsh, " she bears them
meekly."

In two poems, " Sir Galahad " and " St. Agnes'
Eve," Tennyson, like so many of his generation,
further sanctified this unreal sentiment and called it
religion, confusing a fastidious sensuousness, sustained
by perfumes and flowers " that lightly rain from ladies'
hands," with the stern ecstasies of asceticism.

> " My knees are bow'd in crypt and shrine :
> I never felt the kiss of love,
> Nor maiden's hand in mine.
> More bounteous aspects on me beam,
> Me mightier transports move and thrill :
> So keep I fair through faith and prayer
> A virgin heart in work and will."

We may well question the worth of so exquisitely
superior a chastity !

In addition there are one or two not wholly unsuc-
cessful, but clearly artificial, attempts, such as
" Edward Gray," to imitate the Border ballads.

There remain poems partly or altogether devoted to
the versification of topical subjects, political, social,
even commercial. The feminist question first figures
in " Edwin Morris," the contemporary moral dilemma
in " The Vision of Sin," " St. Simeon Stylites," " The
Two Voices " and " Love and Duty." Particularly in
" Locksley Hall " both the manufactured passion,
noticeable in the pastoral and society verses, and the
popular themes and catchwords of the moment,
combine.

This moralising and propagandist vein encroaches
in the later poems even on the province of lyricism.

More and more as the years went by was this topical
and commercial purpose, grateful as it was to popular
taste, to possess Tennyson. His unexampled powers
of word-music were frequently to serve this prosaic
master, and the genius who could pen the great
conclusion of " Ulysses " was to languish in a sultry
Victorian noontide, and only turn from the embroidering of idle virtue or of forced and feverous passion
when, it may be, for moments the face of Hallam
floated up out of the past of grieved remembrance, or
when he heard far off the sorrowing of the sea.

The poems of 1842 are in the light of their successors
a tragic document, because they show the whole range
of Tennyson's powers, and the first stage of that
conflict between genius and the commonplace, which
was to end in so overwhelming victory for the latter.
No critic then had the penetration to see here a poet,
in his highest moments battling from fancy up to
imagination, from particular pleasantries and lovely
airy nothings towards universal sympathy, insight and
experience—in his lowest, stooping to prevent fancy
even from pursuing its own delight, and compelling it
to decorate the ephemeral opinions of the day. We
of a later generation know that this degrading policy
was to become habitual, and the effort of vision the
rarest exception.

We may trace the triumph of the second-rate to
two causes—to the all-pervading influence of public
opinion and to temperamental weakness in Tennyson
himself. His critics particularly applauded him for
insinuating modern problems into his handling of old
myths or legends, or rustic stories, and so encouraged
him to persist in a method which was poetically false.
It is always dangerous for a poet to borrow rather than
create his plot—as Tennyson, with interested detachment, borrowed that of " Dora " from a story of

Miss Mitford's, and of " Lady Clare " from Miss Ferrier—unless he has the power so to possess himself of it, so to pour new life into the material that it is born anew as his own. This borrowing of plots merely for technique to versify became the habit of Tennyson's later years.

In the true handling of a theme, in whatever age, the distinctions of old and new are forgotten. · The little ripples on the surface of time are merged in the everlasting ocean. We do not date the essentials of great poetry; we accept its passionate reality. But Tennyson was induced by popular clamour to desert the universe of passion for the province of platitude. Perhaps it was of himself he wrote the apology in " Edwin Morris,"

> " It is my shyness, or my self-distrust,
> Or something of a wayward modern mind
> Dissecting passion. Time will set me right."

It is possible to dissect passion passionately, and so, while abandoning the instinctive optimism of nature, to retain and even deepen the truths of poetry. Donne and Meredith were masters of this destructively creative insight. It is, perhaps, a necessity for the modern mind; but Tennyson, when he ceased to give himself emotionally to life, could only view her with mild aloofness. He had not the mind or the will to search, with that flaming indignation which is the inverse of positive enthusiasm, into life's secret, and so his modern themes were the fruit, not of individual experience, but of prevalent opinion, and appear like large or small patches of drab upon the brilliance of his lyrical embroidery.

This failure to distinguish between absolute and contemporary values is traceable to a fundamental weakness which Tennyson both shared with his age and helped to intensify—a reluctance, amounting soon to a refusal, to live in spirit, not only virtuously but also perilously. The virtue went out of his poetry, it lost condition and truth and power, because he would not face the danger of an unqualified and unprivileged world, the world of disinterested thought, active passion, and unpretentious idealism. And so, unconsciously, he judged himself when he wrote

> " but something jarr'd :
> .   .   .   .   .   there seem'd
> A touch of something false, some self-conceit,
> Or over-smoothness : "

Or again :

> " Kind nature is the best : those manners next
> That fit us like a nature second-hand ;
> Which are indeed the manners of the great."

Unfortunately " the manners of the great " are a very different thing from the " grand style " of poetry. With simple nature Tennyson was unfamiliar, and he was to spend far too many of his days sacrificing poetical truth to good manners.

The quality of the love mirrored in many of these poems advertises very clearly his weakness. It is conventional, luxurious, even maudlin ; or it sounds a note of forced and hollow passion for this reason— Tennyson feared the flesh. He saw in sexual licence, in every uncontrolled physical act, the triumph of that force which drags mankind down into the mire, and he shrank away disgusted from its animal countenance. And fearing morbidly the animal in himself, he suppressed passion instead of sublimating it. His ideal world was one in which was

> " Every tiger madness muzzled, every serpent passion kill'd,"

but because the conception was negative, the passion which he generally characterised was not the creative force of life tuned by a great intelligence to a noble pitch, but a forced exotic, a weakly sentiment isolated from the free flow of nature and decorated by timid fancy, or merely the excuse for a refined domestic arrangement calculated to replenish English nurseries. For women, despite pretty phrases, were often at heart regarded even in his time as no more than child-bearing chattels. Indeed, by him who fails of love, either through lust or presumption, they must be degraded into some such convenience, since only through joyously admitted equality can two natures share in the true partnership of passion, absolute in itself. Spiritual pride is, therefore, as fatal to true love and true poetry as physical coarseness.

Thus, while morally we must sympathise with Tennyson's loathing of lust, of crude instinct brutally overriding the scruples of intelligence and taste, we are forced to admit that it led him as a poet to flee life rather than interpret it, and to paint—not the vivid, fair and sordid world in which men rise through their passions to the heights where Beauty and Truth are known in absolute purity or are degraded by them to a level lower than the beasts—but an artificial society, where self-righteous lovers struggle discreetly with conscience or condescend to be an improving influence to humble and contrite maids, where a fantastic love-sickness haunts a drooping landscape, and where ladies languish amid gesturing knights and highflown compliments, while passion grows cold with moralising or dies of the fever of romance.

As in his political opinions, so in his view of passion, Tennyson tended more and more towards the negative virtue of discipline, because fear was in his heart. His revulsion from the physical led him from the first to indulge in sentiments which were either pompous or egotistical, or merely fantastic, because they had no deep root in human nature.

It is with a real relish that he traces in such a character as St. Simeon Stylites the Manichean desire " to subdue this home of sin, my flesh, which I despise and hate."

> " Mortify
> Your flesh, like me, with scourges and with thorns ;
> Smite, shrink not, spare not."

Even in the " Morte d'Arthur " the conflict of desire and duty in Sir Bedivere almost leads the dying king into an incongruous homily that breaks the spell, when he tells how it is

> " deep harm to disobey,
> Seeing obedience is the bond of rule."

The condescending patronage of the Lord of Burleigh towards his rustic bride is so intolerable that feeling herself unequal to " the burthen of an honour, Unto which she was not born," she grows faint and dies, providing her lord with a lifelong excuse for affecting melancholy. In " Locksley Hall " not only is the passion forced and metallic, but the assumption of superiority by the jilted lover is almost farcical.

> " Is it well to wish thee happy ?—having known me—to decline
> On a lower range of feelings and a narrower heart than mine !
> Yet it shall be ! thou shalt lower to his level day by day,
> What is fine within thee growing coarse to sympathise with
> clay."

A man might think such things with justice, but he would not give them public expression ; and though it may be argued that Tennyson was representing here a character not his own, yet the note of spiritual arrogance pervading this and many other poems was clearly native to his temperament, and fifty years later, indeed, he was sufficiently ashamed of the sentiments to retract them.

Such lines as

> " I am shamed thro' all my nature to have loved so slight a thing."
> " Woman is the lesser man, and all thy passions, match'd with
>   mine,
>   Are as moonlight unto sunlight, and as water unto wine."
> " I to herd with narrow foreheads, vacant of our glorious gains,
>   Like a beast with lower pleasures, like a beast with lower pains! "
> " I the heir of all the ages in the foremost files of time,"

voice the sentiments of a man who, realising with his generation, perhaps consciously for the first time in the western world, the distinctive aristocracy of man in an animal creation, and that he should be guided by values other than those of brute nature, failed to recognise also that the only true aristocracy must flower direct from the common soil of life, however fair and high it be. Otherwise it becomes a sickly or even a monstrous weed of egotism.

Tennyson's moral outlook is more narrowly imaged in " The Vision of Sin " and " Love and Duty." The former is reminiscent of " The Palace of Art," painting the same surrender to sensuous luxury, but with a more curt and savage hatred. It is a poem full of wormy circumstance, a ghastly caricature of an hysterical hell, in which a creature more fiend than man indulges his " maudlin gall " by mocking at every fair and cleanly thing in the world, and drinking himself into madness. Sin is far more subtle and far less melodramatic than such poetical panic would have us believe, yet the poem contains two lines of remarkable insight :

> " We are men of ruin'd blood :
> Therefore comes it we are wise."

Tennyson learnt, with his generation, that wisdom is bought only at the price of pain, but he flinched before the price demanded. To the healthy and unthinking, wisdom seems even a disease, and, indeed, the first inoculation with thought of the animal man is invariably followed by a period of sickness and disordered faculties until the virus has completed its cure and wrought a higher state of health. The birth pangs of the soul are severe. And Tennyson, in his terrified repression of instinct and his moral distraction figures the transition of modern consciousness from a physical to a spiritual dispensation. But, like Moses, he saw afar the Promised Land without inheriting it.

> " For we are Ancients of the earth,
> And in the morning of the times."

" Love and Duty " was born of his personal dilemma; his love for Emily Sellwood, his desire to realise it in marriage, the duty which he owed to art, and which therefore forced him to " hold passion in a leash." It contained some pompous, rather self-satisfied writing, such as :

> " But am I not the nobler thro' thy love ?
> O three times less unworthy ! likewise thou
> Art more thro' Love, and greater than thy years ;
> The Sun will run his orbit and the Moon
> Her circle. Wait, and Love himself will bring
> The drooping flower of knowledge changed to fruit
> Of wisdom. Wait : my faith is large in Time,
> And that which shapes it to some perfect end.
> Will someone say, Then why not ill for good ?
> Why took ye not your pastime ?   To that man
> My work shall answer, since I knew the right
> And did it ; for a man is not as God,
> But then most Godlike being most a man."

The consolations of self-conscious virtue are a poor alternative for love, as is the belief that in following duty one is avoiding the vulgarities of the demagogue.

> " O shall the braggart shout
> For some blind glimpse of freedom work itself
> Thro' madness, hated by the wise, to law
> System and empire ? "

It is a strange lover who can thus preach to his mistress. Yet in this poem, as later in parts of " Maud," when Tennyson's sincere personal passion is allowed (how rarely) to seize the reins, it speaks with candid nobility, and with a power which helps us regretfully to realise what Tennyson might have been :

> " O then like those, who clench their nerves to rush
> Upon their dissolution, we two rose,
> There—closing like an individual life—
> In one blind cry of passion and of pain,
> Like bitter accusation ev'n to death,
> Caught up the whole of love and utter'd it,
> And bade adieu for ever."

The poems of 1842, then, include much of the purest poetry Tennyson wrote, and amongst the mediocre verses are lines not only of fine descriptive writing, such as

> " The light cloud smoulders on the summer crag "

—felicities which he was to multiply all his life (for he was ever an incomparable master here)—but also such examples of concentrated imagery as :

> " She turn'd, we closed, we kiss'd, swore faith, *I breathed*
> *In some new planet.*"

Even in " Locksley Hall " :

> " Love took up the harp of Life, and smote on all the chords
> with might :
> Smote the chord of self, that, trembling, pass'd in music out
> of sight."

This heightened speech of passion he rarely, if ever, achieved after this time, and no amount of industrious polishing or simulated fire can compensate us for its loss. Of weak lines, however, unenriched by any emotion, and of moral and political jargon, the volume is freer than any of its successors. The revised earlier poems are many of them artistically exquisite, and in the topical poems such lines as

> " What is it I can have done to merit this ? "

or

> " not only we, that prate
> Of rights and wrongs, have loved the people well,
> And loathed to see them overtax'd,"

or

> " There the commonsense of most shall hold a fretful realm in
> awe,"

are comparatively rare.

Tennyson's moral theory of life, we have said, was the defence he raised in fear against the disease of passion. He preached a " sound condition of the soul " as the best insurance against the wastage of illegitimate desires, and to combat the sense of vanity which haunted him in his fanciful activities.

But the ill of dreaded and despised sensuousness, if not as active as in his earlier poems, has not been entirely exorcised by moral seriousness.

Nature still at times resents an arbitrary repression, and there follow

> " The staring eye glaz'd o'er with sapless days,
> The long mechanic pacings to and fro,
> The set gray life, and apathetic end,"

or

> " A vapour heavy, hueless, formless, cold,
> Came floating on for many a month . . ."

or

> " Vex'd with a morbid devil in his blood
> That veil'd the world with jaundice, hid his face
> From all men, and commercing with himself,
> He lost the sense that handles daily life—
> That keeps us all in order more or less—"

His refuge from such a state was in commonplace politeness in the negation of that forward ranging advocated in " Locksley Hall," a thrusting of the old " wild pulsation " and " tumult of life " into the ordered grooves of society. As he wrote in " Tithonus " :

> " Why should a man desire in any way
>   To vary from the kindly race of men,
>   Or pass beyond the goal of ordinance
>   Where all should pause, as is most meet for all ? "

To such comfort he turned from the withering fire of truth.

Yet we cannot help feeling that another motive besides the need of his nature tempted him away from the difficult path of poetical truth into such irrelevancies as the political and religious jargon of the moment, and that at times he was aware of his apostasy with a lurking self-disgust. In " Will Waterproof's Lyrical Monologue " are the lines :

> " I ranged too high : what draws me down
>   Into the common day ?
>   Is it the weight of that half-crown
>   Which I shall have to pay ? "

and

> " Hours, when the Poet's words and looks
>   Had yet their native glow :
>   Nor yet the fear of little books
>   Had made him talk for show : "

The cry of the world was persistent, and without conciliating it he could look only for a long struggle against neglect and popular disregard ; but the world can be bought by any man of talent for a price— the price of treason to his genius. Temperamental lethargy and the inducements of material policy captured in Tennyson the citadel of the soul. The privations and the loneliness inevitable to a persistent assault on the infinite were too costly to be endured.

5

The 1842 volumes served their author's purpose. They conquered literary London.

Through Carlyle's influence the *Quarterly Review*, in the person of John Sterling, made what seemed to

Tennyson and his friends a handsome apology   Yet
to the critical eye of a later age its appreciation seems
almost as damning as its earlier mockery.

"Among the streams and rocks," wrote Sterling,
"he begins to discourse of virtue ; and when he has
risen on the ladder of his vision to the stars, we shall
hear him singing from the solar way that it is by
temperance, soberness and chastity of soul he has so
climbed, and that the praise of this heroic discipline
is his last message to mankind." It is strange to
think that such words were then written and accepted
as praise.

Spedding, in the *Edinburgh* of April 18, 1843, was
minutely enthusiastic, noting, for example, how much
the revised "Miller's Daughter" is "enriched by the
introduction of the mother of the lover," admiring
Tennyson's capture of the spirit of rural England, and
claiming generally that "the handling in his later
pieces is much lighter and freer ; the interest deeper
and purer ; there is more humanity with less image
and drapery, a closer adherence to truth ; a greater
reliance for effect upon the simplicity of Nature.
Moral and spiritual traits of character are more dwelt
upon in place of external scenery and circumstance.
He addresses himself more to the heart and less to the
ear and eye." Spedding added that could Tennyson
find a subject large enough to take the entire impress
of his mind, the result would be astonishing. The
possibility, however, seemed to devout friends remote !

Everyone in short, agreed that Tennyson had
advanced both in his mastery of art and in his comprehension of life. The one opinion was substantially
correct, the other had little truth in it.

Tennyson's new poems embraced more subjects, but
these were neither deeply human nor universal.
Chivalry, duty, love-making, self-control, rustic scenery,

science, philosophy, political theory, patriotism, Liberalism, doubt, suicide, sensuality—certainly the interests
had multiplied ; for the questioner of God he had an
answer, for the curious naturalist he had a phrase
coined of close observance, for the lover a range of
pretty moods and fevered fancies, for the musician a
ravishing strain of pure word melody that put
criticism to sleep as surely as the Sirens did, for the
painter a score of careful landscapes—not stern and
rugged in feature, but rich in ripe pastures, heavy
foliage, well-kept gardens, rose-wreathed homesteads,
and baronial halls.   It was, above all, a comfortable
book.   Even the " heart of unrest " throbbed to a
cultivated measure, and Nature, hiding her fangs,
pretended to a chaste refinement and an indolent
purity.

But it might be asked had he, save perhaps in three
great poems, looked into life any more deeply than
in the youthful days of careless fancy and sensationalism ?   Had he argued his doubt away by searching
thought and bold imagination, or had he only drugged
it now more often with platitudes than before with
sensuous opiates ?   Had he but exchanged a *dilettante's*
sensations for a *dilettante's* sermons ?

These questions, though doubtless they knocked at
times at the door of his own mind, never troubled
his contemporaries.   It was enough that he had
grown in seriousness and had turned to the problems
of the age.

The plaints and vows of country girls and conscience-
stricken lovers had certainly taken the place of
Mermen's music, of Lilian's laughter and the melancholy of abstract goddesses ; but the characters of
" English Idylls " or Eclogues were no more real than
those of mediæval or classical origin, while they were
generally less musical.   Tennyson had come no nearer

to a true humanity; he still decorated fanciful situations with similes, and, without gaining in poetic depth, he had lost something of that natural ecstasy which quickens the fragility of his earlier poems.

A poet, however, with the appearance of a sober message answered the need of a thousand " deephearted readers," as Aubrey de Vere called them, scattered over Victorian England, and an America where Puritanism was beginning to relax its features and breathe a milder piety. Hawthorne, Margaret Fuller, Emerson and Poe on one side of the Atlantic, Dickens, Rogers and Carlyle on the other, welcomed the volumes unreservedly, Rogers saying of " Locksley Hall" that "Shakespeare could not have done it better"; Carlyle that "Truly it is long since in any English Book, Poetry or Prose, I have felt the pulse of a real man's heart as I do in this same"; Dickens that " these writings enlist my whole heart and nature in admiration of their Truth and Beauty"; Sara Coleridge that " The Epic is what might have been expected, not epical at all, but very beautiful. . . . ' The Gardener's Daughter ' is most highly wrought and still more to be admired, I think, than the ' Morte d'Arthur.' " A little later Poe was to write : " In perfect sincerity I regard Alfred Tennyson as the noblest poet that ever lived. I call him and think him the noblest of poets, not because the impressions he produces are at all times the most profound, not because the poetical excitement which he induces is at all times the most intense, but because it is at all times the most ethereal —in other words, the most elevating and most pure."

Few even of the fine minds of the time recognised that though the pure must always be elevating, the elevating may not poetically be pure.

Emerson's criticism is perhaps that with which no one now would quarrel : " Tennyson is endowed

precisely in the points where Wordsworth wanted.
There is no finer ear, nor more command of the keys of
language." To us such words are very tentative
praise ; at the time they seemed conclusive.

But the book, being as it were a Parliament of all the
talents and not unattended by genius itself, attracted
an universal suffrage. The literary world was pleased
to cry with Dickens : " What a great creature he is ! "
Those readers who were captured by the sincerity of
" Ulysses " accepted in the same spirit the meretricious picture of a " nobly simple country girl " in
" Dora," while admirers of the bluster of " Locksley
Hall " were equally ready to languish in the " Palace
of Pleasure," taste the Hebe bloom of the " Gardener's
Daughter," or conduct moral arguments over the heads
of submissive ladies. Finally, the man who noticed
that ash-buds were black in March impressed everyone
as a model of poetical integrity and insight !

Fitzgerald alone found something to criticise. It
was a poem entitled " The Skipping Rope," never
republished, in which Tennyson played the schoolgirl
with laborious facetiousness :

> " Sure never yet was Antelope
> Could skip so lightly by.
> Stand off, or else my skipping-rope
> Will hit you in the eye."

" Alfred," wrote Fitzgerald, " whatever he may think,
cannot trifle." There are men too great to jest, there
are others too small. Tennyson, perhaps because he
believed that all the greatest men had been humorists,
was led at first himself to affect in poetry an occasional
sportiveness. But a broad humanity and a complete
absence of self-consciousness are indispensable for the
jester. Tennyson had neither, and his jesting is
therefore forced with effort from a hollow heart.

"O me, my pleasant rambles by the lake
With Edwin Morris and with Edward Bull
The curate : he was fatter than his cure."

It is heavy-footed raillery! And Tennyson, with a rapid and typical appreciation of what was beyond his powers, realised that from a poet occupied with the serious problems of his age the gift of humour was perhaps fortunately withheld.

But if humour perished for want of air, doubt also began to languish. The self-questioning, the secret arraignments of faith in God and immortality, grew less and less severe. The prevalent belief in an inevitable, if slow, development of life ever upward, from protoplasm to the fine flower of the English middle classes, invited surrender of the human will to a progressive Nature, which it was convenient without examination to call God. So pronounced an "ascent of man" could be no less than Divine!

Rebellion, which had never touched the deeps of Tennyson's being, was over, a fluctuating repose was won. The vistas of evolution comforted him. "Not in vain" did "the distance beacon"; it relieved him of the effort of trying to read the foreground. Of what value was his doubt when a million years were scarce more than a geological moment? Of what value his striving when all things, by their divinely native impulse, tended onward? To argue with doubt when fronted by the apparent certainties of science, was time and energy ill-spent. Wiser was it to bury doubt in the genial poetry of tempered optimism, to believe and hope in the end and not look too closely at the process.

One brave mind only at this time resisted with energy the plausible pleadings of "progress." Carlyle, in "Past and Present," and a few years later in "Latter Day Pamphlets," slashed savagely at the pretty, popular picture, with its vague improving vistas, shattered the goddess which elevated opinion found it so convenient to worship, and in rude tones sketched the ghastly ritual that her temple staged on weekdays, all unknown to the cultured Sunday devotees. His voice troubled the calm of men's acquiescence, but only for a moment ; its very stridency modified its appeal. And then the man was known to be a slave to dyspepsia !

Tennyson was now adequately recognised in all literary quarters. It was significant that his verses became suddenly popular as material for classical students to render into Latin hexameters—the only form of poetic favour indeed which has survived every change of fashion !—and in Oriel Common Room a debating society named " The Decade " discussed the motion that " Tennyson is the greatest poet of the age." Wordsworth, in the eyes of youth, had begun to take a second place. It was in 1843 that he and Tennyson first met at Mr. Moxon's house in London.

Accounts vary as to the exact impression made by the younger on the older poet, but it seems clear that his striking appearance, together with some words of courtly homage, quickened Wordsworth to a more generous appreciation than had the poems themselves. " The large dark eyes, generally dreamy, but with an occasional gleam of imaginative alertness, the dusky, almost Spanish complexion, the high-built head and the massive abundance of curling hair like the finest and blackest silk " cast their customary spell.

" I saw Tennyson," he wrote, " when I was in London several times. He is decidedly the first of our living poets, and I hope will live to give the world still better things. You will be pleased to hear that he expressed in the strongest terms his gratitude to my writings. To this I was far from indifferent, though persuaded that he is not much in sympathy with what I should myself most value in my attempts—namely, the spirituality with which I have endeavoured to invest the material universe, and the moral relations under which I have wished to accept its most ordinary appearance."

In short, to the imagination of Wordsworth, Tennyson's spirituality and morality, the two qualities which seemed particularly distinctive to affectionate friends, were so negligible as to be unnoticed. He approved only the art and craft. Three years later, in conversation with another friend, he said of the poetry of the day : " There is little that can be called high poetry ; Mr. Tennyson affords the richest promise. He will do great things yet, and ought to have done greater things by this time." If he had but known, the greatest had already been accomplished. The years were not destined to bring the deep note of poetic passion for which he hoped.

Tennyson's attitude to Wordsworth was the exact reverse. He lamented a lack of art ; and once, after visiting him, he complained of the " Old Poet's " coldness. He had tried to rouse Wordsworth's imagination, which had been brooding now for half a century upon the truth of man and of God, by a description of a tropical island where the trees, when they first came into leaf, were a vivid scarlet. " Every one of them," I told him, " one flush all over the island, the colour of blood." It would not do. I could not inflame his imagination in the least ! " The scene might have been sketched by Coleridge to illustrate his definition of the difference between fancy and imagination ! We can guess how insignificant an episode an island of sanguinary vegetation would seem to the poet who had lived through the ardours and the horrors of the " Terror," who had been ready to hail

an universal liberty from the ruck of human bloodshed,
had looked lust and savagery in the face, and had
fought his way to faith through the close scrutiny of
despair. He had long learnt the dullness of sensa-
tionalism. Yet, to the fastidious Victorian an island
the colour of blood suggested a fascinating spectacle.
Picturesque violence allured ; it stimulated jaded
senses, it quickened the pulse in perfect security. The
old Romantic's apathy was attributed to the dying
fire of genius.

The response of contemporary taste was very
different. As early as September, 1842, Tennyson
could write to Lushington : " Five hundred of my
books are sold ! According to Moxon's brother I have
made a sensation." Only two years later he was given
prominent appreciation in R. H. Horne's " A New
Spirit of the Age." It contained as a frontispiece the
attractive portrait which Fitzgerald had persuaded
Laurence to do of the poet. The dark patrician
beauty of the face, with its haughty tenderness, which
enthralled every acquaintance, was thus enabled to
speak, and that eloquently, to the public at large.
For the next five years edition followed edition of his
poems. An ardent poetess, by name Miss Barrett,
whose acquaintance Tennyson was shortly to make,
was so spellbound by the " enchanted reverie " of his
verse that, when asked to criticise, she excused herself
on the plea that it is impossible to criticise the divine ;
and if some good-humoured flippancy at his expense
found expression in the " Bon Gaultier Ballads," they
helped to advertise his claims.

Yet, although Tennyson had seized the moment, and
wrung from it by policy and industry a fair meed of
literary applause, he had not yet succeeded in opening
the purse of the general public. His engagement to
Emily Sellwood had been annulled before the publica-

tion of his last poems, and they had agreed even to
cease correspondence, since there seemed little prospect
that circumstances would ever justify marriage. That
this was a grievous disappointment to Tennyson is
certain ; but there is no evidence to show that it
seriously disturbed his equanimity, that it soured his
days, or induced any such restlessness as usually
accompanies the frustration even of a temperate
passion. He was absorbed in his art, in memories of
Hallam, and the elegies which were growing up round
that memory ; and, lastly, in his endeavours to capture
the public taste. Success in this latter attempt would
bring him what in his heart he desired more than the
raptures of love—home life, the companionship of a
gentle, sympathetic woman, the joys and responsibilities of fatherhood. All his energies were therefore
concentrated on these three aims, which conflicted
with each other, but not with an ardent lover's passion,
to which he did not pretend. A catastrophe, however,
was at hand, which seemed to eliminate even the
tenuous hopes of marriage he still cherished.

In a letter to his friend Rawnsley in 1842 Tennyson
wrote : " How the wood-scheme goes on, you ask.
The concern, I believe, is going on very well ; there
are as many orders as can be executed by our old
presses ; we have been modelling presses all this time.
We have dropt the name ' Pyroglyph ' as too full of
meaning . . . and call ourselves ' The Patent Decorative Carving and Sculpture Company ! ' " The wood-
scheme here mentioned originated in a Dr. Allen, who
lived near Beech Hill, and had conceived the idea of
wood-carving by machinery. He was apter in enthusiasm than in foresight, and had persuaded the poet
to invest in the undertaking all his personal capital.
Tennyson's interest in the scheme was not merely
financial. It was the combination of art, machinery

and philanthropy which proved irresistible to him; for the company hoped to reap their profits by producing oak panels and furniture carved by machinery so cheaply as to be within reach of the multitude. To Tennyson an idea which would have thrown William Morris into a passion was fascinating. He was not troubled by scruples as to the possibility of art and machinery agreeing together. He had combined them in his poetry; to do the same in the cottage furniture of the poor gave him an agreeable sense of poetry as an active force in daily life. The masses should have art, and have it cheaply; and he should have his dividends. Æsthetically the scheme was deplorable; from every point of view, except that of the investors, we must deem it fortunate that it failed.

But the complete collapse of the project cost Tennyson all his capital, and some of that of his brothers and sisters. The blow caused acute hypochondria. " I have," he wrote, " drunk one of those most bitter draughts out of the cup of life which go near to make men hate the world they move in." If Lushington had not in 1844 generously insured Dr. Allen's life for a part of the debt due, the loss would have been final, but, the unfortunate doctor dying early in the following year, some of the money was then retrieved. That Tennyson cherished no feelings of animosity against him is attested by the letter addressed to Fitzgerald after his death, containing the sentence, " I had heard the news. No gladness crossed my heart but sorrow and pity: that's not theatrical but the truth."

Previous to this disaster he had varied the monotony of Boxley by visits to Ireland, Mablethorpe and St. Leonards. In Ireland the weather was inclement and his visit short, but he had time to visit Killarney, and

the remembered echoes of a bugle on that "loveliest
of lakes" inspired him soon after with one of the
most haunting lyrics he ever penned, "The splendour
falls on castle walls"; some lines also jotted down in
one of the caves of Ballybunion were to be stitched,
years later, into the fabric of "Merlin and Vivien."
So industrious was he in the manufacture of verse
that few novel impressions went unnoted for future
use in his pocket book. In this he suggests the
painter more than the poet, who is usually content
to absorb rather than tabulate his observations.
Tennyson, indeed, later compared his method to that
of Turner taking rough sketches of landskip to work
eventually into some picture, and gave various
instances of lines and images and the circumstances
which suggested them. There can be little doubt
that this habit, like that of building up a poem
about some melodious or high-sounding phrase, may
prejudice creative sincerity. It was his strength and
his weakness to be a too conscientious artist.

So prostrated was he at first by the financial
catastrophe that his life was even thought to be
endangered. He was persuaded to take a water-cure
such as was then the fashion, but it is probable that
a sudden improvement in his circumstances was the
chief factor in restoring him to health and activity.
Fitzgerald did not accept the situation at quite the
tragic valuation of others. "The course of hydro-
pathy," he wrote, "has done its worst; he writes
the name of his friends in water."

By November of the same year Tennyson was
sufficiently himself again to take an interest in current
literature. "Another book I long very much to
see," he wrote to Moxon, "is that of the superiority
of the modern painters to the old ones, and the
greatness of Turner as an artist, by an Oxford under-

graduate, I think." We cannot help wondering what this undergraduate would have thought of mechanical wood-carving !

The man himself had, without doubt, grown more human and less affected during the fifteen years which had passed since Hallam's death. He had known the consecration of a poignant grief, had been cherishing a beloved memory in secret, and pondering it in verse. Moreover, although he had suffered no rude affront from circumstance, and had not wanted, as others have, food and friendship, cheer and hope, he had known disappointment that touched his heart and had taken to some extent the measure of his powers and of the indifference of the world at large. All this had served to humanise him, to make him more honest and less a lay figure of romance. He is spoken of at this time less as a demi-god, more as a man, gruff and kindly. Always generous, even when himself in straitened circumstances, no man deserving and in difficulties approached him in vain, and his charity was as unassuming as it was real. Savile Norton wrote of him : " I never met a heart so large and full of love " ; Aubrey de Vere spoke of his affection for him as " largely domestic in its character. He was pre-eminently a man as well as a genius, but not the least the man of the world. He was essentially refined ; but convention fled before his face. . . . No acquaintance, however inferior to him in intellect, could be afraid of him. He felt that he was not in the presence of a critic, but of one who respected human nature wherever he found it free from unworthiness, who would think his own thoughts whether in the society of ordinary or extraordinary men, and who could not but express them plainly if he spoke at all."

This testimony to Tennyson's largeness of heart is

that of a later zealot than the early " Apostles," and
it reads differently from theirs.   Tennyson was grown
more human because he had put some of his fear
behind him and no longer felt it necessary to pose
as a silent oracle of truth.   He was ready to accept
the limits of his own mind, because he had learnt that
philosophy and intellectuality play but a small part
in the concerns of men, and that fine sentiment is
the key to general favour.   He felt himself qualified
to be the apostle of a tempered faith ; and in ceasing
to pretend to deeper knowledge he found not only
his natural self, but the audience which he craved.
He surrendered only the hope of attaining to the
intensities of poetry at its highest.

In September of the following year the efforts of
his friends were successful in obtaining for him an
annual pension of £200.   Carlyle threatened Milnes
with damnation on the Day of Judgment unless he
approached Peel on Tennyson's behalf.   Peel had
to choose between the poet and one Sheridan Knowles.
He knew nothing of either claimant, but Milnes made
him read " Ulysses."   It was a wise choice ;   the
pension was forthwith conferred on " one who has
devoted to worthy purposes great intellectual powers."

The allocation of a sum of money towards the
support of a struggling artist is well calculated in
commercial and utilitarian England to excite a public
outcry.   But in this case it was in private quarters
that the grant met with both mistaken criticisms and
unnecessary apologies.   Rogers wrote to a friend
shortly after its bestowal: "Tennyson is by many
thought unfit for a pension ;   but he has many
infirmities, such as to you I hope will be ever unknown,
and such as make him utterly incapable of supporting
himself.   Of his genius I need say nothing, and
have only to wish that I could always understand

him. . . . " Later, Bulwer Lytton, labouring under
the misapprehension that the poet was as well-to-do as
his cousins, the Tennyson d'Eyncourts, bitterly attacked
him in some satirical lines in *Punch* for " quartering
himself on the public purse in the prime of life, without
either wife or family."

Tennyson was led to answer him in a contemptuous
poem. But he was too dignified to delight in the
squabbles of " petty fools of rhyme," save in a moment
of justifiable anger at an undeserved attack. He
regretted his action immediately, and in the very next
number of *Punch* secured himself once again on that
pedestal of reserved magnanimity from which it was
his destiny to look down upon a prostrate public.
An august reputation was certainly too precious to
imperil. It served to remove him from the small
rhymsters " who hate each other for a song," to lift
him nearer " God-like state."

> " Surely, after all,
> The noblest answer unto such
> Is perfect stillness when they brawl."

The bad taste, therefore, of Lytton's attack and the
large charity of Tennyson's later reply to it intensified
in the public mind the aura of remote nobility which
had begun to encircle his mysterious personality.
That the pension had come at a moment when some
such stimulus to renewed hope and activity was
above all things to be desired is certain.

Recovering at this time from " the worst cold I
ever caught since I was a Somersby suckling," Tennyson wrote to his old friend Rawnsley, " I begin to
feel an old man myself." (He was thirty-six !) " I
have gone thro' a vast deal of suffering (as to money
difficulties in my family, etc.) since I saw you last,
and would not live it over again for quadruple the
pension Peel has given me, and on which you con-

gratulate me. Well, I suppose I ought in a manner to be grateful. I have done nothing slavish to get it ; . . . and Peel tells me ' I need not by it be fettered in the public expression of any opinion I choose to take up.' . . . Something in that word ' pension ' sticks in my gizzard ; it is only the name, and perhaps would ' smell sweeter ' by some other."

But if the designation of pensioner ill became the dignity of poet and moralist, its practical uses were quickly apparent.

During 1846 work at a new poem, " The Princess," and at the Elegies was resumed, at first in London, and later during tours to the Isle of Wight and to Switzerland. The latter tour, in the companionship of Moxon, likely as it was to awaken memories of Arthur Hallam, did not prove undiluted romance. " Let it suffice," he wrote, " that I was so satisfied with the size of crags that (Moxon being gone on before in vertigo and leaning on the arm of the guide) I laughed by myself. I was satisfied with the size of crags, but mountains, great mountains, disappointed me." The travellers called on Dickens at Lausanne, and found him very hospitable, but of the summit of the Righi the poet could only write : " Crowd of people, very feeble sunset, tea, infernal chatter as of innumerable apes." The sunrise, however, was more inspiring, and on the next day he enjoyed the company of a " jolly old Radical who abused Dr. Arnold." The Bernese Alps and Lauterbrunnen, " the stateliest bits of landskip I ever saw," impressed him most, and the latter inspired the lyric " Come down, O maid, from yonder mountain height," for which he found a place in his rapidly growing " Princess." Business and pleasure, as usual, were combined.

This poem, planned as early as 1839, and suggested

possibly by a passage in " Rasselas," or by " Love's
Labour's Lost," was to deal with the higher education
of women. Mary Wollstonecraft's brave and solitary
challenge, earlier in the century, to male infallibility
and proprietorship had had little effect on public
opinion in general, and Mills' ardent " Rights of
Women " was yet to come. Tennyson realised that
the time was ripe for a temperate judgment of feminine aspiration, one, in short, which would take the
fancy of the ladies by its polished gallantry without
encroaching in any way on the privileges of the
gentlemen.

Meanwhile the Tennyson family had moved from
Boxley to " a nasty house in Bellevue Place," Cheltenham, and here on his return, Tennyson joined them,
and in a disorderly little room at the top of the house
would entertain old friends and new acquaintances.
Among the latter were Sydney Dobell the poet, and
Frederick Robertson, the popular Brighton preacher
and lecturer of later days. Pipe in mouth he would
talk now less constrainedly than before of men and
things, the meaning of death, and the assurance of a
future existence. Christianity was growing each day
more of a reality to him, as it became more of a
necessity. " It is rugging at my heart," he would say,
and when asked whether he were a Conservative, he
would return the enigmatic answer : " I believe in
progress, and I would conserve the hopes of man."
If he had said : " I like the idea of progress, but I wish
to be comfortable and will run no risks," the statement
might have seemed less oracular.

On occasions memories perhaps of Thermopylæ and
Marathon, or of Roman virtue, culled from the classics,
would conflict with so decorous a Christianity, as,
when viewing passing events in France with indignant
disquiet, he was known to launch the terrifying

challenge, " Let us not see a French soldier land on the English shore, or I will tear him limb from limb."

For a moment the sleepy lion had shown his claws, to the edification of an audience which little then guessed that the ferocious threats of an arm-chair self-righteousness in the nineteenth century should have to be honoured with more than gallery gestures in the twentieth !

Generally, it is true, Tennyson found more gracious and less hysterical ways of advertising his common humanity. An acquaintance who would not rest content with asseverating that it was the greatest honour of his life to have met him, but wore the trite compliment threadbare, was told, after the manner of Wellington, not to " talk d——d nonsense " ; while his sincere fondness for children is revealed in letters which he addressed at this time to Mrs. Burton, the wife of the patron of the Somersby living, to whose youngest baby, named Alfred in his honour, he stood as godfather. " Nothing," he wrote, " could be sweeter than Cathy's Somersby violets, and doubt not but that I shall keep them as a sacred treasure.   The violets of one's native place gathered by the hands of a pure innocent child, must needs be precious to me, and indeed I would have acknowledged the receipt of them and sent her a thousand loves and kisses before now, but there were several reasons why I did not write which it is no use troubling you with ; only I pray you kiss her for me very sweetly on lip and cheek and forehead, and assure her of my gratitude.   I love all children, but I loved little Cathy *par excellence* by a kind of instinct when I saw her first."

Some light also is thrown on the nature of his progressive sympathies by a sentence from a letter written to a lady who had forwarded to him some extracts from a book of textual criticism of the Bible

(in those days a brave adventure !). " They seem to
me," he wrote, " to be very clever and full of a noble
nineteenth centuryism, but whether not too fantastic,
if considered as an explanation of the Mosaic text, may,
I think, admit of doubt. Meanwhile, I hail all such
attempts as heralding a grander and more liberal state
of opinion, and consequently sweeter and nobler modes
of living." To us the connection between biblical
exegesis and a higher culture seems remote ; and yet
such humble sapping of the citadel of obscurantism
was possibly more progressive than the repetition of
vague evolutionary sentiments. It may be that here
Tennyson was right, that in the long run it was through
activities kindred to an explanation of the Mosaic text
that the modern age was first conceived. They served
their purpose, more than poetical pamphleteering, in
emancipating minds from slavish adherence to the
word. The spiritual awakening came later.

Tennyson, living in comparative seclusion in Lincoln's Inn Fields, had now nearly completed " The
Princess," but poetry had to wait on politics and
considerations of publicity. " The papers fibbed," he
wrote late in 1840, " when they said I was about to
publish. What would be the use of that in a General
Election ? " Early in the next year he was correcting
proofs, uncertain whether to publish immediately or
in the autumn, and complaining of the very gratifying
interest shown by the Press as to the date of issue.

He was still burdened with a sense of imperfections,
which was indeed to persist until three editions of the
poem had exhausted his ingenuity in revision ; and his
health caused anxiety, eye trouble, due to a failing
nerve, again threatening. He wrote to his aunt,
Mrs. Russell : " They tell me not to read, not to
think ; but they might as well tell me not to live. I
lack something of the woman's long-enduring patience

in these matters. It is a terribly long process, but then what price is too high for health, and health of mind is so involved with health of body ? "

Shortly afterwards " The Princess " was published.

6

Tennyson's activities during the five preceding years had been directed mainly towards two objects—the perfecting of his art and the capture of a wider popularity.

Intimately personal expression was diverted to the elegies, in which for seventeen years he continued in desultory sincerity to enshrine his grief for Hallam's death.

" The Princess " was a bid for popularity, backed by the two factors he knew to be most powerful in their appeal : his own talent for picturesque descriptive writing ; and the choice and handling of a subject which would satisfy alike Liberal and Conservative, feminine and masculine, opinion, progressive senti- ments and reactionary prejudice.   To sympathise with progress in theory, and at the same time to disprove it, by caricature, in practice, he had discovered to be the key to success.   The public yearned for a poet who would provide it with all the self-satisfaction of Liberal sensations, but relieve it of the self-sacrifice entailed in Liberal duties.   It demanded expression of the compromise between what it knew in the last resort to be right and what it conveniently claimed at the time to be practical.   It wished to be made to feel virtuous without reforming fundamentally its manner of life.

To such a public " The Princess " proved very acceptable.   Questions were increasingly asked in advanced quarters as to the true position of woman in society, the ethics which should govern the relations of the sexes, the right training for female minds and bodies. Projects of a Woman's College were in the air, and it was well to profess advanced opinions on these topics, provided they did not lead to the unsettlement of any young girl's mind or endanger the purity of the home.

Tennyson's poem struck exactly the right, the middle note. He seemed to reconcile without humiliation, a set of pretty ladies in revolt with the " ministering angels," the blushing mothers and submissive wives, so cherished by early Victorian sentiment. There was no rude mastery of the charming rebels by brute force; they swam to surrender on a flood of healing tears and dreams of baby fingers melted the iron in their hearts. And so their defeat—their return to a " sweet humility " before the lordly male after a decorative course of study at an unreal academy, and an orgy of hospital love-making—seemed to the Victorian audience to vindicate the rights of everyone most satisfactorily, while leaving things in truth exactly as they were before.

As so frequently with Tennyson's poetical pamphleteering, his handling of the theme and not the theme itself was false. His virtuous intention was vague enough to be vicious. His view of the need of woman's conversion from a chattel to a conscious soul, distinct from, but essentially equal to the male, was just and nobly expressed :

> " For woman is not undevelopt man,
> But diverse : could we make her as the man,
> Sweet Love were slain : his dearest bond is this,
> Not like to like, but like in difference.
> Yet in the long years liker must they grow ;
> The man be more of woman, she of man ;
> He gain in sweetness and in moral height,
> Nor lose the wrestling thews that throw the world ;

> She mental breadth, nor fail in childward care,
> Nor lose the childlike in the larger mind ;
> Till at the last she set herself to man,
> Like perfect music unto noble words,
>
>   .   .   .   .
>
> Then reign the world's great bridals, chaste and calm :
> Then springs the crowning race of humankind."

As a summary of the ideal relations of the sexes it is a trifle sententious, and not to be compared with such an apprehension of their mingling duality as Shelley achieved in " Prometheus Unbound." But the perception is lofty and true, if not without a hint of the patronising masculinity which, finally, put the lady's scruples to sleep with the comforting words :

> " Lay thy sweet hands in mine and trust to me."

That such a conception, however, was only an indulged sentiment is proved by the manner in which he elaborated it. He would not face the conclusions to which his sentiments should logically have led, but denied woman's right to spiritual emancipation even as he pretended to grant it. Having artificially raised her in the narrative of " The Princess " above servility to man and instinct, with many charming compliments he reduced her to her former state. Princess Ida was content to yield to the Prince's assurance of liberal leanings. For our own part we would prefer candid male brutality, " the virgin marble shrieking under iron heels," to a sensuousness so exquisitely masking its selfishness in hyperbole.

Doubtless if " The Princess " could be treated as purely a romantic entertainment, detached from life, a fantasy " for summer as befits the time," it has many qualities to commend it. The writing in places touches Tennyson's happiest heights, the lyrical interludes between each part (these were added in a later edition, but we are here considering the poem in its final form) are melodiously tender, the unconscious humour of many serious situations is extreme—as when the stately and didactic Princess falls into the river—

> " ' The Head, the Head, the Princess, O the Head ! '
> For blind with rage she miss'd the plank, and roll'd
> In the river.   Out I sprang from glow to gloom :
> There whirl'd her white robe like a blossom'd branch
> Rapt to the horrible fall ; a glance I gave,
> No more, but woman-vested as I was
> Plunged ; "

Stage melodrama and burlesque, " the grotesque, or false sublime," are seldom so blissfully wedded ; as richly ridiculous are " those eight mighty daughters of the plough," the college proctoresses, who

> " Bent their broad faces towards us and address'd
> Their motion : twice I sought to plead my cause,
> But on my shoulder hung their heavy hands,
> The weight of destiny : so from her face
> They push'd us, down the steps, and thro' the court,
> And with grim laughter thrust us out at gates."

On another occasion they were less dignified towards an offender ; they

> " Came sallying thro' the gates, and caught his hair,
> And so belabour'd him on rib and cheek
> They made him wild."

Such incidents in comic opera could be relied on to bring down the house.   In a poem of luxuriant lyrical sentiment, which professes also to propound and solve one of the deepest problems of human life—the essential reality of man and of woman in the high adventure of love—they are almost insultingly irrelevant.   And the unreality, the false romanticism, goes far deeper than the tinselled surface ; it falsifies the moral theory which Tennyson was presenting, and led countless others to take the slippery path of hypocrisy.

The supposed moral of the poem was that woman was not created for the uses of man or merely to satisfy the cravings of appetite or of philoprogenitiveness, but that she had a spiritual and intellectual significance of her own, and that only when she was recognised as the free complement of man could any true love exist between the sexes, or any true marriage be consummated. It is the liberal, if not the prevalent, doctrine of our own day, one with which no idealist could quarrel. But the moral was completely submerged by its setting. The pill, to speak commonly, was so coated with sugar as to lose its value as a pill, neither bringing health nor cleansing opinion of impurities, but leading people to believe that they were cured when they were not, a more deplorable condition than sickness itself.

For the fantastic setting not only begot absurdities ; it meant that the problem was presented falsely. Tennyson first caricatured the claim of women and then disproved his own caricature. He created a flowery Academy amid Elysian lawns, and filled it with " Gardeners' Daughters," drinking for a season at the crystal fountain of abstract knowledge. They were not living women, ardent, open-eyed, pure, but a field of daffodils, of " rosy blondes," fresh and glowing, in which the poet luxuriated,

> " With beauties every shade of brown and fair
> In colours gayer than the morning mist,
> The long hall glitter'd like a bed of flowers,"

or, when danger threatened, they became an exotic spectacle, " a swarm of female whisperers," " some red, some pale," " in silken fluctuation," while

> " from the illumined hall
> Long lanes of splendour slanted o'er a press
> Of snowy shoulders, thick as herded ewes,
> And rainbow robes, and gems and gem-like eyes,
> And gold and golden heads ; "

Elsewhere we discover a tent of satin, embroidered with florid maidens !

The whole poem, even in its moments of violence, is voluptuously perfumed. And if the women are ultra-feminine, so also are the men ; they are the apotheosis of carpet-knights in petticoats, who can address an angry lady thus :

> " O fair and strong and terrible ! Lioness . . ."

The women, even the severe Princess Ida herself, are made to appear such preposterous prigs, or such blushing, melting, panting creatures of instinct, that their surrender to the reiterated appeal of maternity and of wounded masculinity is of no more significance than the conventional marriage of a set of characterless girls newly returned to their homes from a finishing school abroad. Tennyson's girl graduates return in fact, after acting a romantic charade, to the domestic fold which they have really never left. Meanwhile the poet, in his attempt to convince us that his young ladies were in revolt, and needed recalling to Nature's paths, never misses an opportunity of playing, sometimes in sickly fashion, upon the maternal string ; as when the bird

> " That early woke to feed her little ones,
> Sent from a dewy breast a cry for light,"

or as of Psyche :

> " and half
> The sacred mother's bosom, panting, burst
> The laces toward her babe,"

or of Ida herself, who took a child

> " for an hour in mine own bed
> This morning : there the tender orphan hands
> Felt at my heart . . ."

The charming lyrical interludes, too, are meant to serve as reminders to his audience of woman's true function in life, the still small voice of maternal conscience amid the bustle of extravagant opinion ! The child,

dead or alive, figures with a purpose in most of them—
in the cradle-song, to recall the student to the nursery,
in the martial song, to inspire the soldier to strike his
enemy dead, in another, to relieve a widow's grief, in
yet another, to heal a domestic quarrel. And Tennyson originally planned an additional chorus of jubilant
women singing over a child saved from drowning.

Primarily, then, "The Princess" represents the
manufactured rebellion of a number of very normal
young ladies from a marriage contract which they
would by nature have been the first to embrace,
and their artificial reconversion to it through an
aggravation of compassionate maternity. But the
revolt of healthy-minded women has never been
against maternity as such, nor towards a life dressed
with the confectionery of learning and art. The true
revolt was to be directed against the quality of man's
love upon which the privilege and the pain of motherhood were based ; it was a demand for the right of free
and active, as distinct from graciously servile love,
for the passion which will make of marriage the
blended union of two natures finely conscious, each
beckoning to the other from native heights. Marriage
is no less an insult to womanhood when it represents a
family investment than when an act of violent possession. And there was in cultured Victorian England,
behind much mock chivalry and sublime male prostra-
tion, a very material view prevalent of the uses of
woman in the home. The frank animalism of the old
King in "The Princess" probably represented a
considerable body of opinion :

> " Besides, the woman wed is not as we,
> But suffers change of frame. A lusty brace
> Of twins may weed her of her folly. Boy,
> The bearing and the training of a child
> Is woman's wisdom."

Nice sentiment can refine, but it cannot verify any union entered upon primarily for the accumulation of children by men unable to forget themselves in that passionate realisation of love, of which children are the considered, beautiful, but secondary expression. For true love is absolute in itself.

Against such physical tyranny in all its forms women of fine spirituality were eventually to rebel, as against a degradation, no less real because it was praised as a social virtue, received the blessings of the Church, or was dressed in impassioned compliments. Education in the arts and sciences was, therefore, of value to women, as all true education is, not in itself, nor for the *dossiers* of knowledge which it might offer, but as fitting them to develop their powers on an equality with men, to realise their personalities, and so qualify themselves not to droop before mankind " in sweet humility," but to seek a worthy mate with candid eye.

Of such an ideal Tennyson's dainty, bridling Graces are incapable, and thus their picturesque educational experiment is as pointless as it is artificial, while the surrender of the contrite Ida to her convalescent and gently admonishing lover is more reasonably attributed to the strain of hospital duties than either to the abandonment or the realisation of a cherished ideal.

There is something nauseating about a heroine who is made to find " fair peace once more among the sick " :

> " and everywhere
> Low voices with the ministering hand
> Hung round the sick : the maidens came, they talk'd,
> They sang, they read : till she not fair began
> To gather light, and she that was, became
> Her former beauty treble ; and to and fro
> With books, with flowers, with Angel offices,
> Like creatures native unto gracious act,
> And in their own clear element, they moved."

Ida's final admission of wrong-headedness, too, represents an abasement, a humiliation of spirit hard to tolerate. "What pleasure," she chants, "lives in height, In height and cold, the splendour of the hills ? . . . Love is of the valley, come thou down and find him. . . . The children call."

Did ever poet more flagrantly deny his soul than in these lines, more publicly choose the lower path ? It is the fatal compromise which poetry can never tolerate ; and the penalty of such cessation of ideal effort by man or woman is either animalism or that lethargy of the soul, when

> "trust in all things high
> Comes easy to him,"

so easy, in short, that it lacks all reality, as did the high-flown words of the lady lecturer :

> "Better not be at all
> Than not be noble."

Tennyson's reward, however, was inevitable. He gained the world. He lost only truth.

As a whole, then, " The Princess " lacks emotional or intellectual sincerity. It contains passages both of lush and delicate description and of high sentiment, much perfect music, and many lines that throw light upon Tennyson's own attitude to women—his tendency to regard them as mothers in the making rather than souls crying for light and love—and upon his social views, as for example :

> " For me the genial day, the happy crowd,
> The sport half-science, fill me with a faith
> This fine old world of ours is but a child
> Yet in the go-cart. Patience ! give it time
> To learn its limbs ; there is a hand that guides : "

or

> " then the maiden Aunt
> Took this fair day for text and from it preach'd
> An universal culture for the crowd
> And all things great,"

or again, the passage in which, foreshadowing all the errors of Imperialism, he wrotes of how

" those two crownéd twins,
Commerce and conquest, (shall) shower the fiery grain
Of freedom broadcast over all that orbs
Between the northern and the southern morn."

The times, we must admit, did not encourage an author to be honest in his political and social opinions, nor can we in these things judge Tennyson by the standards of our own age; but as a poet we must condemn him for accepting current opinion, whether advanced or retrograde, not merely on questions of the day but on such essential values as love itself and the woman, to whose soul a poet's love should pierce.

The poet should above all bear witness, to a world intent on material gain, that beauty at least can neither be taken by force nor selfishly enjoyed. The beauty and the truth of woman is as impregnable to such tactics as that of hill and wood. Her secret eludes alike the brutal and the indolent egotist : it can only be learnt by a passionate sympathy, by a love one with life in all its ardour and one with understanding in all its subtle consideration, a love which surrenders all to receive all, which realises the absolute harmony of creative life, because it has scorned compulsion and trodden a mean self-satisfaction underfoot.

The great poet discovers truth; he never accepts contemporary standards in his estimation of the realities of life. This, however, Tennyson did; he improved on the standard investing it with an air of nobility; but at bottom the standard remained false. Once again he sanctified sensuousness, he did not sublimate it. The trumpet boast of high intention cannot save such a man from the adverse verdict of a more honest posterity. It is useless for the poet to say grandiloquently :

> " That it becomes no man to nurse despair,
> But in the teeth of clench'd antagonisms
> To follow up the worthiest till he die."

He is not judged by virtuous affirmations, but by the quality of vision, the sincerity of experience revealed in his reading of life. Those who have witnessed during the last thirty years the early stages of that struggle in love's and woman's high service, to rescue the spirit from the flesh, even at the temporary cost of a cherished convention of decency—which, if it sometimes truly symbolised an inward refinement, more often was only a mask that hid the selfish face of falsehood—are driven to dismiss " The Princess " as :

> " fancies hatch'd
> In silken-folded idleness."

The poem lacks truth and passion and brave self-forgetfulness, and is of value only for the sake of a few

> " jewels five-words long
> That on the stretch'd forefinger of all Time
> Sparkle forever."

7

" The Princess " is more reasonably considered " the herald-melody " of Tennyson's failure, of his abdication of the poet's crown, than, as has been said, that of the higher education of women. It is of signal importance in his life as being the first clear announcement of a contented compromise with life. It reveals retrogression in all save art, and henceforth the old self-criticism and self-disgust—which registered in him a desire to

> " Reach the lone heights where we scan
> In the mind's rarer vision this flesh "—

were more and more to be silenced. He accepted defeat at the hands of life and of the lymphatic

elements in his nature, and he thought to turn his
defeat into victory by speaking of it in elevated
language.

Fitzgerald, with the tacit assent of Carlyle, voiced
a lonely protest. He even called the poem "accursed."
"I am considered," he wrote, "a great heretic for
abusing it; it seems to me a wretched waste of power
at a time of life when a man ought to be doing his
best; and I almost feel hopeless about Alfred now."
The contrast between the heroic presence and the
indolent strain of verse which issued from it was to
remain for Fitzgerald an abiding and tantalising
mystery. Even in the lyrics he missed the "cham-
pagne flavour" of former days. His hopelessness was
to be much justified in the after-event, but his criticism
prevailed nothing against the generality of applause.
Three editions followed in quick succession.

Very different was the fate of another volume of
poems issued at this time, of which Tennyson was
apprised in the following letter:

"Sir,—My relatives, Ellis and Acton Bell, and
myself, heedless of the repeated warnings of various
respectable publishers, have committed the rash act
of printing a volume of poems. . . . In the space of a
year the publisher has disposed but of two copies; . . .
Before transferring the edition to the trunkmakers, we
have decided on distributing as presents a few copies
of what we cannot sell. . . . I am, sir,
                    Yours very respectfully,
                              "Currer Bell."

It must surely have been with mixed feelings that one
who had learnt how to woo successfully the public
taste received this produce of its neglect.

Princess Ida remained to Tennyson one of his
favourite heroines, a strong woman, as he wonderfully

deemed her, agreeably tamed, " subduing the elements
of her humanity to that which is highest within her,
and recognising the relation in which she stands
towards the order of the world and toward God " :

> " A greater than all knowledge beat her down."

When we remember that this high-souled heroine had
consciously sacrificed her supposed ideal to what was in
fact brainless instinct, instead of reconciling the two
in any true sense, we can only wonder in what way
Tennyson differentiated God from the brute laws of
Nature.

It was this lack of searching intellectual honesty
which invalidated his doctrine of " chivalrous reverence." In himself the sentiment of chivalry was
possibly a reality, a true contrition of spirit and
delicacy of sense, as when he said : " I would pluck
my hand from a man even if he were my greatest hero,
or dearest friend, if he wronged a woman or told her a
lie." But later, when he preaches " the maiden
passion for a maid,"

> " Not only to keep down the base in man,
> But teach high thought and amiable words,
> And courtliness and the desire of fame,
> And love of truth, and all that makes a man,"

his words betray him. For it is of the uses, not of the
reality, of chaste passion that he writes. A maid, by
the love which she inspires, may enjoy the privilege
of helping to make a man, of teaching him manners,
and launching him upon a successful career. It is a
small, selfish and partisan view of love, however
plausible its expression, just as a chivalrous attitude
could be and often was no more than a courtly fashion
by which men did their best to veil an essential
patronage.

It seems probable, however, that as the poet in

Tennyson deteriorated, the man, personally and socially, improved. More and more he struck the onlooker as a "magnanimous, kindly-delightful fellow," in Fitzgerald's words, because he was content to utter " by far the finest prose-sayings of anyone," and was thus relieved of the irritation consequent on a secret, if ineffectual, struggle against the tide of everyday opinion and his own weaker self.

With the publication of " The Princess," and the fourth edition of the poems in one volume, Tennyson could turn with an easy conscience to the completion of those elegies, consecrated to the memory of Arthur Hallam, over which he had been brooding for seventeen years.

These poems, begun under the imminent shadow of loss, and expressing a poignant personal emotion, had come in the course of time to embrace what were controversial questions of the day—the certainty or uncertainty of a future existence, theological doubts, scientific wonders, and the vision of a reformed society. Yet Tennyson, it is clear, was making no conscious bid for popularity in versifying such topics. They were contingent to Hallam's own speculations, and in discussing them Tennyson sought, as it were, to renew his friend's spirit on earth, and to console his own. His disquisitions proved popular because they were topical, vague and superficial. It was not within his powers to pierce deeper into the great mystery ; but as a sustained expression of a humble and personal emotion, unworthily informed though it was by energy and thought, " In Memoriam " is perhaps unique amongst all Tennyson's writings.

To the finishing of this prized and private task he gave himself for the next three years. His trips to London from Cheltenham were more frequent, and the circle of his friends grew. Miss Barrett, Macready,

the actor, Coventry Patmore, and Thackeray were
of the number. With the two latter he became very
intimate, and acquaintanceship with Macready took
him often to the theatre. Old friends, however, were
not neglected ; he frequently breakfasted with Rogers,
who was apt to prove touchy if his poetical omniscience
were questioned, but was ever kindly at heart ; the
enigma of death was much in the thoughts of both,
and it is probably of this time that Tennyson wrote :
" We have often talked of death together till I have
seen the tears roll down his cheeks." At Rogers'
house he met, among others, Crabb Robinson, the
diarist who rivalled his host in garrulity, Tom Moore,
the poet, and Mr. W. E. Gladstone, a rising young
politician.

The Carlyles saw much of him, and although to
the worshipper of Cromwell and the scourger of cant
" The Princess " must have seemed to justify his
previous Hogarthian description of the poet as " sitting
upon a dung-heap, surrounded by innumerable dead
dogs," his respect for the man underwent no eclipse.
Often they would walk about the streets together at
night, Carlyle vehemently raving, as was his wont,
against the " putrid phosphorescences " of the time,
Tennyson sympathetic but deprecatory. Once only,
it is rumoured, they quarrelled, when the poet talked
of poetry as " high art." For the very element which
Carlyle denounced in poetry was cultivated snobbery,
the elegancies of æsthetic deportment ; and it is plain
that he was drawn to Tennyson, when first they met,
not as an artist, but as a soul " who had almost lost
his way amongst will-o'-the-wisps," a struggling soul
feeling out vaguely towards deeper mysteries even as
he himself was, though with half the power, and
likely, without help, to flounder " among the quag-
mires that abound." But he knew Tennyson's weak-

ness. "He wants a task," he wrote to a friend, "and, alas! that of spinning rhymes and naming it 'Art' and 'High Art,' in a time like ours, will never furnish him."

A Society of Authors which gave a dinner at Hampstead, to which Tennyson was invited about this time, was less critical of "High Art" than the Sage of Chelsea. Sergeant Talfourd, who was in the chair, expressed the feelings of the company when he informed the poet that he was "sure to live," and Douglas Jerrold, seizing his hand in the exuberance of the moment, added, "I haven't the smallest doubt that you will outlast us all, and that you are the one who will live." Strange and a little ironical must these boasts of permanence have sounded to one who for so long had been communing with the apparent impermanence of death! If only, Tennyson may well have thought, he could be as certain, in such moments of gratifying enthusiasm, of other than literary immortality!

The solitary little churchyard of Clevedon, in Somersetshire, where Hallam's remains lay within sound of the waves moaning and fretting about the cliffs near by, must have risen before his mind's eye often in these months, when every day the world seemed to be taking him to its heart more intimately, and the "tender grace of a day" less peopled and popular, but, oh! how much dearer and truer, was being sealed with the incontrovertible sign of death. He longed to prove "no lapse of moons can canker love," but as the years of silence multiplied between them it was not so much over his friend, cut down in the springtide of his powers, that he sorrowed as over his own "widowed" state and the problems which that state so insistently, but so vainly, set him to solve.

Hallam was indeed slipping from him ; the memory of that eager spirit no longer woke the old response, urging upward and onward, fretting complacence with its happy impatience of prosaic levels. And if on earth death did indeed bring division not only between body and body, but between soul and soul, so that a love which was once an inspiration became only a sedate, almost a whimsical memory, part at least of the spirit being veritably swallowed with body in the drift of time, then in a future life alone was hope and reasonable continuity to be found.

And yet the world to come was a dreadful speculation, and in moments of dejection he could only look to his Creator with reverent expectation : " Hast Thou made all this for nought ? Is all this trouble of life worth undergoing if we only end in our own corpse-coffins at last ? If you allow a God, and God allows this strong instinct and universal yearning for another life, surely that is in a measure a presumption of its truth. We cannot give up the mighty hopes that make us men."

Increasingly, as " In Memoriam " neared completion, that terrified denial of pessimism found utterance. Tennyson had dreamed enough of doubt in earlier years, ranged over the whole poignant landscape of his loss, and examined its dread contingencies with a detailed detachment almost morbid. But now, as health returned to him and the world began to smile, it was time to turn to " the larger hope " of that eternal future in which alone he might renew the spirit that seemed to have gone out of him and redeem his vision of the " master-mind " that once was Hallam's.

Whether impelled by a feeling of its proximity to the last resting-place of Hallam or, as he wrote, because " I hear there are larger waves there than any other part of the British coast, and must go

thither and be alone with God," Tennyson, in the early
summer of 1848, made a tour in Cornwall, now bathing
in the clear water of Polpur Cove, now sailing where
he could see " the long green swell heaving on the
black cliff " or hear " the dismal wailing of mews,"
walking through fields of crimson clover and " by
bays, the peacock's neck in hue." The haunted
valleys of the West Country, with its myth-awaken-
ing names, its ruins and relics, its Tintagel and King
Arthur's Stone, its " castles darkening in the gloom "
and marble-veined caves, in stormy weather chambers
of stifled thunder, its Land's End, so suggestive of
" Life's End," consorted well with his mood of mellow
melancholy. Thoughts of his knightly friend and of
this old enchanted world of romance were in harmony,
both having perished out of time, but both preserving
a fragrance as of immortal youth and courage. He
dreamed of devoting himself again to the theme of
" Arthur."

But the tour was not without realistic incident.
" At one place," it is told of him, " where he arrived
in the evening, he cried : ' Where is the sea ? Show
me the sea ? ' So after the sea he went, stumbling in
the dark, and fell down and hurt his leg so much that
he had to be nursed six weeks by a surgeon there, who
introduced some friends to him, and thus he got into
a class of society totally new to him." From this time
on he stayed with little grocers and shopkeepers along
his line of travel, and found Cornishmen very superior
to the generality, and very appreciative of his poetry.
Whereof the narrator of the story remarks : " Thus
he became familiarised with the thoughts and feelings
of all classes of society "—a supposition, however,
which we shall find scarcely verified by his poetry.
But the sea as usual brought him health, if shopkeepers
failed to bring him democratic experience.

One to whose father's house in Plymouth Tennyson paid a visit, during this tour, has left a vivid picture of him, vigorous and voluble, nervous of company, with a " powerful, thoughtful face, kind smile, hearty laugh," and extreme near-sightedness ; of his conversation, too, touching hurriedly upon a multitude of subjects so diverse as Titian, geology, lower organisms, railway engines and Goethe, " the snobbery of English society," and " the wholesomeness of kitchen gardens " ; and of how he confided in this very young lady, a poetical aspirant herself, that he was shy " only with false or conventional people "—among whom admiring young ladies must certainly not be numbered. " I would rather stay with you bright girls," he said, " than dine with Mr. W." With all such he was henceforward gallantly at ease. The shyest maiden who approached him would be received with a gracious benevolence rarely accorded to any youth or man on first making his acquaintance.

Cornwall must have supplied much material for his poetical notebook ; and this was supplemented by a visit to Scotland in the succeeding autumn. Again the sea was his delight, and the " exquisite shapes " of the far hills ; but the lochs disappointed him. He visited Kirk Alloway out of love for Burns ; they were gathering in the wheat, and the spirit of the man seemed to mingle with all he saw. Standing beside the " bonnie Doon," he felt the tears course down his cheeks in memory of that " passionate tormented heart." It was only in tamer hours that he would remark how " dreadfully coarse " the poet Burns could be.

Meanwhile little was added to the Elegies, but Tennyson planned to print some twenty-five copies, the better to judge of their merits, circulating them among his friends.

A German poet had now honoured many of his poems with translation, and Tennyson began to receive those unsolicited expressions of admiration from private individuals which, in the years when self-confidence is still halting, are of such particular value to a writer, even if in later years they may become a burden.

He was again at Mablethorpe early in 1849, revising " The Princess " for a new edition ; and later in the year, on the invitation of Aubrey de Vere, paid a second visit to Ireland, and was there charmed by the modest loveliness of Irish girlhood—with one " stately " maiden, indeed, he was prevailed upon to play in a charade the Prince in his own poem of " The Sleeping Beauty," to another he promised a pocket copy of Milton. He was shocked by the poverty of the Irish peasantry, but the high spirits of the most melancholy race in Europe seem to have infected him ; for he was persuaded by a scolding lady to give up " growling at his amusements in a voice as deep as a lion's," and to dance for several hours on end. The mists which had hung over him for twenty years were at last scattering before the morning breeze of success, and once again, as of old, he seemed to hear " the horns of Elfland faintly blowing." But if in Ireland he could escape from himself momentarily into that realm of faery, where he was ever most at home, outside the radius of contemporary opinion, regaining perhaps something of the old sense of enchantment he knew in care-free days at Somersby—London, when he returned to it, broke the spell.

The burden of the mystery returned to him, the baffling enigma of death. Late every night at this time Aubrey de Vere would visit him, and Tennyson would read from his long, narrow manuscript book in a voice trembling with emotion, or discuss his Elegies till the early hours of the morning. " The tears often ran down his face as he read, without the slightest apparent consciousness of them on his part," and his voice would drop towards the end of a stanza, or at moments when the pathos of remembrance overcame him. For the years had made the grief which he was here recording something far more than personal. Over the restless pain of his own loss Time had begun to scatter her poppy, bringing " the low beginnings of content "; he could now almost have regarded the private tragedy dispassionately, had it not come to signify in his mind something universal—that awful shadow which death casts over every thing of beauty once loved and unavailingly mourned throughout all the world.

" In Memoriam," begun to relieve grief, and as a monument to his friend, growing into a record of past days once bathed in the sunshine of young happiness, had finally become a parable of the soul of man in travail through the night of pain to the dawn of a not too extravagant hope. The " I " of the poem now signified not so much Tennyson himself, as " the voice of the human race speaking thro' him." Loss and lamentation were, alas! all too common, and

> " never morning wore
> To evening, but some heart did break."

It remains to be seen whether Tennyson conquered pain upon this pilgrimage or merely parted company with it when he could no longer endure its presence. To a friend who suggested, later, the addition of a song of triumph to complete, in a third part, a poem in which woe and consolation, but not exultancy, were represented, he answered, " I have written what I have felt and known, and I will never write anything else." It was true. This was perhaps the only poem in which he would countenance no alteration, nor welcome the critical ingenuity of friends or enemies. It was useless for Fitzgerald to write querulously : " Don't you think the world wants other notes than elegiac now ? " In this matter, at least, the world could go unsatisfied. Above policy or calculation, one poem should be his own ; and only because he had become typical of his generation did that generation take it to themselves.

The manuscript, after being nearly lost in a London lodging-house, from which it was rescued by Coventry Patmore, was published anonymously in the early summer of 1850.

8

It is difficult to estimate to what extent Tennyson moulded or was moulded by the opinions of his age. Ideas are in the air, are bartered in private circles, long before they find public expression, and the views on faith and doubt, religion and science versified in " In Memoriam " had doubtless often figured in the discussions of the " Apostles " twenty years before. Tennyson, however, may be said to be so far original as to have articulated these views in very representative terms at least ten years before they were the staple utterance of educated opinion, and in particular of a group of progressive-minded Anglican clergymen. It was not until the appearance of Darwin's " Origin of Species " that men became acutely conscious of a problem, and this did not occur until 1859.

The philosophical idea of evolution was, of course, centuries old, but philosophical ideas do not trouble the popular, nor for that matter the clerical or the scientific, mind. It is true that before 1850 the Darwinian hypothesis had been imperfectly traced in the realm of applied science by such men as Lamarck and the elder Darwin, but Tennyson was among the first to realise the vital and disordering impingement that a physical, as distinct from a philosophical, theory of evolution was to make upon religious sentiment; and his foresight was founded upon no more convincing evidence than Robert Chambers' far from scientific "Vestiges of Creation," also upon a general interest in physics, geology, astronomy and anthropology. But if he attempted to "lay the spectres of the mind" before either he or others had sufficient evidence to estimate their strength, his prevision of the coming dilemma was astonishingly accurate, and mere dates compel us to suppose that the theology of such Broad Churchmen as F. D. Maurice and Jowett was derived, if derived at all, from him.

It cannot be said that either Tennyson or they honestly fronted the attack of science and routed it. Circumstances did not allow them to do that; the assault of mind upon unexamined faith was too sudden. Yet, in the light of our day, they did something perhaps more important. They created a bridge upon which men, with their sacred heritage of humanity and religion, could stand, if uncomfortably, until the threatening flood of materialism had begun to subside; they discovered a compromise to which wise and ignorant alike could cling, until they learnt that the world of human spirit was, in its highest realisation, independent of that of matter:

> " The hills are shadows, and they flow
> From form to form, and nothing stands ;
> They melt like mist, the solid lands,
> Like clouds they shape themselves and go.
>
> But in my spirit will I dwell
> And dream my dream, and hold it true . . ."

It was no small achievement to render faith plausible for the time by a superficial absolution of science.

In so doing Tennyson possibly preserved his generation from being split up into two armed camps of
fanatics, the one excommunicating science, the other
denouncing not only the superstitions but the
eternities of religion. This was, indeed, to prove
noble service to an age which, in spite of the moral
support of such temperate idealism, was only too
ready to prostrate its human spirit before the laws of
physical nature and the science which laboriously
catalogued them.

When "Nature, red in tooth and claw," quite
successfully "shriek'd" down man's intelligence for
a season, the poet who sang "that somehow good
will be the final goal ot ill," and that love was
"Creation's final law," although the words implied
little more than pious aspirations, gave his times a
spar or two to cling to, until a deeper reason returned
and enabled men to see the analysis of physical
science in due perspective, to realise that knowledge, however laborious, was not thought, and that
intellectual vision saw further than the microscope.
Even Tennyson's rather haughty assertion of spiritual
aristocracy was of value in the face of that mechanical
democracy which was to advance across the nineteenth century with science at its head. It helped to
limit the vulgarisation of spirit and of taste whose
occurrence nothing could prevent :

> "Let him, the wiser man who springs
> Hereafter, up from childhood shape
> His action like the greater ape,
> But I was born to other things."

The function of science, we now realise, is to explore
the natural world, to trace the development of life
from the lower organisms up to physical man ; that
of poetry and philosophy is to explore the supernatural world, to trace the progress of man towards

God, his relations to eternity, and the conflict between the spirit and the flesh. The distinction, as even the earlier Romantics knew, is absolute.

The religion of Wordsworth and Shelley, and of Keats in his last days, was a spiritual, as apart from a material, apprehension of what evolution implies. They were not troubled by any threat of physical servitude or any doubt of the reality of the soul or of God, because they saw deeper into life than the generation which succeeded them, and knew that the harmony of which Beauty, Truth and Goodness are the elements, was the state of being to which all evolution tended, and which no scientific statistics could challenge. Spiritual evolution begins where physical ends ; the creative harmony of mind transcends the creative harmony of force. Man is more than the culmination of the beast.

But Tennyson was born into an age which, fearing liberty, confused in its respect for law, the empirical processes of Nature with the finalities of spirit—the facts of an animal world with the idea of a human. The Darwinian hypothesis, even if in point of fact it were proven, does not affect the spiritual values of a modern mind ; it is of physical, not of metaphysical, interest. But Tennyson suffered as much from a lack of metaphysical insight as Coleridge from an excess of it. Feeling he possessed, knowledge he cultivated, absolute apprehension he lacked. He and his generation were enslaved by the relative.

Scientists are bound to the relative, it is their preserved province, and the Victorian theologian, moreover, was an indifferent scientist—religion lacked seership. And so we see in these years the strange spectacle of scientists wishing to believe, but bound by professional logic, and religious men driven to doubt, though tortured by sentimental dogmas.

In the current faith there was much superstition to be exorcised by fearless reason, in the current doubt much small-minded materialism, a confusion, for want of vision, of realism with truth. Tennyson, by common sense rather than intellect, and inclination rather than vision, wrought a unification of faith and scepticism, contriving by limiting himself to generalities and avoiding the deeps of either controversy or experience, to urge men to cherish what was eternal in religion and what progressive in science. But because great poetry does not deal with abstract generalities, but pierces intensely into the heart of life, the topical theorising of " In Memoriam," extremely valuable as it was in its own day in giving a lead to sober opinion, is interesting now only as a relic. Indeed, doubt being a sincerer anguish at that time than faith was a conviction, even the pathetic dilemma of Clough is to-day more poetically alive than the liberal asseveration of Tennyson.

Tennyson's faith was in the long view a more reasonable standpoint, certainly, too, more beneficial to his age, whose nerves were suffering from the first shock of mechanical modernism, but poetically it was less real. For faith then was bound to be an escape from conflict, or, at best, a rather corrupt rearward action. Doubt, on the other hand, did involve a desperate battle, and the omnipresent shadow of defeat.

The synthesis which Tennyson affected was too easy and superficial to excite in him either profound emotion or passionate thought, the two forces out of which poetry is born. He never faced the darkness, and fought his way out into daylight, but rather, remaining safe in the citadel of traditional belief, he invited the less extreme among his sceptical opponents to enter in, and, having composed their difficulties in a general way, to ally with him against the more dangerous forces of disruption.

" This is a terrible age of unfaith," he wrote. " I hate utter unfaith, I cannot endure that men should sacrifice everything at the cold altar of what with imperfect knowledge they choose to call truth and reason."

It is right to be impatient with mere materialists, whether of mind or body, who, trained to facts, are blind to their spiritual significance as ideas. Yet it is only through first daring such a sacrifice that faith and truth can be made one. Tennyson, because he shuddered to expose himself to the material cold, never made himself worthy of the spiritual fire. Formal dogma can be as unspiritual as materialistic science, yet to dogma he clung for its security, fearing always the peril of going out alone into the wilderness beyond the protection of forms, and warning those who so dared that in a world of so many confusions they might meet with ruin " for want of such a type." But only through risking ruin can the soul find thorough salvation. Men and women in general may refuse to take the risk, preferring the passive serenity of the social virtues. It is a poet's duty and distinction to take it.

Many of us can accept to-day, after having stood the searching test of science and discovered its limitations, the first principles enunciated by Tennyson that a God exists revealed at His highest in the quality of self-sacrificing love, that the human will is essentially free, and the soul immortal, that darkness shall in due time be all light, and creative harmony at last, after long discord, be attained.

But Tennyson clung to these principles not so much because he had discovered them for himself, but because they were those upon which " the wisest and best have rested through all ages." His faith on analysis proves to be but a re-statement of the old belief in a Divine Providence, blindly held by the simple, with certain harmless scientific generalities grafted on to it. It is not an advance made upon the stronghold of life, but, so to say, a strategic alliance between an old dynasty too indolent to fight and an upstart too diffident to carry his rebellion to extremes.

Where Evolution seemed to open up vistas of progress from life of " lower phase " to the " crowning race," where it supported the charitable concept that " All is well," it was gladly welcomed by the devout ; where it seemed to ·compel a stricter definition of a so-called Omnipotent Deity, to threaten men's convenient trust in the virtues of Nature and to dwarf the claims of the individual either to survival or free-will in the machine-like manufacture of the type, its evidence was either disregarded without examination or accepted with a grim and absolute despondency for which there was no intellectual justification.

Science makes no claim to a romantic atheism. It is merely neutral ; it seeks practical evidence from physical phenomena, and works on a level quite distinct from that of the eternities to which true religion and art belong. It is not concerned with values ; its morals are those of the machine. It kills superstition, but it cannot touch the truly ideal. It was falsely entitled Reason and opposed to Faith, because Victorian faith was conventional. Science is a very specialised form of applied logic. It is exact only within arbitrary boundaries, and can make no claim to the pure reason of either philosophy at its highest or the creative intuition of art. To pious mid-Victorians, however, it seemed the direct enemy of God, the anti-Christ of the time, a misunderstanding which was very embarrassing to honest-minded investigators, and drove them in mere self-defence to exaggerate the scope of their activity.

"In Memoriam" consoled a wide audience which had begun secretly to fear that God was to be outlawed, not by laying the ghosts of their fear, but by insisting that man could and would not endure the loss of his God. Tennyson's generation was tremblingly determined to hold on to a minimum of faith, which instinctively it dare not surrender, instead of fighting boldly for a maximum consistent with reason. God existed for these men because He was needed, not because He was known, but Tennyson's very inability to penetrate to the heart of Nature or of humanity, to either the essence of the spiritual or the brutal, prevented him from capturing evidence upon which he could convincingly prove or disprove. He neither yielded to materialism nor triumphed through idealism, but he sentimentalised the facts of science, as he did the dogmas of religion, to suit the conclusion he desired, which was, in truth, not the result of passionate insight or logical effort, but merely an emotional preference for the faith of his fathers. At the same time he avoided the charge of obscurantism by appearing to welcome and quote science without really facing the question whether she was foe or friend, or neither, to the higher hopes of man.

His sober faith in immortality springs from the same hungry egotism, not from vision. He claimed that, unless man's soul were immortal, life was meaningless and intolerable, which proves how little Evolution really meant to him and how little he was prepared to sacrifice his identity, if the need arose, to those "nobler types" of the future, which, with all his professed belief in them, he should have been glad, if it were necessary, to serve.

But to be a mere self-effacing agent of progress ill satisfied his egotism. He would not admit that, although belief in an after-life had in the past proved a useful instrument of morality, it was possible to surrender it without man returning perforce to his former " coarsest satyr-shape," " to bask and batten in the woods." In short, he would not grant that a love of the highest might be cultivated for its own sake, and without the rewards and punishments of a conjectural futurity. Yet life is no less a test of truth than death.

To our generation, therefore, Tennyson is neither the poet of Science nor of Religion ; through trying to satisfy both camps (as in his political verse he mixed Conservatism and Liberalism) he compromises, and so lacks poetical conviction. He made faith and doubt live happily together by allowing them only to meet to pass pleasantries about each other.

But to all the men of his time, just because of his compromise, his words proved a very present help in trouble. To industrious scientists who, for no fault of their own, were suddenly burdened with a criminal reputation, it was balm to read :

> " There lives more faith in honest doubt,
> Believe me, than in half the creeds ! "

Moreover, a poet who observed and recorded Nature as through the microscope of his senses, and who welcomed the latest scientific discoveries, was so far more comprehensible than a Shakespeare who seemed to make the world out of his dreams and to move upon a plane where scientific research had no discoverable standing !

It cannot be denied that Tennyson's guarded Liberalism was of great service to an age whose dilemmas command our sympathy. The devout and

the agnostic owed him much.   Faint hope and faint
doubt found in him one to

> " lull with song an aching heart,
> And render human love his due."

He comforted and consoled, and helped to purge the
coming conflict of some of its small-minded bitterness.
Scepticism was to go far beyond his limits, and faith
was to show a far more rueful countenance, but
meanwhile he encouraged tolerance and deprecated
fanaticism, and he had the originality to foresee the
struggle and to prepare men's minds to enter it
guardedly at least ten years before it became acute
or general.

But great poetry is far more than ten years before
its time, and it does not soothe, but liberates and
convinces.   It is clear that later in his life, in moments
of deeper thought, Tennyson's foresight went beyond
the compromise his age invited.   He had glimmerings
of that clearer, more conscious distinction between the
law of Nature and of man, between the physical processes of the life-force and the higher understanding
of humanity which was to be the ultimate reaction
from scientific materialism.   Intuitively he hailed
Creative Evolution beyond Natural Selection, as when
he said, "An Omnipotent Creator who could make
such a painful world is to me sometimes as hard to
believe in as to believe in blind matter behind everything.   The lavish profusion, too, in the natural world
appals me, from the growths of the tropical forest to
the capacity of man to multiply, the torrent of babies."
And " Yet God is love, transcendent, all-pervading !
We do not get this faith from Nature or the world.
If we look at Nature alone, full of perfection and
imperfection, she tells us that God is disease, murder
and rapine. . We get this faith from ourselves, from
what is highest within us. . . ."

Moreover, he came to realise the gulf which for ever divides the realms of matter and of spirit, the gulf which no scientist can ever bridge, because the spirit cannot be tabulated, any more than the wind that "bloweth where it listeth." "No evolutionist," he wrote, "is able to explain the mind of Man or how any possible physiological change of tissue can produce conscious thought." But such confronting of science is not found in "In Memoriam." Here the arguments for religion and morality are either sentimental or utilitarian. "Self-reverence, self-knowledge, self-control," no less than a vague belief in a Benevolent Deity, are preached because, without such faith and discipline, men, it is held, can only sink into pessimism or madness. Certainly the facts of Evolution provided the preacher with picturesque imagery :

> "Arise and fly
> The reeling Faun, the sensual feast ;
> Move upward, working out the beast,
> And let the ape and tiger die."

Sound doctrine, we may allow, but grim matter for the lips of the Muses !

9

Doctrine, however, is only incidental to "In Memoriam." The burden of the poem is the love and grief of one man for another—and that a "soul of nobler tone" than the many. Few, listening to the tale of that sorrow, can fail to recognise the genuine voice of a man tender and great-hearted, one exquisitely responsive to fineness of nature in another—to an aristocracy of spirit—reverent of friendship, patient of remembrance, sincere—if at times morbid—in lamentation, loyal and to some extent self-forgetful as he records an affection in which the elements of worship and understanding so notably united. Only a noble nature could have experienced such a sorrow for " the human-hearted man I loved " as Tennyson reveals in the most intimate parts of his poem.

Yet when we turn from the man, as we must, to the poet, criticism awakes. Tennyson can make us believe that his own sorrow was deep and pro-longed ; but seldom, save in the few high moments of the poem, can he make us share in it. It is not enough for a poet to feel unless he can give to his emotion that unique and concentrated expression which compels response in another. " In Memoriam " is both too diffuse and too mechanical to effect that. There are times when we feel that the poet does literally hold " commerce with the dead," in very truth trading with his emotions to no further end than the accumulation of verses ; the discursive spirit of the poem is well expressed in the invocation :

> " From art, from nature, from the schools,
> Let random influences glance. . . ."

The poem is nowhere marred by the weak sensa-tionalism, the surrender to luxuriant description, so common in his earlier work. " The nerve of sense is numb." His grief is too austere to countenance that. But a want of active creative intelligence is constantly evident ; we do not feel that an urgent emotion is ever demanding new and distinct expression, but rather that the poet is strewing the grave of his friend with endless memorial verses, barely distinguish-able the one from the other, and fashioned consciously to illustrate a sentiment too vague to find form for itself—verses which are

> " Short swallow-flights of song, that dip
> Their wings in tears and skim away."

Or at other times he seems to write for no other purpose than that

> " For the unquiet heart and brain,
> A use in measured language lies ;
> The sad mechanic exercise
> Like dull narcotics, numbing pain."

But poetry is neither a drug nor a substitute for tears.

It is possible, indeed, that Tennyson's grief was too intimate for expression in poetry. The great elegies have rarely had a deeply personal inspiration, for it is difficult to sublimate a private sorrow. Tennyson could not sublimate his ; he could only play variations on a private theme and relate it artificially to abstract problems of life and death. And so at times grief merely

> " Stunn'd me from my power to think
> And all my knowledge of myself."

It made him hysterical—" A weight of nerves without a mind "—or else reduced him to the maudlin

> " My Arthur, whom I shall not see
> Till all my widow'd race be run ;
> Dear as the mother to the son,
> More than my brothers are to me "—

the passage, no doubt, which inspired the historic criticism by one reviewer : " These touching lines evidently come from the full heart of the widow of a military man."

Often he is artificial ; indeed, in the expression of a personal loss, any art of which we are made conscious, any intrusion of technique, however fine, upon the emotion, suggests the artificial, because it implies the degradation of a passionate theme by a manner suitable only for a sentimental. By his choice of stanza Tennyson made it impossible for grief and lamentation to speak spaciously ; their utterance was

bound to be conscious and polite; the surge of life
and of death, of exultation and agony, cannot break
through such a form.   But his artificiality went beyond
technique and its consequences.   He could write:

> " I do but sing because I must,
> And pipe but as the linnets sing "—

as flagrantly false a definition of his method as could
well be imagined, or

> " I met with scoffs, I met with scorns
> From youth and babe and hoary hairs :
> They call'd me in the public squares
> The fool that wears a crown of thorns."

Lapses into " poetic thought " and the prosaic are
too many to call for detailed quotation.   We may
instance

> " How pure at heart and sound in head,
> With what divine affections bold
> Should be the man whose thought would hold
> An hour's communion with the dead."

Or

> " The baby new to earth and sky,
> What time his tender palm is prest
> Against the circle of the breast,
> Has never thought that ' this is I ' :
>
> But as he grows he gathers much,
> And learns the use of ' I ' and ' me,'
> And finds ' I am not what I see,
> And other than the things I touch.' "

Tennyson's mood is happiest when " memory
murmuring of the past " prompts him to describe
scenery and incidents once shared with Hallam.
Here sorrow sheds an inward radiance over pictures
of place and season drawn with that delicacy of
which he was a master.   Such lyrical passages as
" The time draws near the birth of Christ," " When
on my bed the moonlight falls," or " Now fades
the last long streak of snow," are as near perfection

in this kind as the pen of poet can make them.   But
there are moments in the poem when grief rises
above hysteria, morbidity and artifice, when the
stricken spirit of the man launches out bravely into
the deeps whither the spirit of his friend is gone,
and we hear suddenly the tones of the great elegists
sounding above the tinkle of craft :

> " So word by word, and line by line,
> The dead man touch'd me from the past,
> And all at once it seem'd at last
> The living soul was flash'd on mine,
>
> And mine in this was wound, and whirl'd
> About empyreal heights of thought,
> And came on that which is, and caught
> The deep pulsations of the world,
>
> Æonian music measuring out
> The steps of Time—the shocks of Chance—
> The blows of Death.   At length my trance
> Was cancell'd, stricken thro' with doubt."

The trance of imagination was rarely allowed to abide.
It was cancelled quickly not only by doubt but by
the laboured asseveration of faith, the laudation of
" knowledge," by arguments of desperate hope and
self-pity, by the hunger of exact remembrance, and
by the concentration necessary to frequent rhyming.
Possibly Tennyson knew that unless he recorded his
grief consciously, unless he remained chiefly the
sorrowful pedestrian, and bound himself within the
limits of a strict form of verse, he would only lapse
into hysteria. " Let Love clasp Grief," he cried,
" lest both be drowned."   He dare not surrender to
his grief, " like some wild poet," " without a conscience or an aim," because he lacked the intellect
which heightens the hysterical until it becomes the
imaginative.

" In Memoriam " is full of grand and gracious
sentiments—whether personal or, as in " Ring out,

wild bells," or " Strong Son of God, Immortal Love,"
expressive of the noblest religious or social feeling.
Yet the early critic who considered that " a great deal
of poetic feeling had been wasted " was right. The
emotion needs crystallising. " All-comprehensive tenderness " is not in itself sufficient matter for poetry,
nor " heart-affluence in discursive talk," and even a
genuine sorrow can die of mechanical over-elaboration,
until a poet comes only to " embalm in dying songs a
dead regret." The poet need not, or rather, must not,
be a disputant, but he must possess the passionate
insight which pierces immediately to the truth of
things beyond dispute. If he value feeling above
logic, he must be sure that his feeling is profound, and
thus unanswerable, or logic will sneer and trip him up.
Tennyson's feeling lacked concentration, power and
particularity, lacked, above all, a fiery intellectuality.
The " warmth within the breast " and " the freezing
reason's colder part " rarely combine in an apprehension of truth. Working as they do apart, they
neutralise each other's extremes. Once again the
temperamental compromise, which poetry brooks not,
rules the situation, and the result is in the main a music
thin and long-drawn-out, a lack of inevitability, a
sense of weary, laborious and even ingenious
detachment.

10

The qualities of " In Memoriam," however, its wide
range of subject-matter, the slight call it made upon
thought or passion, while simulating both, the tone
of gentle ruminating sorrow, assured it immediate
popularity. To a clergyman such as Robertson it was
welcome as containing " the most satisfactory things
that have been ever said on the future state," to all
who had " loved and lost " it offered for consolation

a mint of subdued reflection, it satisfied the devout, the scientific, the liberal-minded, for reasons already enunciated. Mr. Gladstone considered the poem " the richest oblation ever offered by the affection of friendship at the tomb of the departed."

Anonymity preserved the secret of authorship but a short time. When Wordsworth died on the 23rd of April, Tennyson's verse was in the popular mouth, and his claims to succession to the Laureateship were very strong. Moxon was now able to promise the poet a settled allowance from royalties, his " Poems " had gone into a sixth edition, and with his pension and the life insurance derived from the unfortunate Dr. Allen, he could at last contemplate marriage in safety. On the 13th of June, at Shiplake Church, he was married to Emily Sellwood, the woman for whom he had cherished a loyal affection for over twenty years, during ten of which he had been divided from her. The unhoped-for had been realised. And as if every element of happiness and success were to crowd into this year of wonder, he was appointed Laureate in the following November. Poetry, popularity and officialdom had come to terms. Henceforth he wrote as a public voice. He had conquered his world, he had won his lady. The future stretched assured and prosperous before him, promising the calm of domestic happiness which he craved, and the dignity of a national position and a people's reverence.

Yet as he put thus blissfully into port at the age of forty-one, it may be that for a moment the old doubts and scruples, the old self-criticism of genius, made a last and feeble protest, that the face also of Hallam rose out of the past, gently questioning whether this was indeed the goal of a poet's journeying, and not some pleasant hostel by the way. In life truly he had captured all he wished to capture, but in art, in the recording of vital experience—was there advance and triumph, or had the years brought retreat and resignation, instead of valiant progress ?

" I wish," wrote Fitzgerald, " I could take twenty years off Alfred's shoulders and set him up again in his youthful glory ! " Tennyson himself, we suspect, had no desire to emulate Faust, even if a virtuous archangel had offered him the opportunity.

" Regret is dead," he wrote at the end of " In Memoriam,"

> " but love is more
> Than in the summers that have flown,
> For I myself with these have grown
> To something greater than before."

Greater as man, we are driven to conclude, but weaker as poet, as adventurer in the realms of undiscovered possibilities. For in art, as events were to prove, he had expressed almost all he was to express. Henceforth he ceased to trouble about heights which conscience once had urged him to attempt.

PART III
SUCCESS

PART III

SUCCESS

I

THE ivy-towered church of Shiplake stands, amid
laurel-hedges and cedars, high above the "silent
level" of the Thames, on a promontory overhanging
one of the finest bends of the river. In Tennyson's
life it holds a kindred eminence; it looks out over
forty years of tranquil domestic life, full but leisured,
like the river, and back across forty during which
the poet, whom it welcomed as a bridegroom, had
grown to such stature as circumstances and his imperfect powers decreed. This place, consecrated and yet
homely, mediæval in its ornament and so essentially
English in its setting, was symbolic of the point which
Tennyson had reached in life and in poetry, and
beyond which henceforth he was not to venture.
The doubts and despairs of youth were over, contentment was won; he had possessed himself of "the
wise indifference of the wise."

Long after, he wrote of his marriage: "The peace
of God came into my life before the altar when I
wedded her." Mrs. Tennyson, with her "tender
spiritual nature," her quiet humour, and "faith as
clear as the heights of the June-blue heaven," her
talent for music, her gentle submissiveness, was the
ideal wife for the poet. To her he could turn for
sympathy in times of depression, and even for counsel
in literary matters. "I am proud of her intellect,"

he would say, and together they always discussed whatever work he had in hand. Gradually, as he became a public character, much sought after both by the intellectual and the romantic-minded of the day, he drew into himself, sharing confidences no longer even with the faithful friends of his youth, but only with her who was " Dear, near and true." Fitzgerald was driven fretfully to say : " You know, he never writes, nor indeed cares a halfpenny about one."

To one prejudice, however, Mrs. Tennyson did cling. She held that " doubt was devil-born." After his marriage Tennyson ceased to doubt.

The honeymoon began by a visit to Clevedon. " It seemed a kind of consecration to go there," to bring the two loves of his life together before the gulf widened and his new life carried him further and further away from the still fragrant memories of youth. Husband and wife standing by Hallam's grave, the sacrament of marriage was complete.

They spent some time in Devonshire, rambling through woods and over heather, exploring Exmoor and Glastonbury. Friends vied with each other in proffering honeymoon houses. The Tennysons chose Tent Lodge, Coniston, lent by a sister of Tennyson's old friend, Spring Rice. It possessed a park, considered by Tennyson " as lovely as the Garden of Eden," and a view of lake, wood and hill unrivalled perhaps in Europe. Here they drove, walked and boated with an energy which Mrs. Tennyson may have found a little exacting ; for when Carlyle met them he wrote to his wife : " Alfred looks really improved I should say ; cheerful in what he talks and looking forward to a future less detached than the past has been. A good soul, find him where and how situated you may. Mrs. Tennyson lights up bright glittering blue eyes when you speak to her ; has wit, has sense ; and were it not that she seems so very delicate in health, I should augur really well of Tennyson's adventure." Delicate she was always to remain, but such disability only served to increase the chivalrous devotion of her husband.

Sitting one evening at this time with a friend over a pipe, he let his feelings break through the customary barrier of reticence. " I have known many women," he murmured, " who were excellent, one in one way, another in another way, but this woman is the noblest woman I have ever known." Both he and his Muse were henceforward happily married to nobility.

This was doubtless the quality in " In Memoriam " which won the admiration of the Prince Consort and, supplemented by the Queen's more idyllic appreciation of " The Miller's Daughter," ensured Tennyson the Laureateship. Of his acceptance of the office he wrote : " I was advised by my friends not to decline it. I have no passion for Courts, but a great love of privacy." It was, however, an office which brought him the dignity and stability that he could not but appreciate, without trespassing in any but a gratifying way upon his privacy ; and so exactly were his powers suited to its tenure, so perfect was the blend of poet and publicist, of knight and Victorian gentle-man, that he made of a moribund office something new and vastly impressive, something which met the unspoken wish of the Victorian age—to cherish at least a little longer the pretence that the public life of a modern nation is both moral and romantic.

Certainly, had not Tennyson been Laureate, the Victorian age would lack a perfect figurehead. The acceptance of the Laureateship may not have been as fortunate for the poet himself as for the public. It must have tended to confirm in him that professional conscience, as of one ever singing in a public place and consulting the public ear, to which circumstances had already directed him. Such publicity is fatal to the intimate tones of originality.

Mammon at least was appeased. Henceforth his poems alone brought him in £500 a year, and amid the shoals of verses from every poetaster in the Empire which, as Laureate, he now began to receive, he was correcting all his volumes for new editions.

The Tennysons' first choice of a home was not a happy one. A Copley-Fielding-like view of the South Downs, and " the full song of birds delighting them as they drove up to the door " on a visit of inspection, persuaded them to take an out-of-the-way house at Warninglid, in Sussex. It was discovered when they came to live in it that no postman came near the house, and that the nearest doctor and butcher were seven miles distant at Horsham. The first bad storm nearly brought the house down about their ears. They left in haste, the disillusioned poet drawing away his lady in' a bath-chair. A friend then found them an old Queen Anne house at Twickenham, one which over-looked a couple of parks, and boasted a mitred bishop carved upon its oak staircase, and tall, narrow, ecclesiastical windows. Here they settled in comfort, and here on April 20, 1851, their first child was born dead. Tennyson was deeply agitated, and he hungered after paternity. " Dead as he was I felt proud of him," he wrote, " . . . dear little nameless one that hast lived tho' thou hast never breathed, I, thy father, love thee and weep over thee, tho' thou hast no place in the Universe. Who knows ? It may be that thou hast . . . God's will be done." Three years later the memory was still poignant : " I nearly broke my heart," he said, " with going to look at him. He lay like a little warrior, having fought the fight, and failed, with his hands clenched and a frown on his brow."

About this time, it is worth noting, Tennyson received a book of poems from a young author, George Meredith, containing one poem which he confessed he could have wished to have written himself. It was "Love in a Valley."

In the summer Tennyson rejoiced in the sublime structure of the Great Exhibition, "particularly the great glass fountain," before setting out with his wife to Italy to spend three weeks at the Baths of Lucca, in a house opposite a wood, where they could sit and watch the green lizards at play. They took delightful drives over the mountains, and Tennyson loved the violet colouring of the hills and the picturesque peasants. They visited Frederick Tennyson at Florence, and met the Brownings on their return through Paris, Mrs. Browning welcoming Mrs. Tennyson "as if she were her own sister."

One of the first effects of the Laureateship upon Tennyson was to stimulate his patriotism. This fervour, as was natural, was directed first towards the Queen, in whose honour he was already meditating some reverent lines ; but rumours of war gave it also a sterner character. About this time he sent £5 to Coventry Patmore for the Rifles, "thinking that the more noise we make in that way the better, and the more we practise the less likely are we to be called upon to perform." The fatal game of frightened international bluff had begun, and Tennyson gave both his money and his Muse to forward it. Two "National Songs for Englishmen" were published in the *Examiner* of 1852, "Britons, Guard your Own," and "Hands All Round," both instinct with that plausible patriotism which avowed international sympathies, but by its aggressiveness destroyed them.

" That man's the best cosmopolite
Who loves his native country best,"

was the burden of these songs, and " the Devil take anyone who says that it isn't " was implicit in their manner. The same spirit of arrogant self-righteousness speaks in the lines written later in the year :

" It was our ancient privilege, my Lords,
To fling whate'er we felt, not fearing, into words,'

or

" No little German State are we
But the one voice in Europe,"

or

" We are not cotton-spinners all
But some love England and her honour yet."

Such love and such honour with their challenging complacency invite opposition. Thus, to the accompaniment of sounding phrases was the unassuming spirit of true Freedom harnessed between the shafts of cautious policy in the mid-nineteenth century, and driven to ruin in the twentieth. Tennyson was among the first to wave the whip, not because his intentions were evil, but because here, too, he lacked intellectual honesty and fearlessness. Quite unconsciously he compromised his love of man by his sentiment for his country, his desire for peace by his fear of war, his international tolerance by a certain racial snobbery, hard, indeed, in all but saints and seers to eradicate and likely particularly to flourish in the heart of a satisfied moralist. Tennyson, by his influence, as a poet widely read and reckoned high-minded, gave an undoubted lead to self-satisfied national arrogance. It was not his intention, but it is hard to forgive him the consequences.

Spring and summer in 1852 were more than ordinarily beautiful ; it was a flowery time, and the

BENJAMIN JOWETT

From a photograph

[*To face p.* 174

days passed happily in the Twickenham garden,
where Tennyson lounged, reading aloud to his wife,
or entertaining some of the many callers with frank,
full and varied conversation. Among these were
Mr. Palgrave and Mr. Jowett, both of whom were to
remain very intimate and sympathetic friends to the
end of Tennyson's life.

In June Tennyson paid a short round of visits,
seeing his mother at Cheltenham and meeting the
Carlyles and Sydney Dobell at Malvern, where he
stayed with his friend Rashdall. Though much
troubled with " hay-fever," he went on to the East
Coast, visiting Whitby and Scarborough before journeying south to his brother Charles, where, walking in
the evening through the fields to Grasby and admiring
once again the long-stemmed Lincolnshire wheat,
flushed by the low rays of the sun, remembrance of his
boyhood's days must surely have returned to him, and
thankfulness, not untouched by regret, for all that had
come upon him since. At Whitby he indulged himself
rather characteristically : " I have ordered a carriage,"
he wrote to his wife, " and am going to see Lord
Normanby's park near here," an experience which
was pleasurably enhanced by an old smuggler mis-
taking the poet for Lord Normanby himself !

On August 11th the father in him found peace. A
little son was born without misadventure. Writing
to Mrs. Browning, he said of his wife : " I never saw
any face so radiant with all high and sweet expression
as hers when I saw her some time after."

Mrs. Browning's acknowledgment of the good news
was a challenge of motherliness : " Will you say to
dear Mrs. Tennyson when she is able to think of anything so far off as a friend, how deeply I sympathise
in her happiness, with the memory of all that ecstacy
as I felt it myself, still thrilling through me ? . . .

And there are barbarians in the world who dare to call the new little creatures not pretty, ugly even ! "

Tennyson's affection for children was deep and serious ; he was a father by vocation, not by irresponsible fondness, as Coleridge and as so many poets have been. From the first he watched his little son with interest, and loved to dandle him in his arms. He was awestruck by the solemnity of an infant's gaze, its virgin wonder and worship. And the emotion went deep. The poem " De Profundis," begun in the first pride and humility of this moment, one of the great moments of any man's life who has loved reverently beyond the flesh, is not only a tender welcome to a helpless creature of his blood, the sign and seal of a love long cherished in strait places ; Tennyson hailed also in his child a veritable symbol of God, of the immanent Will, a miracle which spiritualised evolution, a little messenger sent from " that true world within the world we see " ; it might be straight from the arms of Hallam. The oppression of loss so long endured in secret was finally lifted by this birth of a son, the dark problem of death solved by the bright mystery of life. Hallam the child was named.

In November the Duke of Wellington died. Tennyson had never spoken to him, and had, indeed, shrunk from a proffered introduction, but once, " in soldier fashion," the Duke had greeted him " with lifted hand a gazer in the street." The memory of that gesture, of the rugged countenance, and the stiffness but simplicity of carriage, returned to him. The Duke was discipline incarnate, a monument of commonsense and rigorous manhood, sworn foe alike of " brainless mobs and lawless Powers " and strutting Napoleons. He was the sublime servant of the State, he scaled " the toppling crags of Duty." It was an occasion not to be missed. The "Memorial Ode," published on the morning of the funeral, was a fine blend of musical pomp, noble panegyric, and sententious homily. In it Tennyson hymned not only the Duke himself (and this, issuing as it did from sincere personal admiration and regret, was the best part of the Ode), but also

> " That sober freedom out of which there springs
> Our loyal passion for our temperate kings,"

while to those who learnt to deaden " love of self " he held out the exotic prospect of

> " the stubborn thistle bursting
> Into glossy purples, which outredden
> All voluptuous garden-roses."

The Duke, we can only conjecture, would have been sorely embarrassed by so luxurious a recompense for his austerity !

The funeral enhanced Tennyson's pride as an Englishman. " I was struck with the look of sober manhood in the British soldier," he observed ; yet the public and the Press were strangely inappreciative of his Ode. Very soon, when the national temperature touched the fever point of war, they were to learn the value of a professional Laureate who combined, for their encouragement and edification, the qualities of poet, preacher and high-minded politician ; but that time was not yet. The Ode was heartily abused in all directions, and Tennyson was driven even to offer to accept less than the £200 promised him by his publishers. Friends, however, as usual, stepped into the breach. " It has a greatness," wrote Henry Taylor, " worthy of its theme and an absolute simplicity and truth, with all the poetic passion of your nature moving beneath."

Meanwhile the Twickenham house was proving unsatisfactory. In the autumn floods had driven the

family to Seaford and Brighton. The air, too, was
indifferent, sometimes even malodorous; not even
a sculptured bishop could compensate for the smell of
decaying cabbages which at times invaded the rooms.
A change seemed imperative. Tennyson found a house
near Farnham, standing agreeably enough in the
vicinity of a park and just under an episcopal palace,
but it proved too small. A visit to the North during
the summer delayed house-hunting, and at Edinburgh
the poet enshrined his memories of Italy in a poem
entitled "The Daisy," addressed to his wife. It
was not without strained echoes of Browning's
inspired conversationalism, but it closed contentedly
on the note

> "O love, we two shall go no longer
> To lands of summer across the sea."

Autumn approved the sentiment by bringing the
Tennysons a home, from which nothing could woo
them for any considerable length of time during the
next forty years.

The poet, when on a visit to Bonchurch, heard of
a vacant house at Farringford, in the Isle of Wight.
Its situation was beautiful, combining the best of
sea and country, and it was remote. Tennyson was
weary of the nods and becks of society, and was
determined to live a country life of simple, earnest
industry, poetical and. horticultural, welcoming his
friends from time to time as they liked to seek him
out. Mrs. Tennyson was in entire agreement with
him, and Farringford seemed to satisfy these conditions quite ideally. It was not easily approachable
by casual visitors, and the land attached to the house
offered just such a degree of suzerainty over rustic
dependents as Tennyson would be pleased to exercise.

On a still November afternoon the two of them
crossed the Solent in a rowing boat and landed at

Freshwater Bay. Walking inland as the light began
to fail, they passed down Farringford Lane, and so,
by the gardener's lodge, into the natural park that
surrounded the·house. The trees stood so thick about
it that, though almost bare of leaves, they screened
it from view at this point, and not until the Tennysons
had entered the avenue leading directly to the front
door did they realise how close at hand it was. It
was an old house that they came upon, overgrown
with ivy and embowered with every variety of tree,
which in summer would surely nest birdsong and
shadow and fill the drowsy air with a soft perpetual
rustle; a house almost overwhelmed on two sides
by the embraces of Nature. Out to the south, as
they looked through the oriel window of the drawing-
room, stretched a more formal park, undulating about
stately trees, old elms still golden with a few last
leaves, chestnuts and red-stemmed pines. Somnolent
it lay between two shoulders of the downs, and beyond
it, level in the last gleam of daylight, was the sea.
" We will go no further," they said; " this must be
our home."

By borrowing £600 from Moxon it was possible to
take the house immediately on lease, with the option
of buying it later. Thus on the 24th November, 1853,
they left Twickenham and settled in the home which
was to gather about it the privileged associations of
forty years, and which one who knew it intimately
has compared to " a charmed palace, with green walls
without and speaking walls within." " There," she
adds, " hung Dante, with his solemn nose and wreath;
Italy gleamed over the doorways; friends' faces lined
the passages, books fitted the shelves, and a glow of
crimson was everywhere; the oriel drawing-room
window was full of green and golden leaves, of the
sound of birds and of the distant sea."

Here was to be found all that was most pure,
cultured and gracious, in that upper middle-class
homelife of which the Victorian age can rightly
boast the achievement. It was perhaps the one ideal
realised by that age, and, at its best, the one entirely
satisfactory contribution to the art of life. But
because it demanded peculiarly favoured circumstances for its realisation, in fact, a class leisured but
still industrious, economically independent and yet
uncorrupted by wealth, a class brought up to appreciate the humanities by familiarity with the graces and
wisdom of classical literature, and to be reverent in the
face of life by a study of the Bible, the fair flower of
Victorian homelife has perished amid middle-class
economic ruins. The foot of commerce has trampled
it down ; a mechanical age, prizing only money values,
and reverencing only in terms of efficiency and vulgar
enterprise, has driven it to a last degraded refuge in the
gilt drawing-rooms of suburbia.

The homelife of the Tennysons at Farringford is
therefore the more to be treasured by a generation
that can scarcely hope to recapture its charm in
practice. Looking back upon it from the noisy
mediocrity of the twentieth century, we see it like an
emanation of beauty fading ever further away, an oasis
in the desert of life's savagery, a garden full of the
drone of bees, of quiet perfume and shadowed lawns, of
which the high walls have now been broken, and the
neat pathways littered with torn rose petals.

For here during a quarter of a century were found
things lovely and of good report. Peace and refinement reigned over this home, gentleness and consideration, cultured talk, and freedom from any base display.

If within the house all was calm and cloistered,
without Nature wantoned in profusion of beauty. In
spring and early summer the sky was full of the song

of larks, the woods peopled with thrushes and nightingales. Flowers crowded the deep lanes, everywhere
was a lush growth, and on the lower slopes of the downs
the gorse and broom flamed in glory.

Tennyson's second son, Lionel, was born in the
March following their arrival, and the father's cup of
happiness was full. He was always a wise, natural
and devoted father. He loved to watch the wide-
eyed wonder of his babies. They seemed to him, with
their helpless gestures, not only infinitely touching,
but even portentous. They were "prophets of a
mightier race." Yet this evolutionary prescience did
not in any way restrict his relations with them as
they grew to boyhood. He was their guide, philosopher and friend, shared their games, romped or
botanised with them, blew bubbles on festal occasions,
and read them fairy stories or ballads. Above all he
watched carefully over their religious and moral
instruction, yet without a touch of pedantry or
aloofness. On two points alone he was very strict,
truthfulness and courtesy. "A truthful man," he
would say, "has generally all the virtues," and he
would not tolerate rudeness or want of respect towards
the poor or dependent. It was, in short, the ideal of
a gentleman that he held up before them, the καλος
κἀγαθος of the Greek, the belief that a beautiful life
was a good one, and a good one happy.

Mrs. Tennyson was not strong enough to scour the
country with them on foot, but was wont to be pro-
pelled in a garden carriage by her enthusiastic family.
Of an afternoon all would share in the general work of
the garden, brushing up leaves from the lawn or laying
new paths through the shrubs; while both Tennyson
and his wife took an active interest in the small home
farm attached to the house and in the cottagers of the
village. It was a choice nursery for the young, an

ideal " school for husbands," as a friend in later years laughingly named it to himself. Perhaps the most familiar incident in the quiet routine of this homelife was the regular walk on the downs, hushed and companionable in summer-time, but in other seasons often swept by a gusty west wind. Hither Tennyson would take on a late morning walk any of the friends who came to visit him during forty years, talking earnestly on every variety of subject : the politics of the day, the flora of the downs, the geology of the coast ; his cloak flapping in the wind, while " the gulls came sideways, flashing their white breasts against the edge of the cliffs." Mounting a steep chalk cliff, he would work his way along the ridge to its highest point at Farringford Beacon. Here he could look fondly down upon his home in its nest of trees, and far beyond to the silver thread of the river Yar, curving by Freshwater to the Solent ; or turn seaward to the waste of waters, amber in the sunlight, that he loved and understood so well, or he could pass on down the cliff line to the thymy promontory above the Needles, and watch the waves raven upon gleaming rocks, where the gulls perched among tufts of thrift and the cormorants dried themselves on the chalk ledges.

But the calls of such a homelife upon his time were not allowed, after the first distraction of novel surroundings had passed, to interfere with the regular industry of poetry, which he so happily cultivated. Rather a reverent domestic quiet formed exactly the appropriate setting for an activity which now less and less caused that agitation of the nerves and passions customarily associated with poetical effort. His best working days, Tennyson found, were " in early Spring, when Nature begins to awaken from her winter sleep," but whatever the season, the mills of poetry rarely ceased to grind. The air on the downs was at all times "worth sixpence a pint," and under such favourable conditions, the old eye trouble, which had again attacked him early in the year, finally departed.

Upon this round of cultivated duties few disturbing factors encroached. Prolonged absences from home were rare, and friends intruded just so frequently as to divert and entertain without becoming a labour and a hindrance. Thus, in the spring of this new year of wonder, when the daffodils overran the lawns and ruby sheaths showed on the lime-tree branches, came Fitzgerald and stayed a fortnight, sketching and talking by day, and playing Mozart or translating Persian Odes by night, and filling the quiet house with ecstasies of appreciation.

In the island, too, Tennyson soon discovered a friend whose companionship was to prove of more than passing value. Sir John Simeon lived at Swainston and first visited Farringford on the day of Lionel's christening. Tennyson found in him a man of taste and understanding, a very "Prince of courtesy," and a sympathetic listener, and often the two on summer afternoons would "go long expeditions through the lanes and over the downs; then back through the soft evening air to dinner and to the long evening of talk and of reading."

It was Sir John who first kindled the flame of "Maud." For Tennyson chanced to read him the poem "O that 'twere possible," published years before in the *Tribute*, and he found it none too intelligible. He suggested that some more explanatory verses should be added to relieve any ambiguity. Tennyson agreed, and in the writing of these discovered the possibilities of a lengthy lyrical monodrama. To this task he gave himself in the summer of 1854, sitting morning and evening in a hard, high-backed wooden chair in his little room at the top of the house, glancing up from time to time to watch far off the white waves rolling into Freshwater Bay; never was anyone allowed to intrude upon him during the half-hours after breakfast and dinner, the times of his " sacred pipes," when his best thoughts, he said, came to him.

It is notable, however, that both of the ambitious works of his prime, " Maud " and " The Idylls," are not original in idea, but elaborate enlargements of sketches captured in earlier and more passionate years. Original ideas had always been to him as fugitives hard to apprehend and harder still to hold. They were almost complete strangers to the house of Farringford. But, if ideas fled him, the pleasures of craft increased. He pursued the music of words, the felicity of fine imagery, with even more conscious relish because the aim was now uncomplicated. His marvellous technique gave him continual satisfaction. As he ceased to strive after the creative, he became contentedly possessive, accumulating poetry around him, much as a man of fine taste will furnish his house with treasures, experimenting in moods and phrases, sounds and colours.

One who was with him in that still and sparkling summer when " Maud " was being written has told how, in the garden, of an afternoon beneath a cloudless sky, lapped by the soft sounds of June, or upon the cool downs at sunset, or along the shore at twilight, with the moon " marbling " the wet sands, Tennyson would chant his poems newly wrought, repeating them like an incantation as the surest way to discover any defects. In the sound of words, rich-toned and finely modulated, even his moral being melted. Sense, argument and passion came more and more to serve as indifferent instruments through which to interpret this self-sufficing music.

But beyond the Farringford Park, in that brute world to which a nation's Laureate must needs turn his eye from time to time, deeds of glory and of savagery were being done. The Crimean War was in progress, and public excitement was intense. On October 10th the Tennysons read an account of the Battle of Alma, and on the same day " looking from the Beacon and seeing the white cliffs, and the clear sea, their violet-gray shading seemed to us tender and sad." The death-roll was grievous reading, but now, in the inspiration of a common purpose, France was forgiven. No more did Tennyson assail her with angry threats and scarce-veiled insults. Henceforward there should be no other strife between them

> " Than which of us most shall help the world,
> Which lead the noblest life."

For France possibly this invitation to competitive virtue proved even more embarrassing than the poet's earlier assumption of moral superiority.

In November a friend wrote of the charge of the Heavy Brigade at Balaclava : " Our ears were frenzied by the monotonous, incessant cannonade going on for days together." The words seemed to bring the vibration of war very near ; and after reading a month later in *The Times* a description of the charge of the Light Brigade, in which occurred the words " some one had blundered," Tennyson's martial fervour picked up the step of that phrase and galloped with the Six Hundred through the jaws of Death, " to the mouth of Hell," in six of the most vigorous stanzas he ever penned. It was done in a few minutes, and happy as it was in its intention and its execution, it was equally happy in its effects upon the poet's personal reputation. It made him known to a completely new audience, with whom otherwise he could scarcely have gained contact, not only to the soldiers before Sebastopol, to whom, on the suggestion of a Crimean chaplain, it was sent on printed slips, and who inevitably applauded so enthusiastic a tribute (indeed, the spirit of the lines was reported to have cured patients when even leeches had failed !), but also to all the commonplace elements in the nation, indifferent to poetry in general, but ready to embrace a poet who gave expression to a transient mood engendered by war fever. By the publication of " The Charge of the Light Brigade " Tennyson became a revered and representative Laureate. He had won the heart of those mild and respectable masses who nourish in secret dreams of violence and gallantry, and look to a poet to rattle the sabre for them, and to relieve drab days by flaunting in perfect security the banners of war.

" Maud," nearing completion in the height of these hostilities, was bound to echo the Crimean cannonades. A poem originally conceived as the musical tale of an ill-starred love and a morbid lover became crossed with martial music, as morning by morning news arrived of victory or defeat. There can be no doubt that if the Crimean War reduced the combatants to madness it restored the hero of " Maud " to a very sudden and muscular sanity. Providence at the last moment supplied Tennyson with the means by which he could rescue the " poetic soul " of his poem from a morass of introspection, and lose him in the inconclusive gamble of a national crusade.

Early in January, 1855, he had completed the transformation, and April found him copying out the poem for the Press. Meanwhile the world was in more than one direction registering its admiration of his genius. The leader of the expedition into the Arctic regions in

search of the ill-fated Sir John Franklin named a
rock of " imposing dignity " to the north of latitude
79 degrees " Tennyson's Monument," and New
Zealand now boasted a " Tennyson Lake."

Ruskin wrote begging him to name a date when he
would come and view his Turners, that they might
be prepared " to look their rosiest and best." " Capri-
cious they are," he added, " as enchanted opals,
but they must surely shine for you." In May the
project of an illustrated edition of his poems brought
him into touch with the pre-Raphaelites, Rossetti and
Holman Hunt. Millais had already stayed at Farringford in the previous November, and made sketches of
Hallam and his mother in illustration of " Dora."
Tennyson's hatred of modern realism and his love
of the decorative for its own sake made him very
sympathetic towards this school of painting.

In June he received an Oxford Doctorate, and,
though very nervous of the ceremony, met with a
great ovation from the assembled undergraduates,
interspersed, indeed, with ribald questions as to
whether anyone did wake and call him early. Later
Tennyson obtained permission from the Master of
Balliol, whose guest he was, to stroll, clad in his scarlet
robes, amid the greenery of the garden. It is doubtful whether he took more pleasure in the brilliance
of the colour contrast or in the opportunity for
picturesque dignity afforded by the occasion. To be
romantically magisterial was the need and satisfaction
of all his later life, and the gorgeous figure peram-
bulating the high-walled garden of Balliol is surely
a parable in little of the poet who was increasingly
content to be—a Laureate. In the evening, at
Magdalen, he had earnest talk with Mr. Gladstone,
and on the following night took tea with two scientific
professors and " looked at the Nebulæ in Cassiopeia

through the big telescope, the Ring Nebula in Lyra, and also some double stars." It was his business to keep abreast of the times ; telescopes and microscopes were not to be neglected by a professional poet with a modern audience to consider. Later in the year his researches took another direction. He wrote to a friend : " Merwood brought me a lump of snake's eggs, and I picked carefully out two little embryo snakes with bolting eyes and beating hearts. I laid them on a piece of white paper. Their hearts or blood vessels beat for at *least* two hours after extraction. Does not that in some way explain why it is so very difficult to kill a snake ? I was so sorry not to have you and your microscope here." The secrets which microscopes revealed were likely to prove a very satisfactory substitute for those baffling ideas which cost so much trouble to apprehend.

On July 7th " Maud " was sent to the publisher. It was very dear to Tennyson, both as the first-fruits of Farringford and for its high-sounding passages and moody melodrama, which fitted it well for recitation. The hostile reception, therefore, with which it met was proportionately matter for bitterness. Even Mr. Gladstone " doubted whether the poem had the full moral equilibrium which is so marked a characteristic of the sister-works." A more candid critic wrote : " Sir, I used to worship you, but now I hate you. I loathe and detest you. You beast ! So you've taken to imitating Longfellow. Yours in aversion. . . ." The professional reviewers vied with each other in destructive scurrilities. To one " Maud " was an " unreal allegory of the Russian war," to another " a spasm," to a third " a political fever, an epidemic caught from the prevalent carelessness of thought and rambling contemplativeness of the time," to others " the dead level of prose run mad," " rampant

and rabid bloodthirstiness of soul." Tennyson took
his wounded sensibility to the New Forest. "It
is true old wild English nature," he wrote; and
then "the fresh heath-sweetened air is so delicious.
The Forest is grand."

Yet the poem was not without its influential
champions. Mr. Jowett wrote: "I want to tell you
how greatly I admire 'Maud.' No poem since
Shakespeare seems to show equal power of the same
kind or equal knowledge of human nature."

Tennyson dined late in September with the Brownings in London, and met the two Rossettis. He read
his poem to the company, and the bardic, arch-druid
presence worked its usual miracle. "Both of them,"
he wrote next day, "are great admirers of poor little
'Maud'"; while Gabriel Rossetti confided to a
friend: "He is quite as glorious in his way as Browning in his, and perhaps of the two even more impressive
on the whole personality." Mrs. Browning, too,
wrote comfortingly to the poet's wife: "Dear Mrs.
Tennyson, you do not mind the foolish remarks on
'Maud,' do you? These things are but signs of an
advance made, of the tide rising. People on the
shore are troubled in their picking up of shells a little."
Ruskin, goaded by the prevalence of "stupid and
feelingless misunderstandings," expressed later in the
year his sincere admiration, leavened by a little gentle
criticism; while a letter from an unknown but
sympathetic lady in New South Wales, full of reverent
homage and containing the prayer, "God bless the
poet and put still some beautiful words and thoughts
in his heart," touched Tennyson deeply; another,
telling him of a man who had been roused from a
state of suicidal despondency by "The Two Voices,"
assured him of his value to the world. He could
afford to smile "half-pitifully, half-mournfully," at

"brainless abuse" and "anonymous spite"; the heart of the people was the best judge of merit. And the sales of the book justified him in thinking that this heart beat aright. He was enabled to purchase Farringford. In April of the year following the "ivied home among the pine-trees" was his. It was a prize which Spring made more precious than ever, and the voice of hostile criticism was forgotten amid "blue hyacinths, orchises, primroses, daisies, marsh-marigolds and cuckoo-flowers." The lanes were white with blackthorn. The wild cherry trees were in bloom, the park golden with cowslips and flaming furze; elms were budding at the foot of the downs, horse-chestnuts in the glades about the house, and rosy apple trees in the orchard. Thrushes and nightingales vied together in a rapture of song.

"At sunset," wrote Mrs. Tennyson, "the golden green of the trees, the burning splendour of Blackgang Chine and St. Catharine's, and the red bank of the primeval river, contrasted with the turkis-blue of the sea, make altogether a miracle of beauty. We are glad that Farringford is ours."

2

Certainly much of the criticism launched at "Maud, or the Madness," was on a par with that of Tennyson's aunt, Mrs. Russell, who was vexed with it for containing what she took to be an attack upon coal mine-owners. But the critics' instinctive dislike of the poem, though they were generally unable sensibly to explain it, we can see now to have been justified. They were right in spirit, if wrong in method, when they detected something meretricious and refused to be allured by a passionate pretence of passion, however exquisite its presentation. Nor were they so misguided, as has been supposed, in their confusion of Tennyson with the morbid hero of the poem. " Maud," indeed, was a later revelation of the Tennyson of " Locksley Hall," of that strain in his nature which was violent, sensational and weakly introspective, a strain usually withdrawn behind moral righteousness. The fortuitous manner of the poem's evolution is enough to explain what is invertebrate in its structure, the forced virtuosity of much of its style, the sense of brilliant extemporisation we have in reading it, as if it were a string of stones, some precious, some of baser quality, some glittering, some molten-red, and all hung together to form an effective colour scheme. In short, we feel that the incoherencies of such a poem do not spring out of coherent experience ; that it represents a chance aggregation of moods, many of them exploited for the purpose of melodrama, and all enfolded in a sort of sullen fever.

It is clear that, when the suggestion came to Tennyson to build up a story about the single lyric " O that 'twere possible," his thoughts turned to tales of baffled and tragic love with which he was familiar ; for he himself lacked the constructive power that evolves a plot. Chief among such stories was " The Bride of Lammermoor," endeared to him since boyhood. Upon the framework of this plot, modernised as the time demanded, there can be little doubt that Tennyson reared his poem. The Master of Ravenswood and Tennyson's hero are one in circumstance and conduct. Both mourn a father and a fortune brought low by a " grey old wolf," both linger on amid the ruins of their home to fall in love with the daughter of the hostile house. Both loves are fatal, both lovers engage in a duel. But here the similarity ends. " The Bride of Lammermoor " is a great tragic masterpiece, powerfully conceived and passionately executed, of which the plot is possessed and overruled by the emotion. In " Maud " the plot is merely borrowed to give an appearance of form and substance to a series of arbitrary moods. And these moods of exaggerated self-consciousness, although native to Tennyson's own experience, are also to some extent derived from the Byronism and Wertherism so popular early in the century. The hero is a latter-day Werther by temperament, a Master of Ravenswood by circumstance. Lastly, as we have seen, the guns in the Crimea introduced, when the composition of the poem was well advanced, a further element, the initial and final denunciations and rhapsodies— the glorification of war as a purifier of life grown stale and the hysterical cry from a sick and vacillating age, nerve-shaken by the spectacle of a mismanaged campaign, for

> " a man with heart, head, hand,
> Like some of the simple great ones gone
> For ever and ever by,
> One still, strong man in a blatant land
> Whatever they call him, what care I,
> Aristocrat, democrat, autocrat,—one
> Who can rule and dare not lie."

A poem accumulated from such casual and external sources could scarcely possess that spiritual veracity which we demand of a work of art, nor reflect, except spasmodically, the sincere emotion of its author.

In such enraptured lyrics, perfect in art and inspiration, as " A Voice by the Cedar Tree," " Birds in the High Hall-garden," " Go not, Happy Day," and " I have Led her Home," Tennyson, exalted by vivid memories of his own love-making, charmed, too, by the hushed beauty of his Farringford garden and the distant murmur of the sea, sings because he must. The impassioned reverence, the delicate,

courtly sensuousness of a love finely experienced, speak
here with exquisite, if sometimes exotic, truth.

There is a grave and deeply-felt beauty also in the
lyrics which express moods kindred to " O that 'twere
possible," moods of brooding soliloquy or regret,
such, for example, as parts of " See what a lovely
shell " and " Courage, poor heart of stone." In
both of these categories Tennyson sorrows without
theatricality, with a heightening but not a distortion
of Nature. It was natural to him to voice his love
in such humbled hyperbole as

> " She is coming, my own, my sweet ;
>   Were it ever so airy a tread,
> My heart would hear her and beat,
>   Were it earth in an earthy bed ;
> My dust would hear her and beat
>   Had I lain a century dead ;
> Would start and tremble under her feet,
>   And blossom in purple and red."

Every worthy lover has wished at some time to
prostrate himself thus before beauty and the woman
who embodies it for him ; and these lines represented
very fairly the height of selflessness to which Tennyson's passion, never wholly free from a self-conscious
chivalry, could attain.

But if incidentally " Maud " has great beauty,
organically it is false and characterless. Tennyson,
writing in defence of it, claimed that " This poem
is a little ' Hamlet,' the history of a morbid poetic
soul under the blighting influence of a recklessly
speculative age. He is the heir of madness, an
egotist with the makings of a cynic." Another has
named it " A Drama of the Soul set in a landscape
glorified by Love." No descriptions surely could be
further from the truth.

Hamlet is a man of vision, of subtle and penetrating
intelligence, forced into a set of circumstances terrible

and baffling enough to try the sanity of any mind, and yet fighting them all the while with only too large and fatal a surplus of reason. The hero of "Maud" is a victim of erotomania ; his truest enemy is himself ; and that self is so selfishly characterless as to be unreal, and thus fails to excite in us any degree either of sympathy or antipathy. Plainly manufactured, too, is the vague oppressive destiny against which he is supposed to be struggling, a destiny very different from the clear-drawn web in which the Prince of Denmark is caught. The passion of Tennyson's hero is purely selfish ; hope elevates it into an ardent appetite, so perfect at times, it is true, in its expression as to make its subsequent flaccidity artistically improbable. Catastrophe, after it has been arranged with romantic theatricality, reduces such passion to delirium. In short, the soul, of which "Maud" is claimed to be a drama, is almost entirely absent from the poem. It is sensational melodrama, containing a number of exquisitely sentimental songs, to display, as it were, the high notes of the hero's tenor voice.

Neurasthenia, weird seizures and frenzies appealed to a morbid trait in Tennyson ; he had already represented them in "The Princess." But such conditions are of no artistic significance unless they have more than a physical or a sentimental basis. Hamlet's introspection pierces to the veiled intimacies of life and draws forth into the light the entanglements of a noble conscience. Tennyson's hero is self-absorbed, without vigour of mind or of body, incapable of examining the truth of his passion or of life. He loves and hates with weakly abandonment, and the invective which he pours out upon life in general is chaotic, a moody spleen, full of cant phrases and shallow disgust.

Tennyson said that at the last " he was raised to sanity by a pure and holy love which elevates his whole nature." But such startling transformations, outside the pages of a novelette or the walls of a provincial theatre, are not found in the nature of things. Considering the poem as a whole, its hero was no more satisfactorily sane, no more a man empowered with courage and a sense of reality, when he conducted a clandestine romance with a girl of sixteen and swooned in the perfume of flowers, than when, in a burst of hysterical frenzy, he

> " Stood on a giant deck and mixed my breath
> With a loyal people shouting a battle-cry."

The poem lacks either reality or consistency, significant sanity or significant madness. It is a case for pathology. We are as little interested in the jaundiced denunciations of a neurasthenic as in his spurious heroisms. We do not suffer with him in his anguish nor exult with him in his heroics, because we cannot sympathise with a mere hysteria of the senses. We are enraptured by his love lyrics, but we are careful to accept them for themselves, with their charm and ecstasy intact, and to dissociate them from the poem as a whole, which can only degrade them.

Tennyson was highly gratified when a specialist in insanity corroborated the accuracy of the mad scene, but this was, had he known it, a doubtful compliment. It was strange that one who deprecated realism in painting should appreciate its recognition in poetry. The madness which science verifies we can view, if we will, in an asylum ; the madness which is the business of art—that dread state, namely, of spirit darting with naked intuition of truth like a live flame amid the ruins of a " noble mind o'erthrown "—is to be found in " Lear." For neither do we turn to " Maud."

We cannot, however, disengage Tennyson alto-

gether from the ranting phrases in which his hero
cursed a sickly peace and sanctified a dubious war,
as the mood took him. Tennyson was always too
prone not only to think, but to declare his own
nation "the last free race," "the noblest bred"
among men, and the Crimean conflict doubtless
exaggerated momentarily his sentimental aggressiveness, not only on behalf of his own country, but
against those industrial and commercial elements
in it which were coming to displant, so sordidly as it
seemed to him, a feudal society and a romantic standpoint, and to favour the conducting of international
relationships by pacific trade agreements, rather than
by the lances of cavalrymen or the courteous insolences
of diplomats. Wars did at least preserve a measure
of picturesqueness in modern life, where ledgers so
catered for the drab greed of plutocrats. There was
some truth in his aversion towards the " pickpockets "
of commercialism. Democracy had at that time
scarcely begun to force the rudiments of a morality
upon Mammon. The soldier's profession, on the other
hand, did at least entail honour, self-sacrifice, and the
unremunerative business of death, and showed, therefore, in noble, if unconscious, contrast to the life
of those who " prated of the blessings of Peace," the
better to fill their pockets. But the manner in which
Tennyson hailed war as the medicine against a corruption of the public by Mammon, pointing

" to Mars
As he glow'd like a ruddy shield on the Lion's breast,"

was distinctly hectic, nor, so far as we can see, could
the slaughter of some thousands of soldiers in the
Crimea ever effect the purpose which he so fervently
saluted, that no longer should

" Britain's one sole God be the millionaire."

Tennyson himself might

> " wake to the higher aims
> Of a land that has lost for a little her lust of gold,
> And love of a peace that was full of wrongs and shames,
> Horrible, hateful, monstrous, not to be told ; "

he might indulge his fancy with the pretty thought that

> " God's just wrath shall be wreak'd on a giant liar,"

and his senses with the bizarre image,

> " The blood-red blossom of war with a heart of fire,"

but the only discoverable result of the episode which appealed thus romantically to his sentiment was a depression in industry which reduced to an even more grinding level of starvation the toiling Lancashire operatives, without to any remarkable extent encroaching upon their employers' dividends ; an advertisement to the world of incompetent generalship ; a hospital scandal bringing untold agony to wounded men, and a picturesque reputation to a very practical woman who was averse to muddling through ; and a fatal invitation to the British public to tread the paths of provocative Jingoism.

It was too easy for Tennyson's generation to confuse feelings " for their native land " with " the purpose of God," and it was therefore unwise of Tennyson to trumpet the coincidence. He would have been wiser to enquire, as did Lincoln, whether his country was on the side of God, rather than to assume the converse.

Such words, it is true, were attached by Tennyson to a fictitious hero. But when we consider the date of their composition and that they appeared in a volume otherwise martial in tone, when we remember, too, that as English Laureate Tennyson was not the man at a time of crisis to neglect his duties as a leader of the people in the paths of what he thought to be virtue, we are compelled to believe that they expressed their author's sentiments, exaggerated no doubt by the loud frenzy of the moment, to no uncertain degree.

3

With the fall of Sebastopol in the early autumn of 1855, peace returned to the house of Farringford. Anxieties faded, it was no longer necessary to clench the national teeth or brandish a poetic sword. Tennyson was cheerful, vigorous and contented as he had not been for thirty years. In the midst of his family he talked freely and with animation; shyness and morbidity in this charmed circle at least seem to have left him. The short days passed happily in household duties, in the planting of trees and shrubs, rolling the lawn or digging in the kitchen garden. Poetry was not forgotten; the notebook was ever at hand, and the way of bird or of cloud, of wind or of frost, marked down with scrupulous accuracy for future use. Few days went by without Nature's gift of a picture, which he gratefully accepted and laid to his accumulating account. In the evenings, seated cosily with his wife before a well-stacked fire, he would translate the "Odyssey" aloud into Biblical prose, delighting in the resounding phrases and the large adventures of antiquity.

One studying his face in the glow of lamp and firelight would have been struck by the look of splendid maturity which it had now assumed. It still lacked the beard and moustache, which for the remainder of his life were to signify the truly regal and representative bard, at the same time serving to conceal and mitigate the strength of the features. For the chin and aquiline nose in their full development announced a power and a distinction rarely found in combination in modern faces, shrunken and

blunted as they too often are by the constant necessity
of mean calculation. A deep furrow now ran from
nose to chin, conveying something of haughty melancholy, perhaps also a distaste for the crude forces and
the trivial cruelties of the world ; a shrewd observer
might have detected here traces of that conflict with
himself and fortune out of which he had so laboriously
issued. To the mouth and eyes, also, the years had
brought change ; the mouth was no less sensitive than
in youth, but it was fuller, less wistfully determined,
and more serene ;   the eyes seemed to smoulder
a little sultrily beneath heavier lids, so that he had the
look sometimes of a sleepy Viking, resting after some
hard-won and questionable victory.   Lastly, the brow
had attained to its full measure of loftiness and
breadth ; it had promised at one time to become more
decisive in its aspect, but time in magnifying its
proportions had softened its outlines.   It possessed
now the rounded dignity of the antique, and overwhelmed whatever was pensive and puzzled in the face
by its bland and sovereign dignity.

Tennyson had, in truth, reached the happy haven
of maturity. From henceforth he was not troubled
by the necessity of revising an opinion or tracking a
new idea. He had accepted his temperament as final,
and its interpretations of life as adequate.   He
cherished certain moral convictions and certain anti-
pathies ; he could draw two types of women, and
certain variations of one type of man ; he was always
interested to hear of any new discovery of science, and
he followed current politics with reasonable attention.
This was enough to occupy his mind ; his home, his
craft, and his observation of Nature satisfied his
emotions. Poetry was become to him an earnest
hobby, in which he was a master-workman. Each year,
notebook in hand, for two of the summer months he

sought out romantic scenery in Cornwall, Wales, Portugal or Norway. Thus he renewed his depleted store of pictures, returning with a fresh burden of Nature's raw material to prepare for his poetical looms and to weave into a flawless fabric.

His nature, mellowed by contentment, and kept in condition by regular and congenial employment, expanded like a garden in the sun. He became more natural, gracious, and happily detached. " The penpunctures of those parasitic animalcules of the press " almost ceased to trouble him, and of fame he could now afford to say, in the comfortable assurance that he himself had won it : " Fame . . . Next to God—next to the Devil say I . . . What is it ? Only the pleasure of hearing oneself talked of up and down the street." Nor was he any longer ruled by his old need of solitude, or by the self-absorption which had once so frequently depressed his spirits. He enjoyed both the degree of solitude necessary to composition and the kind of company most calculated to prevent dejection, and to fill his life with pleasant, unexacting interests.

He loved the duties of hospitality which it was now his privilege to dispense under such favoured conditions. For his guests were not only invariably people of kindred sympathies and tastes, courteous and charming, bringing life, laughter and talk into a quiet home, but they also accorded him such reverent homage as only the devout can cherish for a genius whose message is well within their powers of comprehension, whose appearance satisfies their craving for the picturesque, and who wears with dignity " the white flower of a blameless life."

To one blessed with an intimate circle of adoring friends and the financial proof of public recognition, fame and criticism were indeed insignificant matters. But certainly, though such admiration may have platitudinised the poet, it called out all that was most kindly and human in the man. His manner as host to those who experienced it could only enhance his reputation as poet.

On occasions he could be remote, wrapping himself, like Merlin, in the mystery of his calling, but as a rule he was simple, unaffected and urbane. On an evening when some friends were leaving, he said : " You are going away—it is taking away a bit of my sunshine ; I've been cutting down trees to let in some, and now you are taking away a bit of it." It was but the plain truth made tender by flattery, yet this happy skill in compliment, no less than the open welcome which greeted every visitor, endeared him deeply to all who met him. The " presence " had discovered a new way of casting its spell ; standing imposingly at the hall door of Farringford, it shed a gracious, fatherly, short-sighted beatitude over parting guests, and wished them a speedy return.

One distinguished stranger, however, was not very happy in the moment of his first visit. The furniture, which after the purchase of Farringford had arrived from Twickenham, was in process of being moved in, when it was announced by a bewildered maid that Prince Albert had called. The confusion everywhere, it was feared, would distress so orderly a mind ; Mrs. Tennyson was in despair, but the view from the drawing-room window saved the situation. It charmed the royal guest no less than it had charmed Tennyson, and the tactful offering of a bunch of cowslips, which he was delighted to take to the Queen, permanently captured his cordiality. Tennyson was much impressed by the quiet, intent seriousness of the honoured visitor, by his modesty, self-repression and accomplished manner. It may be that as the Prince parted from them with his courteous, rather formal

bow, he left with his host a vision of the " still, strong
man " of his desire, realised in the flesh, and seated for
a public ensample in " that fierce light which beats
upon a throne." This surely was the man to convert
" the wretchedest age since Time began " to an
appreciation of sober, industrious manhood ; the
conscientious knight who should restore honour to her
own and wed virtue to romance. England might yet
be saved by such a Prince, supported by such a,
Laureate. In the spring sunshine loyalty begot
strange dreams, nor saw the spirit of Irony, with pity
in her eyes and a sickle in her hand, even then shadow-
ing that earnest figure, as it went on its flowery way to
Osborne.

4

From early years the history of the mythical hero-
king Arthur, and the fantastic scenery of the land of
Lyonnesse and the sacred Mount of Camelot, had
appealed strongly to Tennyson, prone as he was to
delight in a drifting world of dreams, in landscape
delicate and unreal as floating tapestry, in the fine
affectations of chivalry, and in a character which
could be interpreted, by a not too literal fidelity to
legend, as a model of single-minded virtue and valiant
purity. " The vision of Arthur, as I have drawn
him," Tennyson would say, " had come upon me when,
little more than a boy, I first lighted upon Malory."

His study of mythology was never deep or extensive,
Malory and the " Mabinogion " being to the end of his
life his chief authorities ; while in his determination
to find in the " Morte d'Arthur " an ideal character
without spot or blemish, he conveniently ignored the
fact that Malory represents the downfall of the Round
Table as due to an early lapse into lawless passion by
Arthur, of which the issue is Modred, the traitor

knight, who brings the King to his doom.   Typical as
this is of Tennyson's dislike of unpleasant realism, it
does not alter the fact that as a poet he had a perfect
right to accept or reject at will.

But his attitude towards the legends passed through
four phases.

As an impressionable youth without epic or moral
intention he made experiments in the mediæval
manner, elaborating a choice incident or detail with
all the artistic cunning of which he was capable.
"The Lady of Shalott" and "Sir Launcelot and
Queen Guinevere" are both examples of this, and
both were written before 1832.

During the ten years that followed he was engaged,
as we have seen, in trying to enlarge his experience and
deepen the content of his poetry.   Hallam's death
inspired the "Morte d'Arthur," in which the hero of
his dreams and of his life unite.   At the same time he
was formulating an epic which would embrace all the
Arthurian stories, writing fragments of it in prose,
and, after the example of Spenser, working out an
allegorical scheme, in which Arthur was to represent
Religious Faith, Guinevere Christianity, pure and
impure, Modred the sceptical understanding, Merlin
Science, Excalibur war, and the Round Table Liberal
institutions.

But this plan was not pursued, and, instead,
the idea of casting the legends into the form of a
musical masque was seriously entertained, and even
the scenario drafted.   In turn this plan was abandoned,
and the sole direct fruit of his enthusiasm among the
published poems of 1842 was the exotic " Sir Galahad."

Visits, however, to Cornwall and Wales only
increased the attractiveness of the theme.   "The
greatest of all poetical subjects" perpetually haunted
him, and amid the silence and mystery of the New

Forest, safe from a world that was casting stones at his beloved " Maud," he determined to return to it again. But his approach to it now was conditioned by his years and his circumstances. He had deserted both the open arena of life and the active battle of thought in which, with ill-success enough, he had yet struggled to make some advance for twenty years. He was content that his energies should be absorbed by his craft, and his senses satisfied by an increasingly exact and minute observance of Nature. He had become primarily a painter in words of landscape and of romantic incident. " Maud " was his last hectic attempt to be a creative poet ; but if, in the years of frustrated effort, he had failed to grasp vital ideas, he had deepened his instinctive morality, so that it insinuated itself, however unconsciously, even into his pictorial craft. The first principle of that morality was that life is a conflict between flesh and spirit ; that the great and the good man must always master the flesh by suppressing it, being " passionate for an utter purity," and that all evil results from some surrender, if only momentary, to the flesh, which engulfs good and evil alike in its dread consequences. Woman to such a moralist is the sensational figure in human life, upon which the forces of good and evil centre. If she is passively pure she is the ally of virtue, and a worthy mate for the good man ; if she has character or will of her own she is more likely to be impure, or invite impurity, and so prove the agent of evil.

These were the final tenets of Tennyson's morality, which he never during the last forty years of his life revised. They possess truth, but imperfectly as we have already pointed out, because Tennyson's fear of the flesh prevented him from embracing the spirit in its entirety, and so far as his morality affects his characters it detracts from their reality, and at worst reduces them to mere effigies fashioned to illustrate a conventional virtue or an arbitrary vice.

It may indeed be necessary to preach such a morality to a world not yet sufficiently evolved to be trusted with a higher one, a world which would only turn the freedom of spirit, were it granted, to the base uses of the flesh. But the values of poetry are not of the world. They are absolute, or they die with the death of the age which begot them. Arthur is a moral, not a spiritual conception, and true poetry, with its searching candour, must perforce name him false.

Such a morality, then, sentimental rather than ideal, was implicit in Tennyson's nature when in February, 1856, he turned once again to his old love, and wrote the first of what was to prove a chain of episodes— "Merlin and Vivien." Yet it would be wrong, particularly at the beginning of his task, to suppose that he cherished any conscious moral purpose. Doubtless, years later, when all were completed, he could say : " The general drift of the ' Idylls ' is clear enough. The whole is the drama of man coming into practical life and ruined by one sin." At the same time he would affirm : " Poetry is like shot-silk with many glancing colours. Every reader must find his own interpretation according to his ability, and according to his sympathy with the poet."

The truth is that a poet, however merely pictorial his intention, cannot fail to intrude his morality into his art as he works, especially if he be dealing with characters and actions. Thus it was with Tennyson. His morality shaped the incidents, and, being imperfect, weakened the characters independently of his volition. Consciously he was engaged in beautiful writing, in exquisite description, and the accumulation of ornate and splendid imagery. The morality slipped in unaware, and became finally so entangled with the scenery that posterity, in its aversion towards dogma, has even unfairly neglected the art.

It is well, therefore, to note that Tennyson never conceived any new idea, character or situation in the course of the " Idylls." Arthur himself, the flower of perfect knighthood, had blossomed in earlier verses ; the same may be said of the other characters. Men or women, we have met them all before, submissive, erring, contrite, seductive, knightly, sermonising. It is the same with the incident.

What is new is the consistent opulence of style, a style distinct both from the tremulous music of " The Lady of Shalott " and the laboured tones of " In Memoriam," a style of sustained sweetness, luscious as ripe fruit. It is the manner of " The Princess " purified and enriched, and in its kind is the most perfect verse Tennyson produced. We do not place it in the same category as " Ulysses," or with some of the best blank verse written in the last ten years of his life, when he did rise almost to the heights of an impassioned idea. But this luxuriant music, where it occurs, we owe to the concentration of all his talent and sensibility upon art. And when we consider at what cost to his art he had pursued ideas and grasped only moral sentiments, we must feel that his unconscious return to art for art's sake was prudent policy. It was a confession of failure in the highest province of poetry. But he ruled like a King over the lower.

" Merlin and Vivien " is the story of the seduction of a wise man by one of " Satan's shepherdesses." In theme it is another " Vision of Sin " or " Dream of Fair Women." But its theme was of secondary interest even to Tennyson. He wrote it for the pleasure of such phrases as this :

> " So dark a forethought roll'd about his brain,
>   As on a dull day in an Ocean cave
>   The blind wave feeling round his long sea-hall
>   In silence "—

an image borrowed from his Cornish notebook ;
or for the scenery of " the wild woods of Broceliande,"
with which his New Forest notebook was richly
stored ; or for the dainty lyric concerning " The little
rift within the lover's lute." Indeed, we may say
that his descriptive art renders the seduction itself
so attractive that it destroys any moral aversion we
are meant to feel towards the wicked lady.

" Merlin and Vivien " was finished in little more
than a month, and " Geraint and Enid " begun
in mid-April. Here, in contrast to the sage corrupted
by a wily adventuress, we are given the haughty
male, who puts his " simple, noble-natured " wife's
loyalty to various stupid, but highly decorative,
tests. He acts like a knightly boor, but she
suffers all patiently and, like the beaten dog, only
loves her master the more. Enid is in fact a
" Dora," and Geraint is the " Lord of Burleigh " bereft
of his manners, and not unwilling to play the
malingerer the better to prove and enjoy his lady's
despairing attachment :

> " Till at the last he waken'd from his swoon,
>   And found his own dear bride propping his head,
>   And chafing his faint hands, and calling to him ;
>   And felt the warm tears falling on his face ;
>   And said to his own heart, ' She weeps for me : '
>   And yet lay still, and feign'd himself as dead,
>   That he might prove her to the uttermost,
>   And say to his own heart, ' She weeps for me.' "

It is a strange manhood that finds such exquisite
satisfaction in a woman's tears ! The conclusion
of the poem is an inverted " Princess " ; the amorous
uses of the sick-bed and of an interesting convalescence

are once more demonstrated. Geraint was finally, as he deserved, " nigh wounded to the death " :

> " And Enid tended on him there : and there
> Her constant motion round him, and the breath
> Of her sweet tendance hovering over him,
> Fill'd all the genial courses of his blood
> With deeper and with ever deeper love . . ."

And being restored to health, he earned a noble reputation as a " great Prince and man of men,"

> " and in their halls arose
> The cry of children, Enid's and Geraint's,
> Of times to be, nor did he doubt her more . . ."

Once again, therefore, the story and the paltry characterisation are but echoes from the past. The painting of the wilds direct from Welsh scenery, amid which he was staying while he wrote, and the pictorial representation of battle and tournament absorbed all Tennyson's powers. Of " Guinevere," begun in July, 1857, much the same may be said, although in Arthur's address to his humiliated Queen Tennyson proclaims his morality more explicitly and with more emotion than in any other passage in the " Idylls." The moral exclusiveness so often apparent in the Arthur of later " Idylls "—the " lay model" of dispassionate perfection—displays itself in the self-satisfied egotism of parts of this poem ; such lines, for example, as

> " I, whose vast pity almost makes me die,"

or

> " I am thine husband—not a smaller soul."

It was not with such self-advertisement, we remember, that Christ showed pity to a harlot. Yet, with this qualification, many of the King's last words at Almesbury are noble and movingly human ; for this passage embodied the heart of Tennyson's shy, sensitive conviction concerning the world, nourished through many brooding years. For a moment his morality rises to the dignity of a passion ; it is neither querulous, hysterical nor weakly complacent, but intense and constrained. We hear it in the early accusation, cold and taut as Hamlet's " Get thee to a nunnery : why wouldst thou be a breeder of sinners ? " yet raised above the level of any small bitterness :

> " The children born of thee are sword and fire,
> Red ruin and the breaking up of laws,"

no less than in the summary of virtue as originally conceived by the " fair Order of my Table Round " :

> " To serve as model for the mighty world,
> And be the fair beginning of a time."

Tennyson cannot keep this level ; too soon he falls into pompous platitude. Yet it is foolish to allow a natural disgust for the sanctimonious egotism which mars the concluding passages of Arthur's speech to blind us to the dignity and truth of the earlier. Elsewhere, however, Tennyson, as in the preceding episodes, was lost to thought in the " delicious dales " and the " silk pavilions " of his versification.

" Lancelot and Elaine," the other of the first four episodes of the " Idylls " to be written, illustrates a like condition. It contains, however, one creation upon which Tennyson's morality encroaches little, if at all, and so of which the art is the most perfect. The " Lily Maid of Astolat " was, perhaps, preserved from moral degradation by memories of her lyrical prototype, " The Lady of Shalott." She is Tennyson's loveliest fantasy of womanhood, characterless, but pure, faithful in love, and infinitely pathetic. She is above sex and outside the burden of life and worldly interpretation. She speaks as

> " a little, helpless, innocent bird
> That has but one plain passage of few notes,
> Will sing the simple passage o'er and o'er
> For all an April morning."

The moral conflict of one whose " honour rooted in dishonour stood " is conducted beyond the range of her personality, as a catechism cannot consort with music. The intrigues of Guinevere and Lancelot in this episode satisfy all Tennyson's desire to inform his readers how a lawless passion can corrupt love and mar the features. On the maiden he expends his faultless artistry as on no other character in the "Idylls." The guilty Queen is the rose harbouring the invisible worm, but Elaine floats down the stream of murmuring verse a lily without stain. She is the essence of pure art and April innocence.

5

Few were the sorrows or anxieties that intruded upon the " trustful courtesies of household life " at Farringford. In the summer of 1856 rumour came of the probable collapse of the Bank to which Tennyson had entrusted his savings. After the experience of Dr. Allen this was bitter news indeed, but " Alfred," wrote Mrs. Tennyson, " showed a noble disregard of money, much as the loss would affect us " ; and that evening, like a general heartening his wavering hosts by the music of the drum, he asked her to play and sing " the grand Welsh national air, ' Come to Battle.' " The Bank, however, survived the crisis.

In Wales, later in the year, often to his wife's real distress, when the mists swallowed him up and the clouds swept down upon the mountains, he refreshed his spirit amid roaring cataracts and romantic scenery, until sometimes it seemed to him as if the years were annulled, as if it were King Arthur, and not he, who sat in Caerleon and listened to the Usk murmuring by his windows. More and more it was the world and its mean modernity which seemed unreal, the legendary the real. Over Farringford an Arthurian atmosphere brooded, consecrating the simple offices of domestic life and lending itself to an unhurried cultivation of verse as another winter softened into spring.

But the New Year was not to allow the conscience of a Laureate to slumber so pleasantly amid the wild woods and soft pastures of days gone by. In May the Indian Mutiny broke out, and as month followed month with tales of massacre and outrage, of beleaguered women and children and native treachery, a wave of horror passed over the nation, culminating in an hysterical cry for revenge. Tennyson was " stirred to the depths." And yet until late in the year, when public attention became concentrated with trembling intentness upon the siege of Lucknow, he did not suffer a tottering Empire to interfere with his regular industry. India was very far away, and news was uncertain, and probably exaggerated. Meanwhile it was good to welcome Bayard Taylor, the American translator of " Faust," to Farringford, and to listen to his account of a Norwegian forest in winter, " The most beautiful sight in the world," as he claimed, " sheathed in ice, the sun rising over it, and making the whole landscape one rainbow of flashing diamonds." Disastrous rumours dwindled while he made a note of the description for later use and promised himself a visit to a country which offered such scenic possibilities.

July found him at work on " Guinevere," the original first two lines of which, despite their lugubrious content, he gave to his wife as a novel form of birthday present. They read :

"But hither shall I never come again,
    Never lie by thy side : see thee no more :
    Farewell ! "

The illustrated edition of his Poems by the Pre-Raphaelites had now appeared, and brought a sympathetic letter from Ruskin congratulating him upon Rossetti's contributions ; while at Manchester, where later in the summer he stayed on his way to Coniston and Scotland, he not only heard Dickens recite his " Christmas Carol," but was seen studying pictures at the Exhibition by Hawthorne, who, without approaching him, was enslaved by his appearance, writing that he " liked him well and rejoiced more in him than in all the wonders of the Exhibition."

A phenomenally mild winter helped somewhat to distract attention from the struggle in India, which had become matter for acute anxiety as the year drew to its close. Late in November news arrived of Havelock's death, and Tennyson wrote, but perhaps wisely refrained from publishing, a short elegy, of which the concluding stanza contained the comforting reflection :

"Bold Havelock died,
    Tender and great and good,
    And every man in Britain
    Says, ' I am of Havelock's blood.' "

The wild roses, however, were blossoming by scores in the hedges—so marvellous was the season—when on Christmas Day news of the relief of Lucknow arrived. Tennyson was later to interpret the spirit of the heroic defenders, and incidentally the vigorous self-applause of all who, in their city offices and country residences, had, without respite, cultivated the soils of peace, in the bellicose line

"Men will forget what we suffer and not what we do. We can fight ! "

At the moment his professional powers were engaged
on another task, for early in the year the Queen
approached her Laureate with a request. The Princess Royal, scarce yet seventeen years of age, was to
be married to the Crown Prince of Prussia, " Good
Fritz," as Victoria affectionately called him, and the
Queen desired that a stanza should be added to the
National Anthem for a concert to be given at Bucking-
ham Palace on the eve of the wedding day. Tennyson
replied with two stanzas of fervent prayer for the
" hallow'd hour " and loyal farewell to " our England's
flower," nor did he neglect the political aspect of the
nuptials, but made reference to them early in the first
stanza :

> " God bless our Prince and Bride !
> God keep their lands allied,
> God save the Queen ! "

Posterity can only lament that the Deity seems to
have been as unresponsive to this earnest appeal as
to the festivities and the fireworks.

Once more the poet turned to his " Guinevere,"
of which January saw the tentative completion. It
was declared by his wife to be " awe-inspiring." The
labour of writing was from this time rendered even
more delightful by the erection of a little summer-
house that caught the southern sun and made it
possible to enjoy the illusion of heat at almost any
season.

About the New Year two Oxford undergraduates
who were staying in the Isle of Wight called at
Farringford, one of them remarkable for the smallness
of his stature, the mass of flaming hair which crowned
an abnormally large head, and the nervous eagerness
of his gestures and articulation. He confessed to
being a poet, and, on being asked to dinner, proved
so modest and so intelligent a listener, so well versed

also in the Classics, that Tennyson was persuaded to confide in him his special devotion for Virgil and to read him " Maud," for which he expressed the greatest admiration. The visit ended without any attempt on the young man's part to advance any verses of his own, which very favourably impressed his host, blissfully unconscious that the sacred walls of Farringford had harboured for a few brief hours a Bacchanal in demure disguise ; for the decorous undergraduate was none other than Swinburne.

More than seven years had now passed without the publication of a volume, and Tennyson's friends began to grow anxious about the welfare of the Muse. Was domestic bliss proving unfriendly to composition, or did the poet, through that painful sensitiveness " so often combined with real manliness as well as great intellectual gifts," still fear to expose himself to the incivilities of criticism ? Mr. Jowett felt compelled to sound him about his intentions, to confide to him how painful it was for his admirers to feel that they were being robbed of their poetical dues through any false respect being paid to the bites of malignant " mosquitos. . . . . The whole world," he added, " is morbid with dissecting and analysing itself and wants to be comforted and put together again. Might not this be the poet's office, to utter the ' better voice,' while Thackeray is uttering the worse one ? " He hastened to say that he wished in no way to blame Thackeray, that he desired to take the world as it was in this present age, yet that there was need of someone to show the good side of human nature and to condone its frailties.

But neither could reviewers deter Tennyson from publication nor importunate friends hasten the process. He was at peace with himself and with a world which appreciated him and would not let his fame sleep. Had not Lord Dufferin confessed to him in a letter that after twenty years of cold distaste for the masters of poetry in every age, he had been converted to delighted appreciation by a volume of Alfred Tennyson's, " the Orpheus whose music had made the gate of poet-land fly open " ? He would grant the world more of this alluring and educative music in his good time. Delay would but sharpen its appetite and savour his own. Before starting to weave the fine fabric of " the fair maid of Astolat," he turned for diversion to another and simpler *genre* of verse, cultivated with notable success in his youth, and too long neglected—the poem of rustic life which Wordsworth had popularised, but lacked the art, it seemed to Tennyson, to perfect. The joys and sorrows of poor country men and women were very touching, and as Victorian life became more and more upholstered, it was refreshing to be reminded of a class which still clung, if a little hazardously, to the bare breast of Nature.

A companion poem to " The May Queen " of thirty years before was therefore written, and entitled " The Grandmother." It contained an affecting recollection of the little son whom Tennyson had lost at birth, a degree, too, of cultivated pathos, but was otherwise well suited by its lack of vernacular veracity to impress the senior class of a village Sunday school.

He went back with relish to his " Idylls "; not a visit to London, and the necessity of sitting to Watts for a portrait which all his friends found very impressive, and named " the great moonlight portrait of the Bard," could stay his industry. The promised trip to Norway followed, and more than satisfied all expectations. Standing by his cabin door on the passage out, Tennyson multiplied similes. The green sea looked like " a mountainous country," far-off waves with

foam at the top " like snowy mountains bounding the
scene ; one great wave, green-shining, past with all
its crests smoking high up beside the vessel " ; and
then " there came a sudden hurricane and roared
drearily in the funnel for twenty seconds and past
away." As he " drank the large air " his senses
regained their youthful vivacity, and a new poem, to
be named " Sea Dreams," took shape. In this he
mingled sketches of the ground-swell about him that
" upjetted in spirits of wild sea-smoke,"

> " And scaled in sheets of wasteful foam, and fell
> In cataracts,"

with the memory of a man who had once grossly
cheated him of money, and added a dread vision of a
crumbling faith, peculiarly inappropriate to the wife
of a ruined city clerk upon whom it was importunately
thrust.

Later Tennyson was struck by " the magnificent
power " of the water of the Riukan Foss, and by " the
weird blue light behind the fall " ; while a Norwegian
stranger, by his enthusiastic attentions in an hotel, and
the Christiania papers, by their interested letterpress,
showed that even so backward a country was sensibly
honoured by its distinguished visitor.

The following autumn brought the ominous excitement of a comet, to which Tennyson devoted much
attention, observing it from a platform which he had
erected on the top of the house. Of its tail he said :
" It is like a besom of destruction sweeping the sky."
His observance was not wasted. It was to prove of
service to him when later he wrote " Harold."

Meanwhile, as month followed month without any
poetical response to his appeal of the previous year,
Mr. Jowett became more restive. It was plainly
useless to approach the " Bard " ; he determined to
appeal to the conscience of Mrs. Tennyson, and wrote,

therefore, a letter packed with fertile suggestion, in which he again emphasised the insignificance of criticism : " One drop of natural feeling in poetry," he urged, " or the true statement of a single new fact is already felt to be of more value than all the critics put together. . . . I suggested ' old age ' to Mr. Tennyson, a sort of ' In Memoriam ' over a lost child, wandering in soothing strains over all the thoughts and feelings of the aged. . . . Its beauty, its sadness, its peace, its faded experience of life are good elements of poetry. . . . Might not something of the kind be expressed in verse ? If it could, like the ' May Queen,' it would touch the chords of many hearts."

" I wish," he continued, " Mr. Tennyson could be persuaded to put the ' Dogma of Immortality ' to verse . . . an heroic measure suited to manly minds embodying the deep ethical feeling which convinces us that the end of the Maker, though dark, is not here. I believe such a poem might be a possession for the world and better (what a bathos !) than ten thousand sermons. Subjects like blackberries seem to me capable of being gathered off every hedge. . . . Have not many sciences such as Astronomy and Geology a side of feeling which is poetry ? No sight touches ordinary persons so much as a starlight night. . . . Is it not true also that whole periods of history, seen by the light of modern ideas, admit of being described in short passages of poetry ? Representative men such as Charlemagne or Hildebrand seem to me safer than the shadowy personages of the legends of romance."

The blackberries were indeed many, if not all, the finest fruit. Mr. Jowett was convinced that Tennyson could " teach " a thousand " new lessons," more Christian and less barbarous than that, for example, contained in " St. Simeon Stylites," if only he could be persuaded to throw off his sensitive diffidence. To

provide inspiration with solid matter to work upon,
he offered to send books on any imaginable subject.
Mrs. Tennyson's reply, though it informed him that
the poet had for once taken the less safe path of " the
legends of romance," brought him comfort. " I do
not doubt," he wrote, " that the world will be charmed
with the Arthur ' Idylls.' " He proffered, however,
one more suggestion, " that would express the thoughts
of many hearts . . . and afford a solace where it is
much needed. The subject I mean is ' In Memoriam '
for the dead in India. It might be done so as to
include some scenes of Cawnpore and Lucknow ; or
quite simply and slightly ' Relatives in India,' the
schemings and hopings and imaginings about them,
and the fatal missive suddenly announcing their death.
They leave us in the fairness and innocence of youth,
with nothing but the vision of their childhood and
boyhood to look back upon, and return no more."

It chanced, indeed, that early in 1859 old thoughts
of one who had left him in the fairness of youth were
reawakened in Tennyson by the death of Hallam's
father, the historian. It was never Tennyson's wont
to read " In Memoriam " aloud ; " I cannot," he
would say, " it breaks me down," but for one evening
he allowed his memory to linger over that poignant
past, reading much of the poem aloud and dwelling
upon those passages which moved him most.

How remote and mythical those years of youth and
enthusiasm seemed now, how forlorn in that enchanted
late Spring of the century seemed now the figure of
Hallam himself, beckoning his friends forward with
his joyous, improvident glance ! For a few years
Tennyson had gone with him, almost believing that
the world would justify his friend's too generous trust,
too fearless optimism, that it would respond to the cry
of progress at a bound, that the manacles might,

indeed, be loosed and the prison gates thrown
wide.

The vision of his friend venturing forth into a coarse
world on his quixotic errand remained, but he believed
no more in miracles of progress, nor in trusting to the
Divine in foreigners at least, or in the lower classes,
without first taking every reasonable precaution.

In May the European situation was far from satisfactory; more than one Power seemed to threaten
the majesty of England. Tennyson published " Riflemen, form !" in *The Times*, and it "rang like a
trumpet-call through the length and breadth of the
Empire." The international conspiracy of fear, which
was in half a century to reduce to ruins the ordered
house of Europe so painfully preserved in equilibrium
by the scared forces of reaction, was considerably
advanced by a poem widely read, containing the
couplet :

> " Let your reforms for a moment go !
> Look to your butts, and take good aims ! "

To one of the promoters of the Volunteer Rifle Corps
he wrote : " I must heartily congratulate you on
your having been able to do so much for your country ;
and I hope that you will not cease from your labours
until it is the law of the land that every male child in
it shall be trained to the use of arms."

" Riflemen, form !" could scarcely have appealed
to Hallam's taste, but it proved an excellent recruiting
poster, and nervous Victorians slept easier for it in
their beds, happily ignorant of the nightmares they
were preparing for their posterity.

With the completion of " Elaine," the first four
" Idylls " had gone to press, and in the interval before
their appearance Tennyson occupied himself with
" Boadicea," the first of those experiments in classical

prosody, which provided in years to come so happy and musical a pastime.

When early in the summer the " Idylls " appeared, Mr. Jowett's flattering prophecy was fulfilled. The world, with few exceptions, was charmed.

The reviewers, led by Mr. Gladstone, surrendered criticism to appreciation, and even so hard-headed a party man as Macaulay was captivated. Thackeray, enlivened by two bottles of claret, wrote : " You have made me as happy as I was as a child with the ' Arabian Nights,' every step I have walked in Elfland has been a sort of Paradise to me." . . . " How can you, at fifty," he added in a postscript, " be doing things as well as at thirty-five ? " The identity in quality was significant of more than Thackeray implied.

The " Idylls," in fact, as the Duke of Argyll predicted, were " understood and admired by many who are incapable of understanding and appreciating many of your other works." "The applause of the ' Idylls,' " he wrote later, " goes on crescendo, and so far as I can hear, without exception. Detractors are silenced."

The poems combined the sensational and the moral, the two elements in life which make the strongest appeal to ordinary men and women in their moments of leisure. The pleasures to be derived from a religious service and a society sermon, a gorgeous scenario and a tactful unfolding of sexual intrigue, proved, in combination, quite irresistible. Mr. Jowett was in ecstasies. " The Lily Maid," he wrote, " seems to me the fairest, purest, sweetest love poem in the English language. I have not seen any criticism nor do I care about them . . . Of the other poems I admire ' Vivien ' the most (the naughty one), which seems to me a work of wonderful power and skill. It is most elegant and fanciful. I am not surprised at your Delilah reducing the wise man, she

is quite equal to it. . . . I am sure that the ' Grandmother ' is a most exquisite thing."

Ruskin alone expressed a more cautious admiration.
He was not quite happy about " the increased quiet-
ness of style " the poems revealed, and felt the art and
finish a little more than he liked to feel it.   The word-
painting, he thought " such as never was yet for
concentration," but he added : " Merely in the facts
of modern life, not drawing-room formal life, but the
far-away and quite unknown growth of souls in and
through any form of misery and servitude, there is an
infinity of what men should be told, and what none
but a poet can tell.   I cannot but think that the
intense masterful and unerring transcript of an
actuality, and the relation of a story of any real human
life as a poet would watch and analyse it, would make
all men feel more or less what poetry was, as they felt
what Life and Fate were in their instant workings.
This seems to me the true task of the modern poet.
And I think I have seen faces and heard voices by road
and street side, which claimed or conferred as much
as ever the loveliest or saddest of Camelot."

It was the voice of modern criticism, intent on
reality even at the cost of personal pleasure or
edification.   But Tennyson preferred to listen to
Mr. Jowett, to what, in Charles Kingsley's words, " a
gentleman and a Christian ought to think of you and
your work."   The gentlemen and Christians responded
so ardently that ten thousand copies were sold in the
first week of publication, and hundreds more continued
to sell monthly.

Thus encouraged, Tennyson began to study " Pelleas
and Ettarre " and " La Belle Isoude " before leaving
with Mr. Palgrave for an August holiday in Portugal.
Here, however, realism would not spare him.   A
blazing sun, flies and fleas, decided the travellers to

return earlier than they had intended, and the poetical notebook suffered accordingly.

November brought him an early copy, from its author, of the " Origin of Species," which Tennyson studied with great interest and without, perhaps, realising the explosive nature of the material he handled ; but amongst all these signs of enhanced reputation few can have rewarded him so much as a letter from his mother, in which she said of the "Idylls " : " It does indeed give me the purest satisfaction to notice that a spirit of Christianity is perceptible through the whole volume. . . . O dearest Ally, how fervently have I prayed for years that our merciful Redeemer would intercede with our Heavenly Father to grant thee His Holy Spirit to urge thee to employ the talents He has given thee, by taking every opportunity of endeavouring to impress the precepts of His Holy Word on the minds of others. My beloved son, words are too feeble to express the joy of my heart in perceiving that thou art earnestly endeavouring to do so. Dearest Ally, there is nothing for a moment to be compared to the favour of God ! I need not ask thee if thou art of the same opinion."

Words of such saintliness, emanating from so reverenced a source, cannot have failed to temper even whatever exultation Tennyson may have justifiably felt on the receipt of a letter from Prince Albert asking him to be good enough to sign his name in an accompanying volume of the " Idylls," from the reading of which the illustrious writer confessed that he had derived the greatest enjoyment. And indeed the sense of a Divine mission having been entrusted to him seems to have grown upon Tennyson with the years, as in the course of nature he ceased to hunger with so keen and fine an appetite for the pleasures of colour and sound for their own sake.

ALFRED TENNYSON
1860

From a photograph by Rejlander

[*To face p.* 222

One who was privileged to know him intimately
has recorded that he told her " he felt the gift of
poetry to be bestowed on him by his Heavenly Father
as ' a great trust ' . . . that his sense of the Divine
source of this gift was almost awful to him, since he
felt that every word of his should be consecrated to
the service of Him who had touched his lips with
that fire of Heaven which was to enable him to speak
in God's name to his age . . . that to try and find out
what God had made him to be, and then to resolve to
be that very self, and none other, was his constant aim."

Allowance must doubtless be made for the pardon-
able exaggeration of a feminine adorer, yet it is
reasonable to suppose that some such view of his
function as a poet, if only as a consequence of the
public eminence to which he attained, came to colour
his later years.   It is noticeable in the subject-matter
of some of the later " Idylls."

The Duke of Argyll was at this time solicitous that
the theme of the Sangreal should occupy Tennyson's
pen. Tennyson was at first diffident. " I doubt,"
he wrote, " whether such a subject could be handled
in these days without incurring a charge of irreverence.
It would be too much like playing with sacred things."
Time, however, and a tour in Cornwall amid old ruins
and " magnificently coloured seas " diminished his
hesitation. He was well also. One of his companions on the tour wrote to Mrs. Tennyson : " I
expect idling about so long will make his brain so
fertile that, when he gets back to Farringford, he will
do an immense deal of work. He was physically
better, there was no question, for he actually ate
breakfasts ! and partook of tarts not once, but *twice*,
at dinner ! which he had not done before for many
years ; and his face had grown a reddish bronze, a
very healthy colour."

The notebook was as active as ever. At Fowey he remarks : " A cow drinking from a trough on the hillside. The netted beams of light played on the wrinkles of her throat."

On his return he did not immediately turn to Arthurian " Idylls," though a scheme for an enlarged arrangement of them, with the insertion of a number of new episodes, was occupying his mind ; but early in 1861 he made yet another excursion, and with more success than previously, into rustic life with his " Northern Farmer," in which he characterised an old farm bailiff, described to him by a great-uncle years before, and recalled with relish early memories of Lincolnshire dialect. In the summer he took his family on a holiday to Auvergne and the Pyrenees, and had the good fortune to fall in with Mr. Arthur Hugh Clough, already an admired friend, who joined the party, and so particularly endeared himself to all by his gentle disposition that no other title seemed to fit him but " Child-angel," with which, accordingly, he was christened. At Pau they parted from him with sadness, which would have been poignant indeed had they known that within six months malaria was to snatch away all but the memory of a very wistful spirit.

So happy a year, however, was not fated to end in tranquillity. " The foul ways and unhappy diet of that charming Auvergne " upset the health of all the Tennyson family ; and with the autumn, to aggravate a torpid liver, came the threat that " my Freshwater should be polluted and defiled with brick and mortar." " The wholesome hillside," the Laureate's dim retreat, and the prospect from the park itself were threatened by speculating vandals. There was talk of laying out streets and crescents. Yet even such a dread eventuality paled into insignificance before the disaster which befell in December.

The exalted figure who in the life of the nation seemed to promise to exercise so incalculable an influence for good, the self-effacing Prince who had impressed all by his conscientious demeanour when, six years before, he had called at Farringford, was to be cut down in his prime. The death of the Prince Consort not only distressed Tennyson as being a great loss to Britain and the Empire, but it was as if the ideal character of his poem had been erased from the book of life. Sympathy for the Queen, enhanced by loyalty, overwhelmed him. How better could he show it than by dedicating to the Prince's memory the book in which his pure and lofty character was so unworthily mirrored ?

The dedication at least should be worthy of the occasion. It was sent to the Princess Alice with a letter in which Tennyson wrote : " Madam, Having heard some time ago from Sir C. B. Phipps that your Royal Highness had expressed a strong desire that I should in some way ' idealize ' our lamented Prince, and being at that time very unwell, I was unwilling to attempt the subject, because I feared that I might scarce be able to do it justice ; nor did I well see how I should idealize a life which was in itself an ideal. At last it seemed to me that I could do no better than dedicate to his memory a book which he himself had told me was valued by him." He ended : " Though these lines conclude with an address to our beloved Queen, I feel that I cannot do better than leave the occasion of presenting them to the discretion of your Royal Highness."

In the early days of the New Year Tennyson was pondering the Ode to be sung in the summer at the opening of the International Exhibition, that scheme which had inspired the last days of Prince Albert's life with visions of Science, Art and Labour kissing each other, and Peace, as a market woman of ample proportions, presiding with universal smile over a world flowing with milk and bristling with ingenious machinery. He had hoped to make of it a prophetic panegyric in the style of the " Golden Year," but death ordered the insertion of a palinode. He, to whose fertile mind and high intention the world owed a trade exhibition to which the clergy might refer with profit in their sermons, was no more.

> " O silent father of our kings to be
> Mourn'd in this golden hour of jubilee,
> For this, for all, we weep our thanks to thee !
>
> The world-compelling plan was thine,—
> And lo ! the long laborious miles
> Of Palace : lo ! the giant aisles
> Rich in model and design : "

A brotherhood of commerce commended itself as so satisfactory a panacea to all with money to invest. To base peace on swollen dividends, to sanctify the mills and factories which were everywhere making so ugly a blot on the fair English countryside, to " idealize " even the poor sweated country labourer, until one might see in the slums themselves the engines of enlightenment and progress, the hand of a Divine Providence at work—that was indeed a vision pleasant to dwell upon ! Yet it may be that uneasy doubts gathered about Tennyson as he wrote. Did " works of peace " or " works of war " lie in the womb of this accumulating industry ?

> " Harvest-tool and husbandry,
> Loom and wheel and enginery,
> Secrets of the sullen mine,
> Steel and gold, and corn and wine,
> Fabric rough, or fairy-fine . . .
> And shapes and hues of Art divine ! "

The sense of plenty was very intoxicating as the trade list mounted up, and yet was the peaceful issue so certain, even though " ye, the wise who think, the wise who reign," staked their reputation upon it ? Reason made no certain answer.

> " Is the goal so far away ?
> Far, how far no tongue can say,
> Let us dream our dream to-day."

It was thus always that the Victorian Age put its scruples to sleep. Pleasant it was to dream, and perhaps, did they dream but long and fantastically enough, the dream would come true. What need was there to image a dread awakening ?

As on that January evening Tennyson recited his newly completed Ode pontifically to the family at Farringford, the compelling rhythm, the stately music captured their senses. The dream seemed real enough.

The reception of the dedication by the Royal Family had been all that could be desired. " If words could express," wrote Princess Alice, " *thanks* or *real* appreciation of lines so beautiful, so truly worthy of the great pure spirit which inspired the author, Princess Alice would attempt to do it." The task proved far beyond the powers of language. She had, however, transmitted the lines to the Queen, " who desired her to tell Mr. Tennyson, with her sincerest thanks, how much moved she was on reading them, and that they soothed her aching, bleeding heart. She knows also how *he* would have admired them." From the Crown Princess of Prussia came a letter combining fond memories, enthusiastic appreciation, and a request for an autograph. " The first time," she wrote, " I ever heard the ' Idylls of the King ' was last year, when I found both the Queen and Prince quite in raptures about them. The first bit I ever heard was the end of ' Guinevere,' the last two or three pages ; the Prince read them to me, and I shall never forget the impression it made upon me, hearing those grand and simple words in his voice! He did so admire them, and I cannot separate the idea of King Arthur from the image of him whom I most revered on earth! I almost know the ' Idylls of the King ' by heart now ; they are really sublime."

Later, from private sources, Tennyson heard also that the Queen had found much comfort in reading " In Memoriam," and had marked her copy personally. What was professional criticism beside so signal an honour as this ?

In April came a summons to the Presence. It was with considerable trepidation that Tennyson approached his Sovereign at Osborne ; his qualms, however, were superfluous, for the two " Presences " found in each other a perfect harmony. The interview proved very affecting. He told on his return how the Queen " stood pale and statue-like before him, speaking in a quiet, unutterably sad voice," a voice which he knew not whether to love or reverence the more. " There was a kind of stately innocence about her," and she talked with simple and complimentary intimacy. " Next to the Bible," she confessed, " ' In Memoriam ' is my comfort." Of the Prince she brought herself to speak without embarrassment. " He was so like the picture of Arthur Hallam in ' In Memoriam,' even to his blue eyes." The physical likeness had perhaps eluded the notice of Tennyson ; but he declared his conviction that the Prince would have made a great King. " We all grieve with Your Majesty," he added, speaking with quiet dignity, as befitted in some sense the public voice of the land.

The Queen was much impressed with his courtly sincerity. Sorrow and sympathy had of a sudden brought her very close to her Laureate, and Albert had loved his verse. It was enough. The expression of sweetness in her countenance, which Tennyson remarked in this interview, was but the first winsome glance of a favour which was to enfold him in its sunshine for more than a quarter of a century. As immediate heralds of this regal bounty came the promise of two portraits. " Will you say," Tennyson wrote in acknowledgment, " how deeply grateful I am to Her Majesty for the prints of Herself and Him which She proposes to send me, and how very much I shall value Her gift."

Eminence from henceforth was his. Not only a swarming public, but Queens had smiled on his chaste and courtly Muse.

The play, conducted with such admirable discretion throughout, had culminated triumphantly in its third act. It had reached its logical conclusion ; but the curtain was not finally to be rung down upon an applauding audience for over thirty years.

PART IV

EMINENCE

EMINENCE

I

THE Royal favour born so auspiciously on that memorable morning at Osborne, baptised by an interchange of Guizot's edition of Prince Albert's " Speeches," the " Lieder des Leides " of Albert Zeller and the sermons of the Rev. Robertson of Brighton ; confirmed by the various occasions on which the Laureate had been able to exercise his talent to salute the illustrious living, lament them dead, or rouse the heart of the nation to some Imperial end— had culminated in 1883 in the gracious gift of a peerage. " It affords me much pleasure," wrote the Queen, " to confer on my Poet-Laureate, who is so universally admired and respected, a mark of my recognition of the great services he has rendered to literature, which has so great an influence on the world at large." To which Tennyson replied : " The knowledge of Your Majesty's approval of what I have been enabled to do is, as far as I myself am concerned, all that I desire."

Such an avowal contained little of mere courtly exaggeration. The poet's relations with the " Dear and Honoured Lady," whom he was proud to address with more than abstract fervour as " My Queen," had through twenty years become increasingly intimate. Personal intimacy had not detracted from the solemn courtesy, the devout deference, which he offered to her who symbolised the England that he

loved. Yet in his eyes she stood for more even than
this. To him the aristocratic ideal of all the ages rose
to greet him in this little Royal Lady ; even her letters
failed to abuse his mind of the belief that in her not
only every virtue and grace, but the soul of truth itself
resided. The Queen, on her part, appreciated with
far more than official gratitude one who not only
flattered her womanhood with poetic homage, and
consoled her with beautiful thoughts in time of trouble,
but had also known " how to appreciate and so
beautifully describe her dear Husband." Always she
found him " so very kind and full of sympathy," and
it was this same quality, enthroned, which appealed
so deeply to him.

" I will not say," he had written after a visit to
Osborne, " that ' I am loyal,' or that ' Your Majesty
is gracious,' for these are old hackneyed terms used or
abused by every courtier, but I will say that during
our conversation I felt the touch of that true friendship
which binds human beings together, whether they be
kings or cobblers." The sense of simplicity and
kindliness, of impeccable home virtues magnificently
elevated to a position where no unruly Lancelot might
dispute their perfect desirability, was very comforting.
The Crown, in short, by its dignified propriety, stifled
rebellion among the masses, while it consecrated the
unenterprising routine of middle-class life by its great
example. Momentarily all the self-considering virtues
shone with a surprising brilliance. Respectability
ceased to be the cult of ordinary cautious folk ; it
became a majestic, almost a romantic, propriety. The
Don Juans and the Don Quixotes of the world ceased
for a few brief years to rule the stage of life. The conscientious family man with side-whiskers, a dress coat
and an extensive gold watch-chain, usurped the part.
It was then inevitable that the reverence felt by

Tennyson for a Queen who was both a moral institution and a very gracious lady, should be vast. He never questioned the quality of those "lofty and tender sentiments" to which he referred when acknowledging the gift of her "Journal of Our Life in the Highlands"; he never doubted that with her goodness of heart went also a profundity of intelligence. For the Queen and her Laureate shared so many feelings in common; even with his sensitive hatred of indecently intrusive criticism she was in cordial sympathy. "How I wish," she wrote, "you could suggest means of crushing those horrible publications, whose object is to promulgate scandal and calumny which they invent themselves!" Soon she was to sign herself "Yours affectionately."

Twice during the twenty years which had elapsed a Baronetcy had been refused with the nicest tact, but "why," as Tennyson wrote to a friend, "should I be selfish and not suffer an honour to be done to literature in my name?" Moreover, to sit in what he considered "the greatest Upper Chamber in the world," "among the descendants of those who had made England what she is," was a proud and pleasurable privilege. It might be that a revolution were coming in which the gilded chamber and all it stood for would be swallowed up, but, if so, it would be an upheaval "world-wide, the mightiest ever known," and he had no desire to live to see it. The peerage, however, only conferred a public title on an eminence which every year had been growing more impressive.

As a poet Tennyson had become the high-priest of an universal cult. He received letters of fervent admiration and reverence not only from every class in the community, but from communities far beyond the seas, from outposts of the British Empire, from the great new Commonwealth of the West, and even

from lands which did not enjoy the privilege of British
" Liberty." Nor was this admiration confined to mere
pious expression. For though " the Prince of Poets,"
" the Great and Good Poet-Laureate whom everybody
loves so much," doubtless appreciated some few of the
thousand letters which he received from romantic
schoolgirls, " considered fairly advanced for my age,"
as one of them worded it, with their innocent candour
and thinly veiled eagerness for an autograph, yet these
and complimentary sonnets were apt to prove a little
trite after the first novelty had worn away. The
devotion, however, of an American public, which
declared itself in innumerable presents of pipes and
tobacco, or even that of an eccentric gentleman who
sent him loads of firewood, were testimonials to
greatness which it was really satisfactory to accept.

In the immediate circle of his friends, and generally
of refined and educated opinion, criticism was silent.
It was true that Fitzgerald, who had " gone into
darkness " but a few months before, carrying with him
so many memories of " golden hours,"·had remained
unsympathetic towards Tennyson's later poetry to
the end, had, indeed, twenty years earlier, written
rather extravagantly to Frederick Tennyson : " I
think Alfred had better have done singing ; he has
sung well—*tempus silere*." But " Fitz " was admit-
tedly " crotchety " in his taste, and even he had
remarked in one of his most human of Christmas
letters : " I feel how pure, noble and holy your
work is."

Of younger poets, possibly " Master " Swinburne had
proved on occasions less respectful than as an undergraduate he had promised to be. But doubtless he
suffered from that " arrogance of genius " which was
" not necessarily divine," the same demon in fact
which led the poet of " Love in a Valley " to write

about this time : " Why, this stuff is not the Muse, it's
Musery.   The man has got hold of the Muse's clothes-
line and hung it with jewelry ! "

Only on two occasions, however, through all these
years had the public expressed anything but approba-
tion of Tennyson's poetry.   The poem " Despair,"
embodying his hysterical doctrine that only suicide remained for man or woman who lost faith in God, had
been found a little unpalatable, and its conclusion—the
drowning of the creedless heroine, and rescue of the hero
by a minister of religion, and his reconversion thereby
to the faith of his fathers—a trifle unsympathetic
and even unconvincing.   Tennyson's modern village
tragedy, " The Promise of May," had likewise excited
some protest from extremists, and a Marquess had
caused a painful scene at one performance by publicly
denouncing " Mr. Tennyson's abominable caricature
of a Freethinker."   Yet these were exceptions.
Browning continued to be very appreciative, and had
not Longfellow written of him ?—

> " Not of the howling dervishes of song,
>   Who craze the brain with their delirious dance,
>   Art thou, O sweet historian of the heart."

That, surely, was a sufficient answer to " Master "
Swinburne !

Whitman hailed him with colloquial ardour as
" The Boss," and Carlyle even, who had always been
prejudiced against nineteenth century art, considering
it to be at a low ebb, had found " grand thoughts " in
the " Idylls."

The ranks of the " Apostles " had been sadly
depleted by death, Spring-Rice and Brookfield, to
name but two, being gone, but to the end they had
stood faithful, Spedding turning from his long labours
over Bacon to record his admiration of the " Plays."
But now he, too, was gone, leaving behind memories

of fifty years before, when he and Tennyson walked together through fields of daffodils. Mr. Jowett, however, survived to witness one after another of his tentative suggestions satisfactorily realised, particularly " the periods of history, seen by the light of modern ideas," in the " Plays," " the heroic measure suited to manly minds " in " Lucretius " and " The Higher Pantheism," and " drops of natural feeling " showered over many dramatic poems of rustic and fisher life. He did not cease to record his admiration : " I cannot see any reason why Alfred should not write better and better as long as he lives," he confided in a letter to Mrs. Tennyson.

Amid the numerous new and influential friends whom these twenty years had brought into prominence Mr. Gladstone loomed large. In this same year of 1883, Tennyson had gone on a sea voyage with him round the north of Scotland to Norway, and thence to Denmark. Everywhere they had shared a triumphal progress ; together they received the freedom of the Borough of Kirkwall, and at Copenhagen entertained to lunch on board their vessel the King and Queen of Denmark, and the Czar and Czarina, finally steering out of the harbour amid salvoes of applause little inferior to those which greeted Royalty itself. But it was as enthusiastic leader of the chorus of reviewers that Mr. Gladstone exercised so powerful an influence. Writing of the " Idylls " he had said, with that " immeasurable power of vocables " which only he could wield : " We know not where to look in history or in letters for a nobler or more overpowering conception of man as he might be, than in the Arthur of this volume ; wherever he appears, it is as the great pillar of the moral order, and the resplendent top of human excellence. But even he only reaches to his climax in these two really wonderful speeches (at the end of

'Guinevere '). They will not bear mutilation ; they
must be read, and pondered, to be known."

But more gratifying perhaps than the appreciation
of men distinguished in the public eye was the proof
Tennyson continually received that the " masses "
loved him. The selection from his poems, issued in
threepenny numbers, and dedicated to " The working
men of England," had proved phenomenally successful.
The Queen had expressed her cordial satisfaction that
" this admirable selection . . . will be brought within
the reach of the poorest among the subjects of Her
Majesty " ; while the " Enoch Arden " volume, containing the gallant " Welcome to Alexandra," had
sold immediately to the extent of sixty thousand
copies, and was said to have had an excellent effect
upon the uneducated—an effect instanced by the
experience of a district visitor, who so turned the
heads of an assembly of old ladies by reading them
" Enoch Arden," that henceforth they were unwilling
to accept any tract after " that beautiful one " of Mr.
Tennyson's, which had done them such " a power of
good."

It was indeed pleasing for one so aristocratic in
temper to hear that he was now frequently called
" The Poet of the People," as it was for one so
Imperial-hearted to be told by Lord Dufferin how
deeply all in the " True North " of Canada felt
indebted to him for the Colonial sympathies voiced
in the Epilogue to his " Idylls." He was thrilled
with the sense of practical usefulness, as once before,
when he had heard from the Crimea that a book of
his in a soldier's breast-pocket had taken a bullet and
saved an officer's life under fire. Truly an exception
in his favour seemed to be made in that " want of
reverence now-a-days," which years ago he had
deplored, " for great men, whose brightness, like that

of the luminous bodies in the Heaven, makes the dark spaces look the darker."

If greatness was to be judged by reverence, he was great. He could afford to say with impressive unworldliness, " I hate the blare and blaze of so-called fame. What business has the public to want to know about Byron's wildnesses ? He has given them fine work, and they ought to be satisfied."

His own public was satisfied ; but was the " fine work " safe from the hands of future vandals ? Was criticism only cowed by his presence ? He had silenced it long ago, after twenty difficult years ; would it become articulate again when he was gone ? He had a horror of the way famous people were likely to be maligned after their death. Posterity cared so little for contemporary prestige ; it pierced with such cruel curious eyes behind the veil of decency and reticence.

The thought of it troubled him, sitting crowned on the throne of his generation's favour, as his own anxious discontent with easy attainment had once troubled his youth with doubt and tantalised it with visions.

2

Upon Tennyson's home life, at least, no future critic, however malignant his intention or searching his gaze, could cast discredit. No whispered echo of a Byron's wildness could ever in years to come haunt the hushed gardens of Farringford. All here had been wholesome, simple, natural and kind. Everyone, to quote a favourite expression of the Queen, had been consistently " dear and good." And if disrespectful flippancy had been a stranger, there had been no lack of gaiety and diversion during these twenty years. Children's voices had enlivened

Farringford's quiet paths, strains of music, girlish
chatter, gruff laughter, even the sound of "dancers
dancing in tune," had often issued from its deep
windows to die away among the trees. Time had been
bountiful in the rewards of virtue, and Tennyson, on
the morning which brought its sheaves of congratula-
tion from every corner of the earth, had much indeed
for which to be grateful. His home, with its dark
gleaming furniture, its ample upholstery and polished
floors, had become a commodious shrine, visited by
a long line of devout and distinguished pilgrims.
Hither its master had welcomed poets, patriots,
politicians and philosophers; young beauty had
graced its lawns and learning sat at its tables; over
all had love and reverence presided with unassuming
dignity.

Hither Garibaldi came, a romantic figure chanting
Italian poetry, and planted a Wellingtonia tree in
the avenue; the Queen of the Sandwich Islands
took her seat on the throne of ilex wood made for
the occasion, and carried away at parting two
large magnolia blossoms from the garden. Huxley,
" chivalrous, wide and earnest "; " the Great Man,"
Mr. Gladstone; Gordon, with his fanatical eyes and
unworldly bearing; Dr. Martineau, subtle-minded
and mournful; Ruskin, the apostle of æstheticism;
Renan, the fastidious sceptic; Longfellow, " one of
the most enchanting of men "; John Tyndall, the
scientist, whose imagination still survived; Barnes,
the Dorsetshire poet; the devout Mr. Jowett—all
had been guests at one time or another. Here
Turgueneff had played German backgammon, Jenny
Lind had sung " Auld Lang Syne " and parts of the
" Elijah," Joachim had bewitched with his violin,
and Mr. Darwin had assured the poet that his hypothesis did not make against Christianity. Tennyson

had enjoyed welcoming them all, and bidding each
farewell with a dignified gesture and the hospitable
words "Come whenever you like." He had been
peculiarly fortunate, too, in the discovery of interesting
neighbours.

Of Sir John Simeon mention has been already
made—"The only man," Tennyson wrote of him,
"to whom I ever unpacked my whole heart"; and
within easy reach, at Heathfield, was Bradley, with
whom he had stayed when he first took his son
Hallam to Marlborough. Bradley then was Head-
master, and there Tennyson had spent, in turn,
evenings devoted to science masters and microscopes and to poetry readings amongst an admiring
throng of boys. Eventually Bradley settled in the
Island, and Tennyson had often gone botanising with
the little active scholar, setting out armed with
hammer and knapsack for a day's sport among the
fossils in the cliffs; or late on dim August nights
they had talked together of classical prosody, or of
life and death, walking through the dusky lanes till
they reached open spaces filled with the whisper and
smell of the sea. Bradley had introduced him to
another neighbour, W. G. Ward, the metaphysician,
remarkable in that age for his eccentric candour, his
sincere love and knowledge of Shakespeare, and his
failure to appreciate the poems of Alfred Tennyson.
In friendship Ward had proved as loyal as he was
argumentative.

But of less formidable scenes and personalities the
house had in twenty years accumulated many
memories. With each Christmas the familiar festivities had grown dearer to Tennyson—the affectionate
circle about the polished table in the drawing-room
while the wine went round and nuts were cracked,
and he sat in his carved chair convulsing his audience

with a well-tried repertory of stories and anecdotes, or later, over the fire in his study, shared his views on English poetry with Palgrave, or recalled their travels together.

Here, before her husband's death, he had waltzed with Lady Simeon and the Miss Ritchies had charmed his eyes, so like Gainsborough portraits he had thought them in their fresh girlhood, " unspoilt," as he would say, " by the world," and with such inspired music did they fill the drawing-room after dinner. Hither gentle, reflective Anne Thackeray had come, a frequent visitor, and her ardent, appreciative nature, her insight and originality, had made her " the Queen of all hearts " ; and with her was often Magdalene Brookfield, the daughter of his old friend, and so joyous a companion for a walk upon the downs, because she loved and understood his odd humours, his talk of old days, and even responded to graver topics. She had never failed to melt the brusque manner behind which he still at times would veil his shyness by her winning laughter or sympathetic smile.

For from childhood shyness had been almost a disease with Tennyson. Once, in conversation with John Tyndall, he said, " Just feel my skin, a flea-bite will spread a square inch over its surface. The term ' thin-skinned ' is perfectly expressive. I *am* thin-skinned, and I take no pains to hide it." This shyness explained his occasional abruptness in company or with strangers ; but with women he had always suffered from it least. They were sensitive too ; they understood.

Another neighbour, Mr. Cameron, had done much to fill the gap made by the death of Sir John Simeon. A scholar with the appearance of " a grand Oriental chief," Tennyson named him " the philosopher with

his beard dipt in moonlight"; while his merry,
romantic-minded wife, with her untidy hair, her
mania for photography, her wildly extravagant talk,
and the unconventional performances within and
without her private theatre, had been a constant
source of lively entertainment; so impulsively would
she drag Tennyson down from the clouds and only
emphasise his dignity by her pretended disregard of
it. How vividly he recalled dances at her house,
followed by midnight walks amid a bevy of young
people to the sea, its silver mesh sparkling in the
moonlight; and how they promised themselves a
flower-collecting expedition on the morrow; and how
once, because he had said at dinner that to wear their
hair loose was the most becoming fashion for young
ladies, a party of them had taken him at his word!
Still he cherished the picture of their eager haloed
faces, behind them the darkening lawns and a last
low streak of crimson through the trees.

He had enjoyed hard games of battledore with
Butler of Trinity, and triumphed after ferocious
hitting; and but recently, on the first evening after
his return from Italy, he had sat with Miss Ritchie,
as the long July twilight deepened over the garden,
talking of Catullus and the "olive-silvery" Sirmio,
which he had lately visited, until at last candles
were brought, and together, with finger moving from
word to word that his companion, who was an indifferent Latin scholar, might follow the translation,
they had read through some of the loveliest verses
of the "tenderest of Roman poets," lingering over
them, he with tears in his eyes and half-sighs of
delight, as over a lake bathed in moonlight; for it
was always the pathos of beauty which touched him
most.

Of the reading of his poems, particularly "Maud"

and " Guinevere," his favourites, he had a constant
succession of memories. Sometimes it was in the
remote shrine of his high bare attic, alone with an
old friend, whose verdict he valued. Sometimes it
was in his study, to a privileged girl guest, on a bright,
moist evening in spring, when the thrushes and black-
birds sang loud in the " long-fingered cedar " outside
his window, and beyond were fields of hyacinth and
daffodil. Oftenest it was at the end of some long
summer day, when roses filled the red-tinted drawing-
room with scent and very faint through the quiet
evening came the sea's drowsy murmur as it lapped
the rocks. It was then that he loved best to read by
candle-light, seated in his high chair amid a distinguished company, his great head glooming grandly
above a broad expanse of starched white shirt. Once,
too, he had read " Guinevere " to the Upper Sixth
at Marlborough, and once the " Holy Grail " in an
Eton garden. And how reverent and appreciative
every audience had been ! The deep, bell-like voice,
in tone a little monotonous perhaps, but in volume
infinitely changeful and modulated through every
variety of mood from pleading pathos to passionate
power, had never failed to overwhelm all who heard
it, now carrying them away on the tide of its rhythm,
now holding them spellbound as it dropped to a
whisper.

It had brought glory to the eyes of Mr. Gladstone
and reduced George Eliot to tears !

To the poet himself it had become the perfect form
of self-expression. To feel the rapt listeners about
him, to repossess himself of the words which he had
once so lovingly and carefully wrought, to remedy
any inadequacy in them by suggestiveness of immediate emotion, to hear the awestruck silence when the
great voice spoke no longer—all combined to give

him exquisite satisfaction. He realised himself most completely, both as he wished to be and as he wished the world to picture him, in these moments. A player had once said of him, " You are a good actor lost." As he read " Maud " he was not only histrionic, but hierophantic. Actor, preacher and poet were mingled more intricately, perhaps, than he realised.

Truly " the old life," as he wrote, " had been too good to desire change." It seemed to him, looking back, like a dream, like one of those blissful trances, which he could induce by repeating his own name, when he would become lost to reality in an ecstasy of transcendental wonder, and drown almost in the clear waters of sensation.

One agreeable alteration, however, there had been in his domestic circumstances. He had built himself another home. Mrs. Tennyson had been for long a partial invalid, resting for many hours in the day in her garden-chair or on a sofa. Her health had once greatly benefited by the air of Hindhead, and for this reason, and because the privacy of Farringford was more and more imperilled by curious tourists, Tennyson chose Blackdown as the site of a new and commodious house, which on its completion was named Aldworth. The house was built of white stone in the " domestic Gothic style of the Tudor period " ; and in the pavement of the hall and the tile mosaic of the threshold was prominently emblazoned the Welsh motto " The Truth against the World." It stood in a wooded hollow, high but sheltered, hills curving about it on two sides and rising sheer behind it to the north ; but to the south all was wide and open, with a prospect of more than four counties, stretching to the far blue of the South Downs and the sea. The surrounding country was irregular rather than wild. It offered both common-land and deep lanes. The commanding terrace walk beneath the broad windows, the vases full of scarlet flowers set on its balustrade to flame against the blue landscape, the scent of new-cut grass, carnations and standard roses—all contributed to make Aldworth in the drowsy stillness of a cloudless July afternoon no less an English Paradise than Farringford. Seated here on a sheltered corner of the lawn, while the tinkle of tea-cups drew nearer and his family and friends gathered about him, Tennyson seemed not unlike some old Florentine, living anew the days of the " Decameron," in a style more conventionally virtuous indeed, but no less indolent. So brightly glittered the garden beyond the circle of shade in which the little group clustered, so cool and becoming were the ladies' white dresses and large spreading hats, so soft the haze in which the distant weald floated, and so dreamily content the murmur of talk, that a spectator of the scene might have travelled back in memory to that springtide of Italy, in which the spirit of man knew for a brief while how to live at peace with Beauty.

Hither Tennyson would come from Farringford early in July to cure his hay fever, and perhaps his happiest hours were spent by " Wegner's Well " on Hindhead, where he wrote " Flower in the crannied wall," or by the " Silent Pool " beneath the Merrow Downs, watching the " ripply play " of light and colour on the surface of the stream. He loved, too, to rise early and see the sun slowly disperse the blurred ocean of mist, which would often completely fill the wide basin of earth below his window, until hill and valley in turn pricked through the ebbing tide and its last thin trail was gone.

Nor did the hot bath which had been installed fail to prove a luxurious novelty : Tennyson, we are told, would at first take it four or five times a day, conceiving in the rapture of the new experience no higher pleasure in life than " to sit in a hot bath and read about little birds."

Another recorded scene, familiar enough probably to residents in the neighbourhood, was of the poet, a diminutive straw hat decorated with blue ribbons perched upon his head, driving through the Aldworth lanes accompanied by a little golden-haired boy, who sat almost buried beneath the poet's great black sombrero. For by this time, his sons were grown to manhood. Hallam acted as his secretary, Lionel had married Miss Eleanor Locker, and was gone to India. " Golden-hair'd Ally " was the youngest to bear his name—granted, it might seem, by a consoling Providence to silence with his laughter those ghostly voices which had haunted Tennyson after the death of his brother Charles. Thus fondly the poet had written :

> " Golden-hair'd Ally whose name is one with mine,
> Crazy with laughter and babble and earth's new wine,
> Now that the flower of a year and a half is thine,
> O little blossom, O mine, and mine of mine. . . ."

Through all these years the industry of poetry had not languished. Regularly had the eight-o'clock breakfast been followed by the morning pipe and composition. Then came the familiar walk, and in the afternoon the planting of new trees, the inspection of garden or estate, the entertainment of visitors. After six-o'clock dinner the family would take dessert together in the drawing-room, and Tennyson over his pint of port would on most occasions prove a Prince of geniality. Then invariably he retired to his study for a pipe and more composition, later drifting back dreamily to the drawing-room to join in general talk or to read aloud, until the ladies went to bed. And lastly, some favoured guest or guests were invited to his study for confidential discussions, prolonged often until after midnight. The result of this programme, consistently followed out, was inevitably a large body of verse ; while the handling of ballad themes and of rather crude dramatic incidents, to which of late years he had increasingly devoted himself, made him almost as eager to borrow plots from his friends as he still was to wait upon Nature for images. For the quest of new scenery continued year by year.

To Brittany he had gone for the " long lines of cliff," the " red roofs about a narrow wharf," and the fisher folk of " Enoch Arden " ; Switzerland he had visited on two occasions, although the poetical value of the earlier tour had been seriously diminished by the " awful hard beds " at Grindelwald, agonising after the " consenting softness " of those at Farringford, by the heat, by gout, and by an " atrocious odour of decayed cheeses " in a shed by the Falls of Schaffhausen. He had been to Waterloo, to Dresden, to Goethe's house at Weimar, to the Italian Lakes, Venice and Verona, and to Sirmio. There had been voyages when he had watched the moonlight on the sea " like a glorious river rushing to the city of God," and trips with friends to Devonshire and Cornwall, the New Forest and the gardens of Wilton. Latterly, too, he had passed the early spring in London, moving, a remote and striking figure, on the fringes of public life, or enjoying the " good atmosphere of high work " to be found with the Stanleys at the Westminster Deanery.

Always he had been observant and methodical, seldom had he spent himself upon the hazard of thought, or brooded over mysteries too deep or painful to plumb. And so his poetry, though it might seem to have adventured in certain new directions, had in reality only perpetuated a fixed tradition, had, indeed, often become no more than a mechanical act of versification, which not even his wonderful technique could altogether conceal. He had worked a limited seam exhaustively, like the labourer of his poem,

" through months of toil
And years of cultivation."

" Enoch Arden " had been followed by " Aylmer's Field," the " Idylls," enlarged by the addition of a number of new episodes and crowned by the " Quest of the Holy Grail," which he had so long hesitated to attempt, but finally had written in a fortnight. To the " Lover's Tale," composed in his nineteenth year, but laid aside, though breathing in his opinion " the very breath of young love," he had added a gorgeous sequel, " The Golden Supper," set forth in the most sumptuous manner of the " Idylls."

The suicidal end, which he had so often preached as inevitable to every materialistic philosopher who dared to admit the possibility of human extinction, he had once more embodied in " Lucretius," attempting the intimate, but not the colloquial style of Browning.

The vague theism, voiced throughout " In Memoriam," he had concentrated under a sounding title in " The Higher Pantheism."

In moments of leisure between more serious labours he had experimented in classical metres, in translations of Homer into hexameters, and memorial lines to Milton, Dante and others. In many of these his technique, unhampered by any secondary purposes, had shown at its best, while his sympathetic knowledge of Virgil, Catullus, Sappho and Simonides, to name but a few poets of antiquity, enabled him to renew not only the spirit but the dignity, compactness and marmoreal clarity of the classical poetry to a degree rarely, if ever, approached by a modern poet since the days of Milton.

It is only to be regretted that this cleanly exercise

of a classical art in which Tennyson did possess pure genius was treated as a diversion, and its possibilities never thoroughly explored, while those of his faculties which were susceptible to sentimental adulteration were exploited to the point of exhausted platitude.

Later he had ventured into the new field of drama, but still, had he known it, as a lyrical verse writer and not as a dramatist. Indeed, he would confide to friends that " there was one intellectual process in the world of which he could not even entertain an apprehension—that was the Plays of Shakespeare." But as he sketched in " Harold " the conflict of Danes, Saxons and Normans out of which his countrymen were born, or in " The Foresters," the revolt of Barons and people against a tyrant King, or drew Becket, championing the conscience of the Church, or embodied in " Queen Mary " the downfall of Roman Catholicism, the Laureate in him was proud to be the poetical historian of the England that he loved. He was reclaiming history as Mr. Jowett had suggested; but was he renewing it ? He studied his authorities with care, he engineered striking scenic effects, he concocted dialogue on a high poetic level; the result pleased him, many of his friends applauded, and the public showed sympathy. Yet this was not drama, if so he deemed it; for scarce one of his characters has ever come to life. Mellifluous though their printed utterance be, they are shadows, proud, pathetic, sensual or heroic, counselling compromise, practising coquetry, ·or drifting with laborious eloquence across a creaking stage.

Finally, but three years before, in the volume dedicated to his little grandson, he had collected those lyrical dramas of humble and heroic life—some, such as " The Northern Cobbler," little more than happy repetitions of the dialect poems of earlier years—others founded on chance stories that friends had related to him, or that he had heard long ago in Lincolnshire, or in the Isle of Wight, or even, as was the case with " Rizpah," discovered in a penny magazine.

For " The Revenge," one of his most successful poems in the high patriotic vein, one which had evoked even from Carlyle a gruff applause, he had had recourse to Raleigh and Froude.

And if the public had refused to recognise that in his village tragedy " The Promise of May " he had given them, as he claimed, " one leaf out of the great book of truth and Nature," " The Cup," a little play which he wrote because " Becket " had been found too expensive to stage, had made a great success and run for 130 nights—a success, however, which posterity is likely to impute primarily to Sir Henry Irving's acting and Miss Ellen Terry's beauty.

Yet to one considering the verse of these twenty years as texture, unrolling it, so to say, as a choice fabric, it was astoundingly free from flaws. Tennyson's technical powers had become machinelike in their precision. They could always be relied upon. Whatsoever skilful manipulation of word, music, rhythm and images could do, to conceal lack of content or paucity of idea, had been effected. But the result is unsatisfying. There could be no more signal proof of the inadequacy of artistic cunning to sustain poetry of itself. If, however, Tennyson had conceived little new during the thirty years which lay behind him, he had grown older, and this in itself had altered the play of his faculties and modified the quality of his verse, to its advantage in some ways and its disadvantage in others. The poet who had begun to stoop, whose face was deeply lined and head bald upon the top, still maintained the opinions which he had accepted finally at the age of forty-one, still suffered from the limita-

tions against which he had then decided it was useless
to struggle, but the years had added a soberness to
his political, moral and social opinions, and a pathos,
and even grandeur, to certain emotions. They had
tempered the relish of his appetite, and as they brought
death nearer they had compelled him to cling with
even more hysterical insistence to his faith in human
survival. So far as his political opinions were concerned, the Franco-Prussian War had revealed to him
how disagreeable national arrogance might be, and
while still preaching what now—through a blend of
national arrogance and timidity—had become only too
necessary, the need of general military training and
efficient preparedness for war, he was known also to
say : " We rashly expose ourselves to danger, and in
our Press offend foreign Powers, being the most
beastly self-satisfied nation in the world." His earlier
heroics as Laureate had not been calculated to check
such self-satisfaction. But he had begun to learn
wisdom. His belief in progress and reform, in freedom
" slowly broadening down, from precedent to precedent," was also less vaguely assured. He was not
without qualms that some other catastrophe com-
parable to the French Revolution, only world-wide,
might not be gathering to swallow up mankind in a
chaos of Socialism, Atheism and Materialism. He
would speak bitterly of the " Utopian idiocy " of
Communism. His poetry was not at first affected
by this increased tendency to fear extremes in public
and private life, except in so far as it prevented him
from indulging, so much as he had, in the polemics of
virtuous patriotism.

His literary judgments had always shown the
admirable taste of a classical scholar, and the commonsense of one who made no pretence of being able to
follow high flights of imagination, but suspected

extravagance of any kind on principle. Of Shelley, for example, he would say : " He is often too much in the clouds for me," and of his " Life of life," that he seemed to go up and burst.

The poetry of Tennyson's later years, however, differs from that of his earlier not in power or perception, but in an ever-increasing moral earnestness, frequently at the expense of pure art. It has been remarked that his earliest work was almost solely sensational, and even hostile readers will admit that his faculty for exact verbal interpretation of passive impressions has rarely been surpassed in the whole range of literature. But his conscience was uneasy. During the twenty years before and immediately after his marriage, he attempted to deepen his content, he strove for ideas and for passions which his artistic powers might serve to image. The results, significant enough of failure, were " In Memoriam " and " Maud." He abandoned the effort, and once more surrendered himself to sensations, to the fine art of expressing them, and to the morality which was the only fruit of his baffled struggle after ideas. This imperfect morality was for long implicit. As he grew older, it became increasingly explicit. It dominated the situation through the plot, or determined the speeches and actions of the characters ; less and less can we take pleasure in the verse for its own sake.

Tennyson would still say : " An artist should get his workmanship as good as he can, and make his work as perfect as possible. A small vessel, built on fine lines, is likely to float further down the stream of time than a big raft " ; but, at the same time, his conviction of the inadequacy of art in itself was fitly expressed in the line " Art for Art's sake ! Hail, truest Lord of Hell ! " and it was his proud boast that " No nation has treated in poetry moral ideas with more energy and depth than the English nation."

It is true, and it is a glorious heritage. But the tragedy of Tennyson's moral ideas was that they lacked both energy and depth. They were dictated by personal and contemporary sentiment.

The moral ideas which great poetry images are the apprehensions of disinterested imagination; they are absolute and have their foundation in metaphysical truth. Tennyson could talk engagingly of an "Infinity of Worlds," and impress an audience of young ladies with what seemed to be "Astronomical sublimities," he could fill his mind with the latest results of scientific research, keep charts of isothermals and isobars in his room to ensure the exactitude of certain allusions in his poetry to physical science, and he could preach social virtue; but he lacked all capacity for pure thought or its poetic corollary, creative imagination. It is interesting to note that when he became first President of the Metaphysical Society he practised the same stately reticence as in the days of the " Apostles." One writes of him : " I do not remember that the Laureate took any part in the discussion, but his mere presence added dignity to a dignified assembly." Poetry, however, demands more than an impressive presence, and because Tennyson's genius lay in the limited province of the pictorial artist, the more frequent intrusion of a secondary morality into his later work, together with the moral figure-drawing which he practised in lieu of true characterisation, detract considerably from its pure artistic value.

And because he lacked creative idealism, more and more as he grew older, and the necessity of faith grew more desperate, he raised up a false antagonism between Faith and Reason. "Whatever is the object

of Faith," he said, " cannot be the object of Reason."
Faith and Science, we may agree, are opposed to one
another, because Science is specialised Reason. But
intuitive Faith and pure Reason are one. Such
Reason is as opposed to poetic Fancy as it is to
materialistic Science. Although Tennyson did doubtless pierce by intuition to reality in rare inspired
moments, such, for instance, as those mirrored in the
" Holy Grail," when Arthur

> " feels he cannot die,
> And knows himself no vision to himself,
> Nor the high God a vision,"

yet, for the most part, he still believed because he dare
not doubt, with none of the serenity either of the
seer with vision assured, or of the stoical Agnostic,
brave enough, like Meredith, to face the darkness
of doubt, and at the worst comfort himself with the
thought of having served his time and the purpose
of life to the best of his small ability. " I should
consider," he said once in conversation, " that a
liberty had been taken with me if I were made simply
a means of ushering in something higher than myself."
It did not fortify him, as it did Arthur Hugh Clough,
to know that " Though I perish, Truth is so."

Tennyson, as he aged, became in secret more morbidly afraid of personal annihilation and publicly
more loud-voiced in his conviction of survival. For
belief in the survival of the spiritual, as the only real
and true essence in a world of phenomenal matter, was
not enough to satisfy him ; he demanded a retention
of the ego. Of this he could not convince himself
by argument, nor did science come to his aid. " With
country folk," we are told, he loved to converse,
especially seeking out the poor *old* men, from whom
he always tried to ascertain their thoughts upon death
and the future life. He said to his family with deep

feeling one January evening in 1869, "You may tell me that my hand and my foot are only imaginary symbols of existence. I could believe you; but you never, never can convince me that the 'I' is not an eternal Reality and that the spiritual is not the true and real part of me." "These words," his son records, "he spoke with such passionate earnestness that a solemn silence fell on us as he left the room." Yet surely these are the tones of uncertainty affecting omniscience!

But if that religious earnestness for which his mother blessed him five years before her death had assumed a controlling place in the economy of his faculties, trespassing upon his pictorial art, it also in these last twenty years of his life more than once found sincere and artistic expression in itself; for it was, when it ceased to dare the heavens or the earth to say it no, a very gentle, tender and reverent emotion, as was the character of the heart which cherished it. That mood of wistful resignation, as of a quiet twilight settling on a tired world, he had long before grandly recorded in the "Morte d'Arthur," under the first inspiration of a great loss. The passages of truest feeling, and so of most convincing beauty throughout the later "Idylls," are returns to this mood, renewals of the profoundest emotion he ever realised. The yearning hope of some light beyond the darkness of death, of some everlasting spirit beyond a decaying world—this he ever cherished sincerely enough to express absolutely as well as felicitously. He embodied it nobly in various parts of the "Idylls." He concentrated it also in small lyrics. In the hands of such a master of music it takes upon itself a lovely form, and such lyrics as "Flower in the Crannied Wall," "Far, far away," "Merlin and the Gleam," and "Crossing the Bar," because they are sprung from deep personal feeling, whether its origin be in fear or in faith, are of more poetical worth, more poignant in their reflective trustfulness, than a score of passages which boast of future glory or hymn a self-righteous virtue. " I verily believe," he wrote to Mary Boyle, " that the better heart of me beats stronger at seventy-four than ever it did at eighteen." The thought of death had always deepened and dignified his emotion. Fifty years before, Hallam's death had roused that " better heart " to a brief vitality; in two years another poignant personal grief was to test its truth. Nine years more, and death itself was to silence it for ever.

3

Of the poetry, then, and the plays which Tennyson wrote during the twenty years which preceded his acceptance of a peerage it is needless to offer either a detailed account or criticism. They express no new idea nor any sentiment to which reference has not already been made in considering his earlier work. Both the moral sentiments in the poems and the characterisation in the plays have ceased to live or excite interest because both are superficial; the one lacks spiritual intensity, the other deep human insight. The versification and the incidental pictures woven into it are as faultless as ever, the handling of a situation is often clever and ingenious (in " The First Quarrel," for example) ; but often, even in " Rizpah," we are too conscious of the mere effective treatment of a grim plot to be deeply moved, while both plot and sentiment of such a poem as " In the Children's Hospital " are pitifully weak. Many of the dialect poems achieve a gentle pathos or a racy humour. The lines to Milton and Catullus, though experiments

ALFRED TENNYSON

From a painting in the National Portrait Gallery by G. F. Watts, R.A.

[To face p. 258

in quantity, are only less musically perfect than the
later lines "To Virgil," of which they are the pre-
cursors; and such incidental verses as "The Song
of the Wrens" are unsurpassable as lyrics of dainty
sentiment. Yet Tennyson's fundamentally false view
of what comprised virtuous or vicious manhood and
womanhood persists. It leads him to make Sir
Aylmer Aylmer, the sanguine, purse-proud tyrant, an
absurd puppet of villainy who recalls the worst
melodrama of "Maud." "The Promise of May,"
however, advertises the flaw in his thought and
morality most patently, and for this reason deserves
a brief survey. Any but a Victorian public would
surely have risen *en masse* and hissed such a hero-
villain as Edgar off the stage. This creature, whom
some fancied to be a Freethinker—but who in reality
is the conscienceless egotist that Tennyson was too
prone to suppose every rebel against conventional
morality—seduces a girl of fifteen. He wearies of
his victim and, after some evolutionary and com-
munistic vapouring, abandons her; but, to quote
the explanation of the play approved by Tennyson
himself, "her innocence has not been wantonly
sacrificed by the dramatist. She has sown the seed
of repentance in her seducer, though the fruit is slow
in ripening." What a privilege, we cannot help
remarking, is this for outraged girlhood! Years
later, feeling a desire to "make amends," and "his
position of gentleman being forced on his notice,"
Edgar conceives that "to marry the surviving sister
and rescue the old father from ruin would be a
meritorious act. He sets himself to perform it. At
first everything goes well for him; the old weapons
of fascination that had worked the younger sister's
ruin now conquer the heart of the elder. . . .
Suddenly, however, the girl whom he has betrayed,

and whom he thought dead, returns ; she hears him repeating to another the words of love she herself had heard from him and believed. ' Edgar ! ' she cries, and staggers forth from her concealment as she forgives him with her last breath. Then, and not till then, the true soul of the man rushes to his lips ; he recognises his wickedness, and knows the blankness of his life. That is his punishment." The honest father, whose daughters have been so edifyingly sacrificed to these experiments of egotism, is too considerate to add to Edgar's punishment. He forgives a libertinism consecrated by so moral a finale—the wakening of a soul ; and the hero is left to luxuriate in a lifelong contrition.

These are the tones of Rousseau at his worst !

Edgar had demonstrated in speech and action, as in a less degree did the hero of " Maud," that he had no soul to awake, that he was a shallow sensationalist, from whom society should be protected. To engineer a romantic reformation of his character at the expense of two innocent girls is false both to life and morality. The play reveals to what depths of unctuous bathos Tennyson's " moral " intention could lead him.

The same inability to draw a human being, the same moral juggling with decorated types, falsifies the matter and even degrades the manner of many of the " Idylls." The various episodes of this cycle of poems, it must be remembered, were built on no original plan. As with " Maud," and less noticeably with " In Memoriam," each new narrative was at first added more by happy chance than by design, until Tennyson, seeing the possibilities of a complete cycle illustrative of his moral theories, inserted the later episodes with considerable constructive ingenuity. The unity, however, of such a cycle could hardly be organic.

We have already noted the egotism of many of
Tennyson's knights,

> " glancing like a dragon-fly
> In summer suit and silks of holiday,"

and enslaving the hearts of innocently adoring
maidens by their schoolboy arrogance. Arthur himself is claimed to be

> " Ideal manhood closed in a real man."

But such we do not find him. He is an edifying
voice ; the reality of his manhood convinces us as
little as it did Guinevere. The symbol kills the
man. This is the more to be regretted because the
ideal of courtesy, singleness of aim and self-reverence
for which Tennyson meant Arthur to stand is a noble
one, if it be also wedded to power and vision ; and
Tennyson's inability to make it live and his adulteration of it by traits of sublime superiority have tended
to discredit not his ineffectual drawing but the
ideal itself. Far from revealing how shameful is the
sin of adultery by Lancelot's and Guinevere's guilty
love, he has persuaded us that it can under certain
conditions be more beautiful and true than matri-
monial complacence. Lancelot and Guinevere live
more than any other characters in the poem ; their
humanity, rooted if it be in romantic dishonour, is
at least positive. To be told by Tennyson that in
the end Lancelot " died a holy man " is of less importance to us than to know that he lived a true, faulty
and fearless one. The consequences of their sin
against convention—for it is impossible to sin against
such a shadow as Arthur—are drawn disastrously
enough, but the plot is too fantastic to carry any
moral conviction. In any case it is with essential
personal and not social values that poetry should
deal, and Arthur has so little personal value as scarcely

to exist. Tennyson's attempts to enlist our sympathies on his behalf by tracing the ruin of the Round Table to a single domestic infidelity—which any man possessed of Arthur's beauty and eminence could have prevented had he not suffered from spiritual pride, before which a woman was too self-respecting to prostrate herself—are bound to fail. Arthur alienates sympathy because he is too passively dignified to play the man, too morally self-complacent to assert himself when morality demands he should. A knight should surely be ever justifying his lady's loyalty; Arthur is content to assume it, as an unquestionable tribute to his own perfection.

Moreover, we are little more convinced of his spiritual than of his physical reality. In truth, he is the text-book Prince of Family Men, conscientious, scrupulous in his habits, high-principled and mild. He has all the negative virtues sublimely. But towards intense and active spirituality, towards the pursuit of the Grail itself, his attitude is that of all family men towards imaginative adventures. From his arm-chair he speaks of those who have failed :

> " Was I too dark a prophet when I said
> To those who went upon the Holy Quest,
> That most of them would follow wandering fires,
> Lost in the quagmire ? "

While of Galahad he says :

> " And one hath had the vision face to face,
> And now his chair desires him here in vain,
> However they may crown him otherwise."

In short, he may have attained to the seventh heaven, but he has neglected his family obligations ! The Victorian gentleman was apt to presume that all who struggled after visions beyond a middle-class ken were either fanatic or dissolute. Such, they argued, had not been content to invest their energy in the bank of the home and the social virtues, with its moderate but safe returns. They had speculated, and they would be sure to come to a bad end. Typically, Tennyson made the Quest of the Grail signify the fever of a decadent society already sapped by sin and not the culmination of a noble life. But Arthur knows no such fever. He is always temperate-blooded, and is therefore generally commonplace.

The world, we may admit, would be a wilderness without its invaluable millions of passive men and women. It has ever been religion's function to commend these and " idealise " negative virtues, but the poet, though he respect mediocrity for its quiet worth and its inoffensive uses, cannot pretend to find in it an ideal without denying the creative truth for which he stands. For poetry puts morality to an acid test. The negative virtues which succeed are inferior in the eyes of imagination, even to the pure and positive passions that fail.

Tennyson, in the " Idylls," once more compromised, as did his generation. His moral values may have been necessary to his time, but the years, in disproving their quality, reduce his plot, with the sympathies upon which it depended, to ruins. If Tennyson could have drawn men and women, his morality could not have so overwhelmingly depressed the plot ; if Sir Perceval stood before us as a living man, we should not need to be told that he represented virtue attacked by nineteenth-century doubt. But Tennyson did not understand the complexities of personality, and though he could in Sir Gareth, for example, or in Enid suggest in a general way " the eternal youth of goodness " and even make it attractive, more often his types repel, or make no impression at all save one of splendid costumery. Yet we cannot dissociate the knights and ladies from the plot and the moral purpose, as we car, for instance, the " City of Camelot," which we accept gratefully as a fair picture, and care nothing that Tennyson meant it to symbolise " the gradual growth of human beliefs and institutions and of the spiritual development of man."

> " Far off they saw the silver-misty morn
> Rolling her smoke about the Royal mount,
> That rose between the forest and the field.
> At times the summit of the high city flash'd :
> At times the spires and turrets half-way down
> Prick'd thro' the mist, at times the great gate shone
> Only, that open'd on the field below :
> Anon, the whole fair city disappear'd."

Where it is possible, therefore, to read the " Idylls " as " art for art's sake " or for descriptions of nature (as of the thunderstorm in " Vivian "), they survive in all their beauty ; where, too, Tennyson expresses that poignant personal feeling, to which we have already referred, of the spirit which pervades the world, and which encourages one standing on the threshold of death to cherish a quiet confidence, he has written for all time. But where the secondary morality intrudes they offend and even disgust. No modern critic derides Tennyson's love of virtue ; we quarrel with him, not because he was moral, but because poetically he was not moral enough. Throughout the " Idylls," except for moments when he was working at white heat and so reconciled his moral intention with life, we miss imaginative reality. We feel that he has sacrificed truth to edification, and often patronised life instead of understanding it, a presumption which no amount of virtuous intention can condone. Tennyson has not succeeded in illustrating, as he wished, that eternal battle between soul and sense which is the dilemma of human life, because he himself had not the courage to enter it unarmed by conventional morality. And so he has confused the two in a timid compromise,

sentimentalising sense and calling it soul, and the
result is not a culmination of life but an escape from
it. Arthur as a symbol, as a supposedly perfect soul
presiding over an imperfect allegorical world, is an
edifying abstraction ; as a human King and husband
he is either a fool or a prig, a flower of manhood
perhaps, but such a one as does not exist outside a
hothouse.

Thus it is not against Tennyson's virtuous but his
false handling of life that we rebel. We dislike his
picture of man's love for its complacent condescension,
and we disbelieve in a reading of woman which can see
no alternative to an innocent, compliant and characterless Madonna but a Magdalene or a Lilith. Tennyson rejected passion because he had not the intellect
to direct it, he avoided the coarse by cultivating the
luxurious, he decorated sentiments instead of imaging
ideas and characters. The " Idylls " are therefore
a useful document for gauging the mid-Victorian
outlook on love and virtue, but as a whole they lack
the passionate disinterestedness, imaginative intensity
and æsthetic purity, which we claim of poetry in its
truth.

4

Only two months before he received the peerage at
her hands Tennyson had had a touching interview
with the Queen " in dearest Albert's room for nearly
an hour." " He is grown very old," she wrote in her
diary ; " his eyesight much impaired. But he was
very kind. Asked him to sit down. He talked of the
many friends he had lost, and what it would be if he
did not feel and know that there was another world,
where there would be no partings ; and then he spoke
with horror of the unbelievers and philosophers who
would make you believe there was no other world, no

Immortality, who tried to explain all away in a miserable manner—we agreed that were such a thing possible, God, Who is Love, would be far more cruel than any human being. . . . He said : ' I am afraid I think the world is darkened ; I daresay it will brighten again.' . . . when I took leave of him, I thanked him for his kindness, and said I needed it, for I had gone thro' much, and he said : ' You are so alone on that terrible height ; it is terrible. I've only a year or two to live, but I shall be happy to do anything for you I can. Send for me whenever you like ! ' "

Tennyson, however, was fated never to meet his Queen again ; yet had it been ordered otherwise, had she, indeed, summoned him to comfort her spirit in its solitude, it is not likely that he could have added anything to these words of consolation. For this interview embraces almost all the themes over which he brooded during the last ten years of his life. The fanciful spectator might, indeed, consider it as a special epilogue prepared for the last Royal performance of that poetic life-drama which was now drawing to its end. The epilogue with which the public at large were favoured lacked such sovereign brevity as this, but its essence was that which the poet had confided to his Queen in this last hour of intimate talk.

Memories of the past and of the friends who had so lovingly peopled it, doubts and fears for the future of the world, a sense of darkness gathering in the present and clouding over long years of gracious sunlight, above all a passionate assertion of personal Immortality—these were the moods and topics through which he lived, until the great silence fell.

But gradually the burden of mortality displaced all other questions. Not so much speculations

concerning life after death as asseverations of the
soul's destiny and of the reality of God monopolised
his attention. It was the culmination of his lifelong
egotism. He must and would survive. All his days
of happiness and industry, the fame he had won, the
poetry he had compassed, the beauty he had known,
became no more than Dead Sea fruit if anywhere a
faint doubt lurked unconquered, whispering that
death was the end of his distinctive personality. Not
" golden music " itself could make him forget " the
darkness of the pall." In such moods he could write :

> " O slender lily waving there,
> And laughing back the light,
> In vain you tell me ' Earth is fair,'
> When all is dark as night."

Without this certainty religion was no more than
a mocking shadow and God himself a conjectural
fiend. The old dualism which had haunted him all
his life, between his personal desires and an unsympathetic universe, was now centred in this demand for
survival. In youth the conflict had been between
Pleasure and Conscience, between an idler in the Palace
of Art and a struggling, unceremonious world, into
which he felt that he ought to descend. He had
been able then to effect a compromise, silencing the
protests of life by guaranteeing beyond question the
morals of his artistic retreat. But the conflict now
was between pleasure and a nightmare of extinction,
and he could not rebut the challenge of death, as he
had the reproaches of life, by any display of conventional virtue. Compromise therefore being at last
impossible, he was forced to dare an absolute conviction, and his poetry profited accordingly.

His assurances of God, Free Will and Immortality
may be philosophically arguable, but to him they
became in these last ten years poetically urgent, and

thus real—to a degree never equalled even during the months subsequent to Hallam's death. Moreover, as his egotism became concentrated on this theme, the pettiness which he had so often been led to display in his handling of other topics, the selfish sentiment, the arrogance, even the secondary morality, tended to disappear from his poetry and his life. He had ceased to hold so jealous a stake in the world of men ; his vision was set on worlds to come, and so even his political and social judgments reveal a width and a depth, a candour, too, which before they had so often lacked. Even his joy in Nature grew less possessive, so that he could write of her as the pure artist spectator rather than as the devotee with a purpose.

The evening of Tennyson's long life is, therefore, pleasant to contemplate ; the quiet sunset, if it cannot vie with his youth, while the dew was still upon it, is without the mystified cloudiness of his life's later morning, the theatricality and fever of its midday hours, or the sultry opulence of its lingering afternoon. As so often happens in the spectacle of a noble evening sky, above the central glow are to be discovered many tender and ethereal hues, transparent as is the atmosphere in which they float and which for so long has been veiled and oppressive.

All that was most magnanimous in Tennyson shines forth as never before. Even the self-gratifying instinct, the guarded idealism, in which he had lain all his life becalmed, are consecrated and dignified by age. The large sanity of the man, his justice of mind, command increasing respect as they cease to represent a timid compromise with the radical forces which he feared, becoming a courageous conviction for which he has to fight. The Tennyson of these latter years may voice less Liberal sentiments, but at last we feel him to be sincere. He is not expressing the safe and politic opinions of every nice-minded Victorian but those personal to himself. His poetry is, therefore, valid ; it wakes our hearts to sympathy. Indeed, it might seem as if he had determined to rewrite under different titles many of the poems of his youth, weaning them of triviality and enriching them with the deeper feeling and experience which the years had added. The " Death of Œnone " is an old man's answer to the " Œnone " which was long ago conceived in the Pyrenees with Hallam, " St. Telemachus " to " St. Simeon Stylites," " The Ancient Sage " and " Tiresias " to " In Memoriam," the second " Locksley Hall " to the rant and complacence of that of fifty years before. Moreover, the humour of the last dialect poems is incomparably richer than that of the earlier ; the poems, too, of sentiment, even such a one as " The Leper's Bride," are less strainedly artificial ; while amongst the blank verse are passages as noble in manner and almost as full and fervent in content as the inspired " Ulysses."

The old poet at last assumed those grand proportions which for so long he had only affected. He had passed beyond the reach of small anxieties. Still taking that middle path of commonsense along which he had trodden for half a century, he no longer, for the sake of seeming to be in the van of progress, pretended to sympathies which at heart he did not feel.

Tolerant though he remained towards all who cherished dreams of a coming Utopia, he purged himself of that easy optimism which had comforted his middle years. It might be, he would admit, that the world was destined to embrace a new form of society, but he saw now that no amount of mechanical, scientific or engineering cunning could make it virtuous unless the heart of man was set on higher things and the taste and judgment of the crowd educated. Sometimes a vision came to him of the disaster to which the Victorian world was surely moving, as a slow and stately stream moves with scarce a hint of danger to the sudden falls. Behind the outward courtesies of life, the lofty sentiments expressed, behind man's boast of increased knowledge and power, he heard

> " Too plainly what full tides of onset sap
> Our seven high gates, and what a weight of war
> Rides on those ringing axles ! Jingle of bits,
> Shouts, arrows, tramp of the horn-footed horse
> That grinds the glebe to powder ! Strong showers
> Of that ear stunning hail of Arês crash
> Along the sounding walls. Above, below,
> Shock after shock, the song-built towers and gates
> Reel, bruised and butted with the shuddering
> War thunder of iron rams."

Tennyson's generation had not so much created as accumulated a great, rich and ill-distributed material Empire, and its national policy and morality were dictated by an anxious desire to preserve what was already possessed and what increased so satisfactorily at Compound Interest. The vulgarity of this possessive passion they had veiled even from themselves in fine and lofty sentiments and in what they thought sincere enough professions of virtue. The upper middle classes, which had profited most by this economic inflation due to the industrial revolution born of machinery, had evolved a culture on lines kindred to their morality and politics. It, too, was possessive rather than creative. But the material forces which had expended themselves in mill and multiplied themselves in slum to provide the upper middle classes with the luxury of an expensive culture, a patronising morality and foreign policy, were already showing signs of revolt. The machine-ridden masses had endured exploitation long enough, and they began to weary of the pious progressive sentiments behind which their masters sought to retard industrial reforms ; for it was noticeable that while the middle classes proclaimed themselves superior to the physical forces of nature, they were quite ready to accept as inevitable the play of those economic forces which represented only the laws of nature translated into terms of finance. The educated Victorian was too exquisite a gentleman to be capable of the vulgarity or licence of nature, but he had lived long in comfort on the vulgarity and licence of a " natural " industrialism. The spiritual darkness of a commercial age had, in short, clouded the heaven of the cultured, even as the smoke from factory chimneys hung grey above the neighbouring countryside.

But the volcano upon which the Victorian gentleman had built his over-furnished mansion, which had been for years a source of ample income and had enabled him to be both as refined and as arrogant as ill-earned wealth will make a man, was only too soon to erupt. " The madness of our cities " was awake. Tennyson felt the first vibrations ; but he was too old to suffer panic. Catastrophe would not come in his time. Yet he was a little ashamed, as he looked back on the shallow enthusiasms of younger days. How he had welcomed trade, and knowledge, freedom and progress, as if by such titles as these the world was necessarily advanced one step on the way to betterment ! Carlyle, he remembered, had been very unpopular for his persistent refusal to see how progressive the Victorian world was.

" I myself have often babbled," he wrote in the most conservative and courageous poem of his life — which therefore much displeased Victorian taste :

> " Is it well that while we range with Science, glorying in the time,
>   City children soak and blacken soul and sense in city slime ?
>
>   .   .   .   .
>
> Yonder lies our young sea-village—Art and Grace are less
>   and less :
> Science grows and Beauty dwindles—roofs of slated hideous-
>   ness !
>
>   .   .   .   .   .   .
>
> " Nay, your pardon, cry your ' forward,' yours are hope and
>   youth, but I,
> Eighty winters leave the dog too lame to follow with the cry."

We may say that these sentiments are reactionary ;
what matters is that they are honest. Tennyson's
eyes were opened too late. He was too old to vision
that true freedom which might come, when democracy
and science had learnt by bitter experience that it was
necessary to direct matter by the light of eternal
values, and not merely to accumulate, exploit or
examine it. He could not see the true " forward "
prospect, but he was grown sufficient man to turn
and rend the false. The sleeping lion in him was
roused ; he no longer felt it necessary to pander
politely to progressive cant. By the side of the gilded
picture of a divine free-trade, which he had so often
painted in the past, he hung now a more sombre
scene :

> " Desolate offing, sailorless harbours, famishing populace, wharves
>   forlorn : "

and Knowledge, that god of days gone by,

> " is the swallow on the lake
> That sees and stirs the surface-shadow there
> But never yet hath dipt into the abysm."

Freedom, too, and patriotism, those twin impulses to
uneasy lurid sentiments, awoke now a music humble
and austere :

> " My son,
> No sound is breathed so potent to coerce,
> And to conciliate, as their names who dare

For that sweet motherland which gave them birth
Nobly to do, nobly to die. . . . their examples reach a hand
Far thro' all years, and everywhere they meet
And kindle generous purpose, and the strength
To mould it into action pure as theirs."

His conversation reveals a like sobering of opinion. With Newman he shared a profound distrust of Democracy, as being at heart but a system of political materialism. His distrust was doubtless more due to temperamental distaste for the " mindless mob " or the " loud world's bastard judgment day " than to considered judgment. He saw the ugliness which commercialised knowledge was bringing into the world, nor did he realise to what extent the materialism of Democracy had been created and exploited by the class to which he belonged, for all its boast of refined and religious sentiment.

Yet he was sagacious enough to foresee the inevitability of future industrial strife, were not some such equitable measures taken to prevent it as arbitration by mixed tribunals. This enlightened moderation governed all his later views on national and Imperial topics. His essentially compromising mind had no sympathy with party politics, which depend either upon strong convictions or strong prejudices. Tennyson had neither : he entertained a benevolent but cautious belief in gradual progress, which preserved him alike from Radicalism and Toryism. In fact, a deserving, but tame commonsense tended to make his political and social opinions as inactive but as high-sounding as was the morality which he grafted on to his art. As he aged, however, he grew ever more conscious of his own and human limitations, and compromise, as we have said, became a far more convincing creed because he scented real catastrophe. In the Queen he found a sympathetic listener. To her, too, " the fatal cry of party " was very tiresome, if only because so often it meant parting with a favourite Minister.

" Change must needs come," Tennyson wrote to her, " but I wish that statesmen would oftener remember the sayings of Bacon : ' Mere innovations should imitate the work of time, which innovateth slowly but surely.' " These are true words, but they were welcome, we suspect, to the Queen and her Laureate not so much because they were true as because they were comfortable.

But on other subjects Tennyson began to reveal a refreshing candour. The brutalities of science were no longer tacitly condoned. " I have been reading," he said, " of the horrible and brutal experiments in Italy and in France ; and my whole heart goes out to a certain writer in the *Spectator*, who declared that he had yet to find out mankind was worth the cruel torture of a single dumb animal."

Though doubtful of the future, and clinging tenaciously to the old faith and manners which in a long life had become second nature to him, he preserved in public at least a fair measure of open-mindedness. For him " The true old times were dead," but " You must not be surprised," he would say, " at anything that comes to pass in the next fifty years. All ages are ages of transition, but this is an awful moment of transition. It seems to me as if there were much less of the old reverence and chivalrous feeling in the world than there used to be. I am old and I may be wrong, for this generation has assuredly some spirit of chivalry." The chivalry of which he lamented the passing bore, we must admit, but a bastard kinship to that which Burke summarised in a famous passage : " But the age of chivalry is gone . . . the unbought grace of life, the cheap defence of nations, the nurse of manly sentiment and heroic enterprise is gone ! It is gone, that sensibility of principle, that chastity of honour, which felt a stain like a wound, which inspired courage whilst it mitigated ferocity, which ennobled whatever it touched, and under which vice itself lost half its evil by losing all its grossness."

For still the pleased patron in Tennyson believed that women must continue to owe their intelligence and virtue almost entirely to the impressive characters of their menfolk : " Especially do I want people to recognise that the women of our western hemisphere represent the highest type of woman, greatly owing to the respect and honour paid to them by men, but that the moment the honour and respect are diminished the high type of woman will vanish."

Inevitably, too, in the religious scepticism of the day he read only falsehood and not the birth of a healthier truth. Yet it was with the dignity of one whose thoughts were already set on another world that he recorded " the curse of blindness and unbelief." " An Iron Age," " darken'd with doubts of a Faith that saves " was rising on the " Age of Gold," through which, in a more material sense than he implied, he had lived in peace and prosperity. In moments of weariness, ever more frequent as year followed year, he " would that his race was run." His day and all that it stood for was passing, and he knew it. Yet he was not angry or embittered, but rather tired, tolerant and wise, as only the old can be. His later poems are full of this tender, stately resignation. It ennobles their highest moments, it purifies their meanest by raising him above the pettier appetites of life.

> " Raving politics, never at rest—as this poor earth's pale history
> runs—
> What is it all but a trouble of ants in the gleam of a million
> million of suns ? "

He began to see life from the eternal standpoint, and all that jarred upon his courtly nature in the vulgar and yet so just demands of democracy, seemed, after all, very trivial beside the mystery of death and the approaching wonder of the hereafter. Even the tragedy in 1885 of that " noble hero Gordon," to use the Queen's words, whose pale blue eyes lived in Tennyson's memory as those of a child who had never yet learnt to suit his measure to the world's, did not rouse him to indignation as once it would have done. It all sounded unreal and like a sad tale told by a romantic novelist of a weary desert far away; for death, through these last ten years, was always with him : " the world was dark with griefs and graves."

In April, 1886, he lost his son Lionel, who was returning from India. It was " a grief as deep as life or thought." The boy had always been so affectionate, unselfish and capable; a bright, useful future lay before him, and the thought of his lonely moonlight burial in the Red Sea, with all the waste of manhood it implied, and the unuttered farewells of a father's love, haunted the dreams of Tennyson. " It tears me to pieces," he would say; and yet he was too old for prolonged agony. His sorrow only served to make him more patient and more unselfishly thoughtful for others. The pain and the promise of life rid him of all mean melancholy; but alone in his study he could write pathetically enough :

" Poor old voice of eighty crying after voices that have fled !
All I loved are vanish'd voices, all my steps are on the dead.
All the world is ghost to me, and as the phantom disappears,
Forward far and far from here is all the hope of eighty years."

For the loyal friends of past years had vanished one by one. Always now he feared, as he said good-bye to any who still survived, that he was parting from them for the last time. Soon Venables, Browning,

Ward and Allingham were to cross his threshold no
more. He was left alone with sad memories and
eternal hopes. Above all, he thought of Fitzgerald,
whose shrewd affectionate letters had meant so much
to him for thirty years, and whom but yesterday, it
seemed, he had greeted, as he sat in his garden at
Woodbridge in the sunshine beneath his roses, with
his grey floating locks, his humorous-melancholy
expression and his pet doves perched upon his shoulder
—" Fitz," who so hated all things crude and loud and
formless. Now " the gate was bolted and the master
gone " ; sometimes he could almost fancy that in
these friends, so scrupulous in their tastes, so sensitive
to refinement and beauty and virtue, the principle of
aristocracy had begun to perish out of life, gulfed in
a rising tide of indiscriminate vulgarity. In such
moods he could only write, as the tears fell upon his
hand :

> " But for me,
> I would that I were gather'd to my rest,
> And mingled with the famous kings of old,
> On whom about their ocean-islets flash
> The faces of the Gods—the wise man's word,
> Here trampled by the populace under foot,
> There crown'd with worship—and these eyes will find
> The men I knew . . ."

Yet these moods were but transient ; nor did Tennyson's faith ever suffer such dimness as had beset
Carlyle's in his last years, nor his memory afford any
such matter for recrimination. He had lived too
prudently, he was always too sound in mind and
body for querulousness to disarray his faculties or
trespass on the faith which had preserved him, if
hazardously, for so long against doubt and dread.
Rather age deepened and certified it as the claims of
knowledge and science dwindled before the imminent
mystery. The " Ancient Sage " was still too ready

to assume that all who disbelieved in a hereafter must necessarily waste their days in riotous living, but his reply to the young materialist shows a strength and assurance lacking to the poet of " In Memoriam " :

> " Thou canst not prove the nameless, O my son,
> Nor canst thou prove the world thou movest in,
> Thou canst not prove that thou art body alone,
> Nor canst thou prove that thou art spirit alone,
> Nor canst thou prove that thou art both in one.
> Thou canst not prove thou art immortal—no,
> Nor yet that thou art mortal,—nay, my son,
> Thou canst not prove that I who speak with thee,
> Am not thyself in converse with thyself,
> For nothing worthy proving can be proven,
> Nor yet disproven : wherefore thou be wise,
> Cleave ever to the sunnier side of doubt,
> And cling to Faith beyond the forms of Faith.
> She reels not in the storm of warring words,
> She brightens at the clash of ' Yes ' and ' No,'
> She sees the best that glimmers thro' the worst,
> She feels the Sun is hid but for a night. . . ."

The best arguments for faith, as Bishop Blougram knew, have always been the contentment which it ensures and the failure of doubt to prove its case.

> " Who knows ? or whether this earth-narrow life
> Be yet but yolk, and forming in the shell ? "

That Tennyson's conviction of a hereafter was not absolute is clear from the nervous inquiries he so constantly addressed to friends, acquaintances, and even simple rustics, and the gratitude he felt towards those whose faith reinforced his own creed. He was greatly comforted, for example, when Tyndall told him : " God and spirit I know, and matter I know ; and I believe in both " ; as also by Mr. Jowett's answer of " Yes, certainly," to his question whether his faith in God was more earnest than it had been. The subject occurs frequently in his correspondence with the Queen, the immortals being even pictured

as thrilling in sympathy with the ovations of a loyal
public : " If the dead, as I have often felt, tho'
silent, be more living than the living—and linger
about the planet in which their earth-life was passed—
then they, while we are lamenting that they are not
at our side, may still be with us ; and the husband, the
daughter, and the son lost by Your Majesty may rejoice
when the people shout the name of their Queen."

Yet in these last years that Life after death
which had always seemed to Tennyson the cardinal
point of Christianity, took upon it a new and lovelier
aspect. " What matters," he would say, " anything
in this world without full faith in the Immortality
of the Soul and of Love ? " And as he talked, we
are told, his face lighted up and his words flowed as
it were from inspiration. The assurance of a transcendent Love more and more enlarged a merely
egotistical need of survival. That Logic could not
touch the central problems of life and death became
less important than that in Love was life eternal
verified :

> " What the philosophies, all the sciences, poesy, varying voices
>   of prayer ?
> All that is noblest, all that is basest, all that is filthy, with all
>   that is fair ?
> What is it all, if we all of us end but in being our own corpse-
>   coffins at last,
> Swallow'd in Vastness, lost in Silence, drown'd in the deeps
>   of a meaningless Past ?
> What but a murmur of gnats in the gloom, or a moment's anger
>   of bees in their hives ?
>   .   .   .   .
> Peace, let it be ! for I loved him, and love him for ever : the
>   dead are not dead but alive."

" Every heart," as he wrote elsewhere, " that loves
with truth is equal to endure." Love steeled him with
patience, it stilled his fear, it reconciled his doubt

with his faith. The "embattled wall of unbelief" fell before its radiant assault; it turned the face of Death towards the Sun of Life, and in the last considerable poem he wrote, "Akbar's Dream," it filled his mind with a vision of a world in which there were neither the rancours of castes nor creeds nor pugilistic patriotism nor commercial-minded brotherhood,

> "But loftier, simpler, always open-door'd
> To every breath from heaven, and Truth and Peace
> And Love and Justice came and dwelt therein:"

"It is hard to believe in God," he would say, "but it is harder not to believe. I believe in God, not from what I see in Nature, but from what I find in Man." And again, "Love is the highest we feel, therefore we must believe that 'God is Love.'" In this large charity he found peace after long disquiet. No more did he try to rank himself with those "thin minds, who creep from thought to thought." He was grown too wise to relate his mind to any progress save that of the after-life. He had found the "Eternal Now," which should ever be the poet's new discovery, but which had escaped him for so many industrious years. Sometimes he visioned this immanent reality in a remote future with those whom he had loved. It came as "a breath, a whisper—some divine farewell —desolate sweetness—far and far away." Sometimes it shone forth in the simple beauty of earth, more particularly as each spring brought the crocus and the snowdrop and the missel-thrush, and he wondered wistfully whether he should live to see another. In "Persephone" he hailed her

> "Faint as a climate-changing bird that flies
> All night across the darkness, and at dawn
> Falls on the threshold of her native land,"

but in one small lyric he greeted the age-long miracle of new birth in words of purer ecstasy, nearer to the universal note of life and the delicate wisdom of art, than any perhaps which he ever wrote. There is no whisper of intrusive egotism in the stanzas which begin

> " Once more the Heavenly Power
> Makes all things new,
> And domes the red-plow'd hills
> With loving blue :
> The blackbirds have their wills,
> The throstles too."

Death was indeed discovering to him the crystal purity of life at its fount. That heightening of sense and quickening of spirit by which suddenly the clouds are lifted and we look enraptured upon a world new made, a world whose bright leaves and running water had never yet so sparkled in any morning sunlight, came upon him in old age with a more fresh and naked revelation than had ever gladdened his youth. For the first moment perhaps in his life he looked unaccountably beyond the rich verdure, the heavy foliage, into the heart of life. Its vivid eager spirit ran out to meet his own. He was a happy fugitive at last from the body which had grown too weak to hold the spirit any longer in comfortable captivity. Later, in the lines " The Progress of Spring," dedicated to one who stood with him " so close to that dim gate," he traced with " a loving humility " all the detail of the flowering year, until in the deep joyousness of intimacy he knew himself one with the Life " which is Life indeed."

Thus as the end drew near he rose above the cloud and shadow which had veiled the light ever since " Arthur vanish'd, I know not whither,"

> " And broader and brighter
> The gleam flying onward,
> Wed to the melody,
> Sang thro' the world :
> And slower and fainter,

Old and weary,
But eager to follow,
I saw, whenever
In passing it glanced upon
Hamlet or city,
That under the crosses
The dead man's garden,
The mortal hillock,
Would break into blossom.
And so to the land's
Last limit I came—
And can no longer,
But die, rejoicing,
For thro' the magic
Of Him the Mighty,
Who taught me in childhood,
There on the border
Of boundless ocean,
And all but in Heaven
Hovers the Gleam."

His spirit had climbed towards Hallam's at the last.

5

Outwardly the man changed little. His habits and his interests remained the same. Still, if less frequently, he would, as Laureate, tender the nation's sympathies and congratulations to the Crown, or direct the public along the paths of duty. For the occasion of Princess Beatrice's wedding at Whippingham, in July, 1885, he wrote some ceremonial verses, though confessing to the Queen "a fear that the power of poetry was faded or fading in me." The Queen, on her part, revealed no waning of poetical enthusiasm in her reply. "I wish you could have *seen* the wedding," she wrote, " for everyone says it was the prettiest thing they ever saw. The simple, pretty, little village church, all decorated with flowers, the sweet young bride, the handsome young husband, the ten bridesmaids, six of them quite children with flowing fair hair, the brilliant sunshine, and the blue sea, all made up pictures not to be forgotten." That Age, to which the Queen gave her name, had, indeed, offered an endless crescendo of the prettiest sights ever seen !

In the *rôle* of poetical patriot, however, Tennyson certainly benefited by the " fading of power." His lines to " Freedom " and those on " The Fleet," which Cardinal Manning said " ought to be sung perpetually as a National Song in every town of the Empire," are purged of almost all the vicious national egotism which before had too often degraded sentiments quite laudable in themselves. He sang now less of cannonades, and more

> " Of knowledge fusing class with class,
> Of civic hate no more to be,
> Of Love to leaven all the mass
> Till every soul be free."

He had realised that even patriotism can become a sin through " Brass mouths and iron lungs," and his distaste for rant in any form now agreed with his love of the finely polished in art. " I delight," he wrote, " rather in the consummate flower of a writer than in the whole of him, root and all, bad and good together." Yet in his human relationships he withdrew with less frequency to those awe-inspiring heights upon which he had been apt to pose ; he seemed more simply and naturally a man, and a great one. His thoughts dwelt often on the Lincolnshire of his boyhood, on " those old homes, which, though now far away in the morning twilight, are not forgotten," and he took peculiar pleasure in re-embodying the racy humour, which still lived fresh in his marvellous memory from the rustic lips that coined it. As he wrote " The Church

Warden " and " The Spinster's Sweet-Arts," he would rock with laughter.

His home life at Farringford and Aldworth continued to offer the same charmed sanctuary of beauty and affection. Many new friends diverted the evening of his days, and in Miss Mary Anderson, who came at first to discuss the two of his plays in which she was to act, he found still another, and, perhaps, the most lovely of those gentle spirits, the very " flower of girlhood," who throughout his long life had so inevitably offered him their devotion and charmed him with their grace. The years, too, had been kind to him; it seemed as if they were loth to cripple one who had always taken such regular exercise, who had never overtaxed his energy, and had absorbed the beauty of life day by day with sober appreciation. At the age of eighty-two he would defy his friends " to get up twenty times quickly from a low chair without touching it with their hands, and perform the feat himself." So serenely muscular an old age is perhaps only possible to one whose constitution has never had to bear the strain of severe mental or physical effort.

Upon a deep and gentle stream of affection and reverence he had floated contentedly for forty years, cheered and soothed by happy glances and quiet voices, and a love cloudless as soft afternoon sunshine. In such an amiable atmosphere few lurking irritations or morbidities could survive. Nay, so strong was the presumption of greatness universally accorded to him that to act the gracious, the high-minded, part to so sympathetic an audience required the minimum of effort.

Always he had lived with prudence and in comfort bodily and spiritually. He had never struggled with taut nerves and straining sinews for things too high and hard for normal minds to compass. He had

walked impressively in the van of progress ; he had
not adventured in the void.   And so he grew old with
the quiet dignity of some prosperous patriarch of
antiquity, and until the moment of death preserved
the even faculties, the calm equability, of Nature in her
health.

Almost to the last he continued those familiar walks
on the cliff at Freshwater or in the lanes of Aldworth.
The various talk never faltered ; still he remained
mentally alive to every object around him, halting in
mid-sentence to listen to a blackbird's song, to watch
the sunlight flicker on a butterfly's wing, to examine
a flower or to go on his knees to a bed of violets.
The eyes, which tired now somewhat easily over print,
never wearied of Nature, and only by imperceptible
degrees did the more frequent use of his carriage reveal
the encroachment of time.

His interest, too, in science persisted.   In August,
1887, an eclipse of the moon, which he watched with
Professor Jebb from the balcony of his sitting-room,
roused him once again to a high enthusiasm, in which
he visioned a great future for the spectroscope !

In the same year he offered his last gift of panegyric
to his Sovereign :

> " Nothing of the lawless, of the Despot,
> Nothing of the vulgar or vainglorious,
> All is gracious, gentle, great and Queenly."

So he pictured his ideal, the ideal which the upper
middle class stamped upon the century—that ideal so
noble in intention, so conveniently limited in application, so guarded in its holiness.   Dignity and good
manners had been allowed to rule the lives and dictate
the deaths of men for a season ; the decencies of family
life had been preserved in the villa and outraged in the
slum, and the day of retribution was at hand.   Even

over this Ode of Gratitude and Retrospect the storm-
clouds hover. Tennyson hailed them afar :

> " Are there thunders moaning in the distance ?
> Are there spectres moving in the darkness ? "

Spectres, indeed, there were, gathering about the van
of progress, raised by a generation which had divorced
virtue from truth in a time of decency, and destined
to be laid by their children's children in a time of
blood. " The Jubilee of the Ages " was in bitter fact
to prove no such pleasant and imminent dream as
Tennyson's loyalty inspired him to associate with the
reign of Victoria. The Ode was, however, given forth
by a full orchestra on May 11th, was greatly admired,
and Tennyson was rewarded by yet another photograph of the Queen.

The summer months were refreshed each year by
cruises, generally along the Cornish coast, in yachts
put at Tennyson's disposal by friends. Thus, like his
Arthur, he put out to sea in the twilight of his days,
and, landing once at Tintagel, " old memories and
visions of the ' Idylls ' came upon him and he regarded
the whole place with a kind of first-love feeling."

Each post continued to bring its batch of appreciative letters, but many handwritings long familiar were
welcomed no more. One friend, however, survived,
indefatigably admiring and suggestive. In a letter
to Lady Tennyson during a Cornish cruise, Mr. Jowett
wrote : " I hope you have good accounts of the
travellers in the *Stella*. They have had a charming
season for their voyage. Besides the gain to health,
many new thoughts will have been suggested by it.
I always wish for Lord Tennyson, not that he should
cease to write, because he has written so much and so
well, but that every year he should find something
suited to his genius, and that all his friends should urge

him not backwards but forwards. This seems to me
the best for himself and for the world. His memory
and his powers are so undiminished and his experience
so increased, that I think he might even now surpass
himself. I should like some poems in which the truth
of things or some side of the truth is clearly expressed,
' a last vision of things.' " Four years later, lying on
what he knew might prove his death-bed, and when his
friend had passed his eighty-second birthday, Mr.
Jowett's fertile mind returned once more to the
attack : " The doctors," he wrote to the poet's son,
" seem to think that I am seriously ill, and although
I think that I am very likely to recover, I should like
to send my most grateful love to your father and
mother for all their kindness to me. At such a serious
time some of my old projects come back upon me.
One of these is that your father should write a few
hymns in a high strain, to be a treasure to the world
and to the Church, and to come nearer to the familiar
thoughts of men than ' In Memoriam,' which is a
very great work of its kind, but not suited to be sung
in churches."

The suggestive encouragement of friends had during
Tennyson's long life almost seemed to compensate for
a want of invention in himself. The strain, however,
of this last injunction, towards still another side of the
truth, proved literally too high. Mr. Jowett's fore-
thought was not fated to enrich the English Hymnal.

In the early autumn of 1888 Tennyson suffered a
severe attack of rheumatic gout. He drew " as near
death as a man could be without dying," but, after
two serious relapses, recovered rapidly. His illness
revealed with what a homely reverence the English
public now cherished its Poet-Laureate. Tokens of
affection and anxiety were universal, from the Queen
herself down to the well-intentioned strangers who

wrote prescribing burnt cork to be placed under his bed, or a diet of snails.

With a joy more intense perhaps than ever before, because he had known for the first time the thrill of life endangered, he returned to the world and the sun, and sitting in his summer-house at Farringford talked of hopefulness, feeling again, but with a delicacy unrealised in the security of middle-age, " the kiss of the future " on his cheek ; and listening attentively to the different notes of the thrush, finished his song of " The Throstle," begun in the same garden so many years earlier. As " the girlhood of the year " tripped on, shedding her flowery mantle of primroses and cowslips, and the turtle-doves " purred " in the garden, he regained strength, and after a short sea voyage his cure was complete. His eightieth birthday found him cheerful, well and happy in the many congratulatory letters and telegrams which he received. The Queen's " best wishes " were three days late, but the delay was. explicable. " My time," she wrote, " has been so much taken up by my grandson, the Emperor of Germany's visit, that I have hardly been able to write." Yet it seemed as if the invocation addressed to the Deity in those appended verses to the National Anthem long ago had met with a favourable reception ; for the Queen added : " My grandson the Emperor of Germany's visit went off very well, and much cordiality between the two countries was shown on both sides." " I know," wrote Tennyson later, " that your Majesty has a perfect trust in the Love and Wisdom which order the circumstances of our life, and in this alone is there comfort." Once again, as on a day at Farringford thirty years before, the Spirit of Irony must have smiled a little wanly.

The old walks were resumed, fresh work pondered, and no dimming of Tennyson's powers was apparent.

MRS. TENNYSON

From the portrait at Aldworth by G. F. Watts, R.A., by kind permission of Lord Tennyson, Mrs. G. F. Watts, and Messrs. Macmillan & Co., Ltd.

[To face p. 288

Indeed, for two more years he was to walk regularly
for an hour and a half on fine days, and on stormy ones
would pace up and down the music-room, or practise
gymnastic exercises with his legs and arms.

Increasingly during these last years thoughts of her
with whom for forty years he had lived in wedded
sympathy filled his mind. Over all that long reach
of time never had she failed him in his need, never
proved anything but the valiant, self-effacing, sweet-
tempered woman, who had brought him peace on that
far-off day in Shiplake Church. Over every physical
disability her courageous will had triumphed. He liked
to linger fondly in memory over the early days of that
courtship, which at the time had seemed so improbable
in its issue.

> " Rose, on the terrace fifty years ago,
> When I was in my June, you in your May,
> Two words, ' My Rose,' set all your face aglow,
> And now that I am white, and you are gray,
> That blush of fifty years ago, my dear,
> Blooms in the Past, but close to me to-day
> As this red rose, which on our terrace here
> Glows in the blue of fifty miles away."

In spirit she had aged less than he, for she had never
even conferred with doubt. And so as he watched her
in her familiar soft grey cashmere gown, lying in her
garden-chair on the lawn, with her saintly resignation
and her patient eyes, ready at any moment to brim
with welcome, it mattered not that the auburn-brown
had faded from the silken hair—she seemed the same
bright spirit, whose gentle instinct for belief had raised
him above the dilemmas of days long past,

> " With a faith as clear as the heights of the June-blue heaven,
> And a fancy as summer-new
> As the green of the bracken amid the gloom of the heather."

Once she had said to him : " When I pray I see the
face of God smiling upon me." He did not doubt it.

Of her he remarked to a friend, when twilight
invited the confidence: "It is a tender, spiritual
face, is it not?" The deep, calm music of her
voice, her unobtrusive dignity and trustfulness, her
delicate and alert intelligence, all had combined to
mould

> "A spirit, yet a woman too! . . .
> A creature not too bright or good
> For human nature's daily food; . . .
> And yet a Spirit still, and bright
> With something of angelic light."

Often her disinterested love, the uncompromising
Christianity of her views of life, which neither political
economy nor class distinctions could modify, had made
him feel that she was higher than he.   Perfect had she
proved as wife and mother, with that genius for tactful
management which only a good woman can exercise; perfect, too, in sympathetic criticism, in quiet
encouragement and applause.

Many of Tennyson's poems at this time, such as
"Demeter" and "Romney's Remorse," embody
types of beautiful motherhood or self-effacing wifehood.
It was the last tribute of his chivalry to the little Lady
who had satisfied all his sentiments.

On June 13, 1890, they kept their fortieth wedding
day, and the poet gave his bride "a pretty posy of
roses, rosemary and syringa," and was merry as on the
day on which he had driven away from Shiplake
Church, to consecrate his love by Hallam's grave.

All Tennyson's life now seemed rounded and
complete.

The sea, to which he and his brother Charles had
carried the first-fruits of their sensibility on that far-off
afternoon at Mablethorpe, called to him with an ever
more subtle and insistent voice, as the months
darkened round him, "among new men, strange faces,

other minds." On an October afternoon, when
travelling from Aldworth to Farringford, deep
answered to deep, and he settled finally his account
with life and death, as he wrote " Crossing the Bar."
Never more could doubts torment him nor hungers
irk. He gave himself to the unseen Pilot, serene in
hope as one weary after a long and lovely day of
summer will give himself to sleep, and dream of the
dew in the eyes of to-morrow's dawn. The end,
however, was not yet.

His walks along the cliffs, and at low tide among the
green rock-pools on the shore grew dearer than ever.
Browning's death removed still another of the
generous-hearted men whom he had known. He and
Mr. Gladstone and Mr. Jowett seemed sometimes
rather forlorn survivals ; he consoled himself by
reading Thackeray's novels ; they proved a " delicious
and mature " antidote to days so full of haste and
menace. In 1890 influenza weakened him seriously ;
but again the splendid constitution withstood the
attack. He sat to Watts for another portrait in the
spring, and a year later, in a friend's yacht, he visited
his brother Frederick, the Italian exile now come home
to Jersey, and they talked together of Somersby days
and of Hallam still young in memory, parting with a
sense of wistful finality. Many friends visited him in
the summer at Aldworth, and often he would take
them to the top of Blackdown to lie on the heather and
watch the sunset, while with Princess Louise he walked
three miles uphill to the Beacon and back, talking
vivaciously all the time. The death of the Duke of
Clarence in January, 1892, roused the Laureate in him
to a last ceremonial effort, but he was unwell, and the
strain told upon him severely. The Queen's gratitude,
however, was reward enough ; she " spoke with tears
in her eyes of the beauty of the verses . . . on this

terrible tragedy, which is a real misfortune. . . .
They are most affecting."

"Akbar's Dream" of a new Jerusalem, a Platonic
Republic, reared upon justice, wisdom and tolerance,
occupied much of his thought during the last spring
which he was to enjoy at Farringford.

The apple and pear blossom, the white lilacs and
purple aubretia bloomed this year with more than
ordinary luxuriance, and Tennyson delighted to sit in
his summer-house talking of days past and wonders to
come, and of that veiled spirit vital in all matter to
which he ever drew nearer; or he would stroll at
intervals about the garden so familiar and yet so new,
as only Nature can be new to one who has seen eighty
springs and none the same. The long labour of
conscious professional observance was now at an
end. At last he could delight in glimpses of meadows
through the avenue of elms, or in the giant fig-tree, for
their own sake. The poetical notebook was put away.
"What joyous things," he said, "are those larks in
the spring sun!" Never even in his youth had he
realised so unguardedly, with such open, unfearful
eyes, spring's unveiling, Persephone leaping in her
naked beauty, unashamed out of the clutch of death,
which could not soil her virgin grace.

He celebrated his eighty-third birthday at Aldworth,
and few of the letters of affection and remembrance
which he received can have touched him more than
that of Lushington, who wrote: "May the day be
blest to you and all who are dear to you, and may the
year bring more blessing as it goes forward, must be
the warm wish of all who have felt the knowledge of
you and your writings to be among the greatest
blessings of their life. Year after year my deep love
and admiration has grown."

But it was not to be. Soon Farringford was to

know him no more. The tide of life within him was beginning its last journey seaward, yet with no urgency, but with a gradual settling as a tired body will settle itself comfortably to sleep. In death no more than in life was there to be any hasty or rude gesture. It was at Farringford that exhaustion first halted him after a walk longer than he should have attempted. He was glad to be inside his garden gates again, and sat down trembling to rest upon a melon frame. To a companion he spoke sadly of his age, and of what he must expect; for it was hard, indeed, to bid farewell to earth, did he stand on the threshold of the most miraculous hereafter. So fair a Paradise had his home been to him for thirty years, so charged was it with love and kindness, with memories of old friends and sage thoughts, of happy voices calling through green glades, and shapes of beauty moving about quiet lawns.

Later at Aldworth the tide of life seemed once more to turn towards him; momentarily his strength returned, and with it the regular walks; but it was noticed that day by day the distance dwindled, until he was content to sit in one of his summer-houses, gazing out across the Sussex Weald at the long line of Leith Hill and the far-off Kentish Downs shimmering in the afternoon haze, or to watch the sunset deepen over the pine trees of Blackdown and the purple heights of Hindhead. Rarely now after dinner would he take a friend up to his den to smoke and talk. He wished to rest. At midsummer he paid his last visit to London, seeing the Royal Academy and allowing speculation to play for the last time about the ichthyosaurus in the Natural History Museum. Thoughts of God and the mystery of life were seldom absent from his mind, as the early tints of autumn began to trespass on the foliage of an indifferent summer. The bounds of earth would often fade away from him as he sat, the horizons of life grow dim. "Matter is a greater mystery than mind," he would murmur. And then again: "What such a thing as a spirit is apart from God and man I have never been able to conceive. Spirit seems to me to be the reality of the world."

The kingly presence which had for so long ruled with easy majesty every room, every company of men or women, into which chance had brought it, was beginning to lay down the sceptre. Once again, late in August, he was prevailed upon to read "Maud," "sitting in his high-backed chair, fronting a southern window which looked over the groves and yellow cornfields of Sussex." Once again the high-priestly voice performed its overwhelming rite, breathing out its oceanic incantation, filling the room with its reverberations, ebbing and flowing, rising and falling, monotonous but infinitely varied, like the eddies of wave and ripple on the constant undertone of the sea. Against the sunset clouds, seen through the western window, the outlines of his high-domed head showed dark and stately like a Rembrandt portrait. For a last time he stormed the first canto with the old passionate, rhythmic restlessness, and the deep mellow voice trembled with the intensity of a half century of remembrance over

> "I have led her home, my love, my only friend,
> There is none like her, none."

Once more the veiled eyes flashed and a look of heavenly ecstasy lit up the features, as he raised his head and chanted the invitation

> "Come into the garden, Maud."

Once more, with a slow and forlorn solemnity, more poignant perhaps than ever before, he lingered over the broken-hearted lyrics, "Courage, poor heart of stone!" and "Oh! that 'twere possible," until the deep voice passed through the harsh notes of delirium to the trumpet-call of the finale.

But a performance which in the years that were gone had always left him exhilarated and purged, exhausted him now. It was time for the old actor to quit the stage. " He often now longed for the quiet Hereafter where all would be made clear ; " for physical disabilities were increasing. Early in September he complained of pain in his jaw, and had difficulty in swallowing food. On the 29th he was driven to Haslemere, and, pointing out his accustomed haunts, said : " I shall never walk there again." Soon he was glad to keep to his bed, day by day growing more drowsy, and his breathing more uneven. A volume of Shakespeare he had always within reach, though he read but little.

On Tuesday of the week following the last drive to Haslemere, he woke at noon, and the beauty of the world, which he had so much loved, flooded his heart. " I want the blinds up," he said, " I want to see the sky and the light : the sky and the light." Beneath his window lay the Weald of Sussex bathed in brilliant sunshine. The afternoon brought him a telegram of anxious enquiry from the Queen. For a last time the loyal and affectionate servant returned thanks to his dear and honoured Lady. The joy and favour of this world passed from him with the fading of that day's sunlight. " Have I not been walking with Gladstone in the garden, and showing him my trees ? " he asked later, after a short sleep, and next day to his doctor he said : " What a shadow this life is, and how men cling to what is after all but a small part of the great world's life ! "

Death came to him tenderly and reverently, as he would have wished. Throughout Wednesday the torpor deepened, though consciousness was slow to fail. Towards evening, gathering himself suddenly together,

he whispered to his doctor : " Death ? " The doctor
bowed his head, and he answered " That's well." For
the next few hours the full moon, shining through the
oriel window, filled the room with a clear but spectral
light, while the watchers gazed with fascinated awe
upon the great figure stretched motionless as marble
upon the bed, from which the breath was slowly depart-
ing. The grandeur of the antique was written plain
upon the sharpened features ; there was no smallness
left in them, no hunger, scorn, or fear. All was at
last staged heroically. He was realising his dream of
a stately passing. His dignity had mastered life ; it
was commanding death as well. He looked the noble,
peaceful man he ever wished to be, as he lay clasping
his Shakespeare in one hand—the monument of the
conscience and the poetry of more than half a century.
Yet if any visions floated through his clouded mind
during those last three hours of deepening coma, we
can fancy that they were not visions of virtue or of
moral strength.

Perhaps to his dying sense there came faint and far
away, through the mists of seventy years, " the mellow
lin-lan-lone of evening bells," and before his glazing
eyes there rose the picture of that blithe young circle
gathered on the Somersby lawn, as sunset faded and
the bats began to flit, Emily with her harp, Hallam
with his "Dante," the murmur of talk, the low laughter,
the long serenities of silence, the scent of roses, the
stars paling over the hill. Love and remembrance like

> " Music that gentlier on the spirit lies
> Than tir'd eyelids upon tir'd eyes,"

stole over him, loosening the frayed knots of mortality,
consoling, inviting. . . . Gently as a ship that at
twilight, without wind or wave, slips its moorings,
he drifted out to sea.

EPILOGUE

" I cannot praise a fugitive and cloistered virtue, unexercised and unbreathed, that never sallies out and sees her adversary, but slinks out of the race, where that immortal garland is to be run for, not without dust and heat."—JOHN MILTON.

THE verdict of that impartial and subliminal critic, who judges the work of each generation by the light of pure intelligence, upon the great poet, who had stood so publicly for the culture and conscience of the mid-nineteenth century, would inevitably differ much from that of even the most acute among the hushed congregation which gathered in Westminster Abbey to pay its last homage to the Laureate of the Victorian Age ; for in Tennyson's funeral we see the preliminary obsequies of a century which the pomp of the Queen's passing was a little tardily to conclude.

Nor can we after this brief interval pretend to a much larger measure of omniscient equity. Pain and death in recent years have, it may be, prejudiced our minds and hearts as much as sentiment and association did the heart of his contemporaries.

Yet our verdict must be spoken, our experience must register its reaction. This, then, we would say, was a man good, noble and true according to his lights, but his lights were dim and often clouded. A great English gentleman of high-bred manners, wide knowledge, refinement and kindness of heart, a magnificently normal man, simple and frank, open-minded, too, beyond a certain limit of sacred unquestionable topics, often grand and formidable in outward mien, but at heart always tender and human—so we picture

297

him in his everyday life. As a more than Virgilian
weaver of words, a painter of rich scenery, a singer of
delicate airs, an interpreter of the exquisite pleasures
or the troubled moods of the senses—he was a master
unassailable. When he wrote as a pure artist he has
written for all time. None ever was finer craftsman,
few more gallant and generous in intention, more
desirous of righteousness or more industrious in the
perfecting of great talents. Consistently throughout
a long life he revealed temperance and self-respect in
conduct, kindliness in private act, dignity in public
bearing.

But what of his spiritual significance to his own time
and to ours, to that " truth " whose name he so often
and so piously invoked ? Had he, to use Mr. Gladstone's words, " raised the intellects and hearts of his
fellow-beings to a higher level ? " Was that moral
atmosphere of his time which Froude named " pesti-
lential " indeed purified by his verse ? Had he enriched
the blood of the world ?

To these questions we can make no enthusiastic
response. Tennyson had lived a favoured and cloistered life, such as is granted to few, protected from the
harsh winds of Nature and the brutalities of man. It
had not been to his profit. It had encouraged a vein
of weakness, a tendency to self-gratification, an
avoidance of honest thinking, which prejudiced the
heart of almost all he wrote. We have only to consider
how few of the sentiments in his poetry were more than
the measure either of his personal need or gratification,
to be convinced of this. He dreamed away his life in
the sun, lost amid the fancies of beauty and the
formalities of virtue. Consequently his morality was
a mere projection of his senses, seeking to justify
before his conscience a state of pleasure which he
wished to perpetuate. It was not the offspring of

disinterested reason and emotion. It lacked a true basis. Both he and his age wanted moral altruism. They made the fatal substitution of a " high-souled " for a true-souled creed, and the degree of influence exercised by the one upon the other is hard to estimate. Tennyson had always enjoyed the privilege of a gracious, well-informed and comfortably endowed society. No grievous economic burden had ever pressed upon his spirits, nor cruel want hardened him to endure. Not even for a few short years had he to struggle forward in the cold unfriended. Always he had had an enthusiastic bodyguard. Yet it was significant that he had not borne too well the small and transitory disappointments which had fallen upon him; for a too guarded life had softened his fibre and rendered him over-prone to a weak self-pity, too sluggish for battle and enterprise, too fearful of a loss of dignity or grace to dare the world's disdain for the sake of truth. In the constant relaxation, no less than in the affected passion and morality of his poetry, we detect the reverse of " a man all lucid and in equilibrium—his intellect a clear mirror—imaging all things in their correct proportions—healthy, clean and free, and discerning all round about him."

And, therefore, his morality, so earnestly preached and containing, indeed, elements of that ideal which it is the poet's office to abstract from life, depreciated his art without adding finally to the account of virtue. It satisfied for a time the selfish instincts of the favoured class to which he belonged, but it cannot bear the candid scrutiny of a generation which has reaped the bitter fruits of high-sounding egotism and whose hopes have almost perished with their fears. Sadly, too, has the failure of this false morality tended to discredit true virtue in the eyes of foolish men ; for because Tennyson wed art to a false morality, and

the two have perished together, not a few have been
quick to claim both that art should be without
morality and that morality itself is only the convenient weapon of a class which wishes to perpetuate a state of swollen dividends. Such men do not
realise that it was a false morality and not morality
itself which has been disproved, a selfish art and
not Beauty herself dishonoured. The dishonesty of
Victorian virtue, in short, incited men to abandon
principle altogether, to be honest even at the cost of
blackguardism. A compromised Idealism invited a
reaction, not to art, but to " Art for Art's sake," not
to virtue but to Nihilism, of which the issue is not yet.

For this Tennyson, as a more than representative
voice, cannot escape a certain responsibility. He had
not vindicated the ways of God to man, but the right
of the upper middle class to maintain a social and
domestic Deity which pleased them very well. He
had sought, not universal, but local truth. His
morality, we repeat, was dictated by his personal
needs. It was a policy of fear and selfishness, pretending to truth. Behind his stately affirmations of
virtue there lurks a meanness. Vision he lacked and
power and the courage to wrestle with life alone and
speak for all mankind. He voiced many high, gentle
and elegant sentiments ; he championed not a few that
were petty, while to a pure idea beyond the flux of
time and fashion he scarcely ever attained. Rarely
did he fill the perfect chalice of his art with the crystal
waters of truth. Rather he reconciled art and
popularity by compromising truth ; he encouraged
men to restrain their passions, but only at the cost of
indulging their sentiments, to refer the duties of
brotherhood to a providential Deity, to boast of their
superiority to the brutes without shouldering the
burden of a true humanity.

In him the virtues and vices of the Victorian Age
are for ever writ plain. Victorian peace and culture
failed because it was the result of a passive reaction
from Napoleonism, the flower of exhaustion and not
of new birth. There is scarcely a creative idea,
certainly not a fundamental change of heart to be
found throughout all the middle and late nineteenth
century. Both in life and art the age accumulated
a great material Empire ; its primary impulse was
acquisitive. It possessed itself alike of trade and
knowledge and provinces with almost mechanical
greed. And without questioning the essential value
of these things, it named the tenure of them " progress." In art it created little new because the
persistent egotism by which it adjudged everything in
terms of personal desire prevented it from perceiving
life in its essence or entirety ; it was therefore content
to refine technically upon the results of earlier creative
impulse. Of this Tennyson is an outstanding example,
and of his debts to the earlier Romantics we have
already made mention. But beneath the veneer of
middle-class cultivation, the smoke-veiled world of
industry spread further and further its tentacles over
the green land, nourishing as never before the germs
of those two fatal diseases of modern civilisation,
Industrialism and Militarism. Both these scourges
represent surrenders to that licentious nature to which
in his private morals and culture the gracious Victorian
professed to be so superior. But publicly he did little
to oppose the play either of Economic or of Physical
forces which, unrestrained, were leading straight to
disaster, except to affirm the excellence and the
comfort of virtue. For lack of generous imagination
he failed to see how essentially brutal were many of
the practices which he not only tolerated but championed, and behind a vague catchword of " progress,"

he relaxed that individual moral effort upon which alone can civilisation be securely sustained.

The result of such idle high-mindedness was the catastrophe of savagery and folly which we have known, and the decimating of a generation, young in hope and generosity, which had of itself willed no such things.

Once, listening to the choristers in the Abbey, whither he was brought at last to rest, Tennyson said, " It is beautiful, but what empty and awful mockery if there were no God." On the fields of Flanders there was no God, and the mockery and squalor of it all was relieved by no white-robed Choristers, voicing a consolatory strain.

CHRONOLOGICAL LIST OF TENNYSON'S PUBLISHED BOOKS.*

Poems by Two Brothers. 1827.

Timbuctoo. 1829.

Poems Chiefly Lyrical. 1830.

Poems. 1833.

Poems. 2 vols. 1842.

The Princess. 1847.

In Memoriam. 1850.

Ode on the Duke of Wellington. 1852.

Maud. 1855.

The Charge of the Light Brigade. 1855.

Idylls of the King. 1859.

Ode for the Opening of the International Exhibition. 1862.

A Welcome [to H.R.H. The Princess of Wales]. 1863.

Enoch Arden, etc. 1864.

The Holy Grail. 1870.

The Window, or the Songs of the Wrens [1867]. 1871.

Gareth and Linette. 1872.

Queen Mary. 1875.

Harold. 1877.

The Lover's Tale [1830]. 1879.

Ballads and Other Poems. 1880.

The Cup [1881] and The Falcon [1879]. 1882.

Becket [1879]. 1884.

Tiresias and Other Poems. 1885.

Locksley Hall Sixty Years After, etc. 1886.

Demeter and Other Poems. 1889.

The Foresters [1881]. 1892.

The Death of Œnone, etc. 1892.

---

* Many of Tennyson's poems, indeed most of his later works, were put into type soon after composition and a few copies printed off for the author's use. In some instances these poems were not published until years afterwards. Where possible the date of these earlier issues are given in square brackets.

INDEX